Reader Reviews

Gunnar's approach, coupled with his unbridled enthusiasm, will challenge you to get moving and reach for the stars! He is a gifted teacher who leads by example.

Ben Sterling, Southern Philanthropy, Inc.

Gunnar does a great job at explaining leadership in such a way that is interesting and thought provoking. I enjoyed the history lessons and the personal stories that he shared. It is truly a great lesson on everyday leadership in the workplace. Thanks for providing such a great resource for leaders so that we can improve.

Deborah Allen, Confidence Life Coach for
Teens at Mega Learning with a Twist

It is my great pleasure to read Gunnar's book. I have only known Gunnar for a short time, but in the few days we have shared, I can tell you he is the real deal. Gunnar's expressions of faith and belief are practical as well as important in a dying world. I enjoyed the explanations that accompanied his faith and belief stories. In a dying world, he gives a ray of sunshine. To find that the younger generation is looking at and discovering the true meaning of life and life after death is truly a blessing. Thank you, Dr. Gunnar T, for sharing your message with us.

Charlotte Canion - Award-Winning Author

Dr. Gunnar Thelander attempts what I called a "Unified-Field Theory of Life." Many authors address one or two aspects of a person's life (e.g., health and money), but Gunnar attempts to offer his remedies on most of a person's life concerns. On the whole, the book is optimistic: He reminds the reader of the importance of individuals trying to change the world for the better (ignoring today's mindsets, that used to be the norm, not the exception). In addition, he stresses that change is difficult, important, and possible. The author quotes his favorite philosophers and visionaries, and he tries to get people to look up from their own navels (a daunting task indeed).

Frank McEvoy, M.Ed., Editor and Screenwriter

The Ergonomics of Life surprises with deep wisdom at its root and innovative strategies on every page. Offbeat witticisms sneak themselves into each chapter as Gunner's broad background connects wellness with success in every area of life. Forget rigid notions you have about ergonomics, nutrition, and productivity. The Ergonomics of Life empowers you to live the life you want to lead with balance and finesse, not drudgery and stress.

Sherry Prindle - Certified Master Coach Trainer

Corporate Training, Coaching, and Consulting

Founder of the Professional Coach Academy

www.ProfessionalCoachAcademy.com

I like what you have put together. It will be a great gift and resource for folks when you speak or on its own. I really like the approach to attitude with antidotes related to your own experience throughout your book. From discomfort in the form of a crown to the life lessons of the centenarian woman Okinawa, the book's continued scientific support made it work for me. It's a surprisingly easy read.

Ben Farmer, Mojo Mindset Consulting

Gunnar Thelander, in his book, "Ergonomics of Life," goes in much detail and great wisdom of how people can be the most efficient and productive in all areas of life. From relationships to money to time, stress, and faith, Gunnar covers the gamut of all aspects of the human experience to create an easy to read, how-to manual for virtually anything in life you may be struggling with and need a little help.

The applications at the end of the chapters make a great way to apply the knowledge of the information in each chapter and do some inner work and reflection for personal growth. I highly recommend "Ergonomics of Life" to anyone who wants practical help and guidance to live an extraordinary life!

Dr. Carla McGowan, Author, Speaker, and Executive Coach

The Ergonomics of Life

Enhancements you can apply to your
life in stress-management, your body,
your time, money, leadership and more

Gunnar Thelander, Ed.D.

GKT Ventures, LLC
DALLAS, TEXAS

Dedication

This book is dedicated to my wonderful mother and father, who are now in Heaven. You have both inspired me through your lives to write this book!

Acknowledgments

MANY THANKS TO those who have helped me write this book! I could not have done it without you!

Also, thank you for politely laughing at all the missed humor I put into my writing. That didn't go unnoticed!

First to my good friend Ben Stirling, who has introduced me to the John C. Maxwell Team, and now I am a proud member. I now have a greater plan of adding value to others!

To Dr. Keith Mankin, for helping me with all of my misspelled words that spell-check didn't catch and forgetting the difference between nouns, verbs, and adjectives.

To Jeff Klein, for showing me how to become a better speaker.

To Sherry Prindle, for introducing me into the coaching business and sharing all your secrets to success!

To Wallace J. Rutland, for being a great friend of my father and a great friend to me. Your email blogs help keep my faith grounded. The Lord shines through you brighter than anyone I know!

To my sister, Lisa Dudley, thank you for your rigorous secondary editing. It's because of you this book took so long to write. It's flawless now!

To Dr. Angela Massey, thanks for formatting this book to perfection.

To Dwight Craver, I'm grateful for your creativity on the cover of this book, and all the fun video projects now on YouTube. You are a great friend!

And to my mother, Karen Armer, who sadly passed away within the twelve days of Christmas 2007. She showed me that with persistence and prayer, anything is possible! I will never forget it!

Contents

Note to Reader

"The best way to predict the future is to create it."
Tom Peters

ERGONOMICS IS A big buzzword in today's working world, isn't it?

We all want our chairs to be like zero-gravity recliners so we can lean back and picture ourselves somewhere tropical. We want unlimited coffee and refreshments anytime we want it. We even want our trash cans to be within arm's reach or at least within shooting distance for our crumpled-up papers. Two points!

Yet, we are unhappy and even miserable when we park our cars at the office at the start of the workday. Even though many of us go to work environments that are scientifically designed to contour with our bodies to be more productive at work, the opposite is often true.

Somehow, we get stress-induced knots and aches in our neck and back regions, yet our furniture is designed for the opposite outcome. Why?

In this book, we delve into what causes stress in our lives. We have lots to be stressed about at work, with our families, and especially with our money.

The challenge to all readers is to apply proven strategies to redesign our thinking and habits to be ergonomically in line with what God intended. He didn't intend for us to be stressed-out but rather to be joyed-out! This book is for those readers who want to learn strategies to overcome stress in their lives and live above their circumstances.

I have thoroughly researched the foremost thought leaders and found the best-proven strategies that work! And I have tried to pack the fruits of all my years of learning and practices in this book for you. Just as the study of ergonomics is to increase productivity in the office, per se, this book intends to increase productivity within you!

At the end of each chapter, you will find an exercise that you can apply to help you overcome stress in that area covered. Each chapter is independent of the other, so you may read any chapter and still find it fulfilling.

Lastly, pass it on. Every person on this planet has a stress-area to overcome. That includes your spouse, family members, friends, and co-workers. Even if you just verbally share what you discover in each of the chapters, you will have helped someone else live a more abundant life!

Life is what we make it. This book is for the individual who is currently living and breathing. It is for everyone! I invite anyone who wants to live a life with less stress and more joy to read and apply the principles of an ergonomically redesigned future. Yours.

Introduction

ERGONOMICS. YOU HAVE probably heard that word mentioned when it comes to the chair you sit in or the desk where you perform your daily tasks. After all, the very definition of the term applies to the work environment itself.

Wikipedia defines *Ergonomics* as "a branch of science that draws on engineering, physiology, and psychology. It is a made-up word created by joining the Greek words 'ergos' (work) and 'nomos' (natural laws)."

The contribution of Ergonomics has gone way beyond our work environments. Think about how this one word has impacted everything we do:

- Our Automobiles – Our cars today look quite different today than the super wind-resistant Model T Ford. Our cars today contour *with* the wind, not against it, so that we can get places faster and save more gas. Our seats adjust to any height and position, which makes us nice-and-comfy on longer road trips. The seats have a lot of cushion in them to help your neck and back muscles relax after bouts of road rage. All these improvements are ergonomics – the ergonomics of driving!

- Let's not forget about our GPS systems! Not only does the whole system prevent the need to fold and unfold paper maps, but the GPS screens are positioned, so you rarely take your eyes off the road. Heck, that is even more advanced than the Model T Ford, which didn't even have windshield wipers! All this is ergonomics as well.

- Our Phones – One day in the late 80's I remember sitting in my grandfather's car. We were on a pleasant drive in Sugarland, Texas, when we heard a strange ringing from the center console. He opened it up and took out his bulky "portable" phone complete with a long cord dangling from the vintage device. Never did I ever imagine then that this would be the start of cell phone technology. Now with ergonomics firmly in mind, the phones have no cords and fit comfortably in your pocket or purse so you can answer any time it rings. You can say that this is an ergonomic "upgrade" since calling anyone you desire has been made so simple and practical.

- Our Television Sets – Our viewing is ergonomically enhanced by larger but light screens that are flat or even curved inward to provide better head and eye function. Not only that, but I have a shocking statement to our younger generations that they will not believe, which I assure them is very true. If you were born sometime before the 1980s, there were no remote controls. In the days of big-box TVs, if you wanted to change the channel or adjust the volume, you had to get out of your seat and turn those dials on the TV set itself. I know you are probably thinking, "No Way!" Way. And you thought your life was hard now!

- Our Coffee Houses – Starbucks started in 1971; today, it's a $20 billion company. It was a bold move back then. "Nobody will ever go to an establishment to buy a coffee, and definitely not for more than a dollar." After all, when Starbucks began expanding across the US in the late 1980s, the cost to make a single cup of coffee was only $0.32 per cup! How is that for healthy margins? All in the name of the convenience of finding a well-brewed cup of Joe whenever we need it? Is that ergonomics too? I say, *yes*! Just keep in mind that I'm a coffee-lover![1]

- Our Offices – Of course, this is what made ergonomics so, well, "ergonomic-al." We have specially designed workstations like never before. Our desks are at adjustable heights, our chairs are uber-comfy, and our screens are eye-friendly. A lot of scientific research has gone into our workspaces to make them productivity friendly. We want our workers to be comfortable. We want them to be injury-free from repetitive strain injuries, or RSI (much more on this later). Everything is adjustable so that everyone can be as productive as possible.

In the early days of office ergonomics, chairs were designed to be sturdy and hold the worker in a rigid correct posture. However, these chairs proved hard to sit in for long periods. Usually, these chairs were made of wood with small seat cushions, resulting in the rapid onset of lower back pain. New technology has made them more comfortable, flexible, and tolerable while still maintaining a good sitting posture.

Like television sets, computers of the 70s and 80s were just huge boxes sitting on our desks, with the keyboards attached. The angle of a worker's hands and arms was set by the computer's position, which made the posture unnatural, resulting in upper back pain and carpal tunnel, a result of repetitive strokes such as keyboarding and holding the wrists in a downward flexed position for long periods. Now the computers, just like our phones, are light and portable, and the keyboards and mice are wireless (and sometimes not even there). The deskbound worker can be in any comfortable position, or posture-correct or ergonomic if they only knew how.

Therefore, the science of ergonomics has gone a long, long way to minimizing physical stress in the office. We ask our employees to work eight-hour days (or more) and be productive in that time, requiring focus and concentration. Who can concentrate and perform well when they have an irritating knot in their neck? We all still get those knots at times, but not nearly as fast as workers did in the days before real ergonomics was taken seriously.

Although the aches and pains may be less frequent than earlier times, research proves today we have more office stress than ever before. As a result, we still get headaches, aches, pains, and even more serious physical diseases or even cancer.

So how is this possible? Why has our physical stress gone up while our work environments are ergonomically designed to *reduce* that stress? Unfortunately, the studies demonstrate that even as our physical stress is going down, our mental and emotional stress levels have risen critically. Is each of the physical, mental, and emotional states of stress intertwined together?

Ladies and gentlemen, that's what this book tackles!

What if we could use the same approach that has been done on our physical stress and discover how to ergonomically redesign the way we think and the way we act in every area of our lives? I challenge you to expand your mind. If Ergonomics has improved our working environments for better productivity, we can change the way we think of this four-syllable word to improve everything we do. What will be the outcome of this book's great experiment? That's up to you.

Let me show you an example of how our experiment may come out.

My well-to-do grandfather would often ask me, "How is your financial situation?" which mildly annoyed me in my younger years as a schoolteacher and coach. However, it's one we must always ask ourselves. I've encountered so many individuals who tell me they never balance their checkbook or monitor their bank accounts on a daily basis. Then they are shocked when a transaction at the local mall comes back as 'insufficient funds." Therefore, if Ergonomics was applied here, what changes would you make? To ergonomically improve our finances, we need to start saving. We need to get out of credit card debt. We need to have a plan. We will expand in chapter 7 to help you develop an ergonomically sound plan to live above your financial circumstances, including some great stuff by Dave Ramsey.

That is just one example of understanding *The Ergonomics of Life*. The purpose of this book is to help you maximize your life while living on this planet. We will cover the ergonomics of your time, health, managing your stress, and a plan for personal growth that is all ergonomically-sound. I have accumulated tips and advice from top experts in all these areas, including my training and experience in years of solving ergonomic problems for clients and students. I am confident that everything we will discuss in this book will help you in every area of your life if you apply them. Just imagine if you were able to learn proven techniques to de-stress every area of your life. The result would be a life filled with abundance in joy, relationships, and productivity in work and private time. Your attitude will reflect how you handle your stress level, and that is the factor in the equation, which is entirely up to you.

This book has been through multiple revisions, and that takes time. I'm glad for it. Why? In the timeframe of doing the revisions, the Coronavirus COVID19 impacted the entire world brought it to a screeching halt. It wasn't just hard times; it was the hardest of times. As we all know, the virus affected the entire world, crashed the markets and filled the hospitals.

For such a time as this—here's *The Ergonomics of Life*. We will experience stress at all levels in our lifetimes, and the Coronavirus Pandemic was a real stress test for all of us. I will share with you insights on how to get through the tough times and sail through the good times when things are rolling along.

Read. Enjoy. Laugh. Rejoice. Rest.

One last word of warning! I have a very witty, slap-stick sense of humor. I love telling stories, and I promise this book is full of them! Please wrap-up this book and send it back if you ever experience boredom while reading it. No yawning or day-dreaming is allowed! You will hopefully laugh and probably perform lots of eye-rolls, but I do this because of a wise statement made by Maya Angelou, "I've learned that people will forget what you said, people will forget what you did, but they will never forget how you made them feel." I want to inspire you!

You will feel better when you wake up every day because of the changes you are making in your life! Well, and let's not forget that laughter *is* the best medicine!

So, get ready, buckle your seat belts, and enjoy the ride!

Oh no, wait a minute! Never read and drive. I'm sorry if I just now motivated you to read this book while driving your car. You may, however, read while sitting at red lights. The car behind you will always let you know the light just turned green, of course, in a very polite manner!

Gunnar Thelander, Ed. D
Dallas, Texas

CHAPTER ONE

Ergonomics of Stress

THE WAY OUR bodies are designed is simply astounding. Think about all we put our bodies through on a daily basis. Every day we manage our lives at home and work. We do all we can to live a balanced lifestyle. Those who realize nobody is perfect yet strive towards perfection every day will most likely receive the greatest outcomes in life, while those who don't strive for anything will receive lesser outcomes. Just check out these crazy stats from Statista.com[2]:

> *PEOPLE IN AMERICA ON A YEARLY BASIS:*
>
> *Spend 159 billion hours in the car; or 17,600 minutes per person per year*
>
> *Spend 3 billion hours online, or 116,800 minutes per person per year*
>
> *Give 800 million status updates*
>
> *Sit in 19 million meetings*
>
> *Send 144 billion emails*
>
> *Watch 4 billion YouTube Videos*

Get 2 billion hours of sleep or less than 7 hours per night per person

Drink 1.6 billion cups of coffee

Get 50 million hours of Exercise

Have you noticed that sleep and exercise rank lower than all the above activities? The worst part of the list above is the amount of sitting we do. In fact, six of the activities on this list involve sitting. My new favorite saying is that nowadays *sitting is the new smoking!*

All of this activity, especially the lack of exercise and movement, has a significant impact on America's stress levels. Here is what is going on in our bodies when we get "stressed out," this is what the scientists and doctors call the "physiologic response to stress:"

Cortisol and Adrenaline – These are the "fight or flight" chemicals of the body. These chemicals saved our ancestors when they stumbled upon a grizzly bear in the woods. Cortisol and adrenaline increase your pulse rate, make your heartbeat stronger, raise your blood pressure, make your blood pump faster to the brain, and a whole bunch of other responses that will help you in a short-term crisis. In fact, more than fourteen hundred known physical and chemical reactions happen in our bodies in fight or flight! All stress is the same to the body, regardless of whether it is mental, physical, or emotional. Therefore, facing deadlines at work, traffic jams, financial pressure, and negative relationships result in basically the same body or physiologic reaction to stress as stumbling upon a bear in the woods. The big difference here is one is short-lived, and the other is usually more constant. If you see the bear and it eats you, the good news is your stress is officially over. Permanently. But in day-to-day life, the stress goes on and on. We go to bed with prolonged stress pumping a steady stream of cortisol running through our veins as we are filled with anxious thoughts and then wonder why we can't sleep.

Serotonin – This is the "antidote" to cortisol. It allows the heartbeat and blood pressure to relax and the brain to calm down. But serotonin and cortisol do not co-exist—only one can work at a time. You are either feeling great because serotonin is fully active in your body, or you are stressed and on edge with cortisol filling you up like a gas tank. The good news is that serotonin is instantly activated with any pleasant or comfortable activity. Serotonin is always available in our bodies when we hug someone we love, accomplish a task, and help someone else in need. We need more of this in our lives! Imagine if everyone in your office focused on helping everyone else rather than themselves? It's impossible to worry about yourself when you are focused on helping others.

However, cortisol is playing the dominant role in our society today. Too many of us are so stressed that we ignore other's needs and put our own first, and the lack of good stimulus only makes the cortisol levels higher. We even ignore what our bodies tell us with sore necks and back pain. In my effort to help others, I co-founded a corporate chair massage company called *Massage Kneads & Wellness*, based in Dallas, Texas. We offer chair massages for employees who need them and lead workshops that instruct them on almost every aspect of well-being. This service is well needed in our corporate world today. According to research conducted by the American Institute of Stress,[3]

83% of US workers suffer from work-related stress

75% of workers believe they are more stressed-out than previous generations

Stress caused sleep deprivation for 66% of American workers in 2018

Workers say that stress and anxiety affect their work productivity and coworker relations more than any other factor

Work-related stress causes 120,000 deaths and results in $190 billion in healthcare costs yearly

43% of all adults suffer from adverse health conditions related to stress

75-90% of all doctor visits are for stress-related symptoms

An estimated 1 million workers are absent on an average workday due to stress-related problems and complaints, which also accounts for millions of workdays lost due to absenteeism.

Americans consume 5 billion tranquilizers, 5 billion barbiturates, 3 billion amphetamines, and 16 tons of aspirin every year. All these medicines are taken to relieve stress-related symptoms.

Chronic stress has been linked to many leading causes of death, including cardiovascular disease, cancer, lung ailments, accidents, and even suicide.

What is happening here to our bodies when we get stressed out? What is stress in the first place?

The dictionary defines stress as *"mental or physical tension or strain."* One expert in the medical field describes stress as *"the pressures of life and how one perceives, reacts, and copes with those pressures."* It may be your perception, reaction, and coping that leads you to an ergonomic path to stress relief.

I want to share a story (you have been forewarned) from my high school days when my mother taught me a critical lesson about stress. I love Drama. No, I'm not referring to the kind that most folks say about someone they dislike, such as "She is drama!" I'm referring to Drama Class when I was a sophomore in high school. I wanted to be one of the main supporting roles in the class play, a one-act adaptation of *Pride & Prejudice*. However, the role was already filled, and I was placed on the "waiting list" to fill in just in case something happened. Well, something happened. And I got the role! The bad news was that I got the part only three days before the show's opening and I had a lot of lines to memorize. Everyone else had months to practice, and I had three days!

I studied like I've never studied before. I was so excited to be on the stage in front of a live audience. I wanted to be the star, even though I was just a supporting star. Wow, maybe a big Hollywood producer would happen to be in my small little high school audience, discover me, and put me on the silver screen. Just maybe, right?

I now know the stress I was feeling was cortisol and adrenaline rushing through my veins—the good stress that causes us to be productive and focused. This is how we get results, and hopefully, ones can be proud of for years to come.

So back to the story, and it didn't end well. Not even close. This particular play, my fellow actors and actresses had a lot hinging on my opening lines as I walked across the stage to hand a girl a letter. I had a long speech, literally a paragraph, which would set up all the action in the scenes to come. So finally, my big chance came! I walked across the stage and handed the girl the letter, and then my mind went blank. Completely blank like a brand-new dry erase board. I looked at her with that look that all actors dread, muttered "Here" as I gave her the letter, and then hurried off the stage. All the other actors suddenly had to become very creative improvisers. As it turns out, they all were great at improv, and the play went well despite my one-line or rather one-word debut. Heck, I even received an award called "Honorable Mention" I suppose it's because I mentioned something on the stage?

As anxious and upset as I was by my flubbing the lines, I remembered one of the most important things my mother taught all of us in the family: *"Life is 10% what happens to you and 90% how you react."*

I forgot my line in my moment on stage, and that's the 10% happening to everyone else. How everyone reacted was what actually saved the performance! That was the 90%! Good job, everybody!

How about you? What is happening right now in your own life, and how is your *reaction* affecting your stress?

While we reflect on important homilies that our parents have taught us, how about this familiar statement?

"Life is short."

Surely it is much too short for tension headaches, depression, ulcers, fatigue, and panic attacks. All of which are associated not just with stress-inducing events, but even more with how we are *reacting* to those stressors in our lives!

Now it's time for a little test called the *Life-Event Stress Test* or also known as *The Holmes & Raye Stress Scale*, borrowed from the American Institute of Stress.[4]

Remember, it's not the event itself, but how you react to it that makes all the difference. Just check the items as they apply to your life at this time.

THE LIFE-EVENT STRESS TEST

	Death of a spouse or child	100
	Divorce	73
	Marital separation	65
	Jail term	63
	Death of close family member	63
	Personal injury or illness	53

	Marriage	50
	Fired at work	47
	Marital reconciliation	45
	Retirement	45
	Change in family member's health	44
	Pregnancy	40
	Sex difficulties	39
	Addition to family	39
	Business readjustment	39
	Change in financial state	38
	Death of a close friend	37
	Change of position at work	36
	Apply for loan or mortgage	30
	Son or daughter leaving home	29
	Trouble with in-laws	29
	Outstanding personal achievement	28
	Spouse begins or stops work	26
	Starting or finishing school	26
	Change in living conditions	25
	Revision of personal habits	24
	Trouble with boss	23
	Change in work hours, conditions	20
	Change in residence	20
	Change in schools	20
	Change in recreational habits	19
	Change in church, social activities	19
	Loan for minor purchase (car, furniture)	17
	Change in sleeping habits	16
	Change in eating habits	15
	Vacation	13
	Minor law violations	11

(Notice that good, as well as bad things, are on this list. Good things can cause a stress response as well as depending on how you react to them.)

Now add up your points of all the items you checked. Your total score is_____

According to statistics, if your score totals 300 or more, you have a nearly 80% chance of getting sick in the near future. If you scored 150-299, then you have a 50% chance of illness. If you scored less than 150, you stand less than a 30% chance of illness.

So how did you do on this life event stress test? Was your score higher or lower than anticipated?

Remember, even if your score was in the good range, how you *react* to the stress event makes a significant difference!

When writing this chapter, I took this important test and scored a 155. My stressors were the trials and tribulations of growing a speaking and coaching practice. Why did I choose this path? I love helping others reach their own well-being goals, and we all need a nice reduction to our physical and mental stress, don't we? My profession is as much psychological as it is physical, so finding the right balance between the two is often a challenge. Also, I recently lost my Aunt Frieda and good friend Cody in the same timeframe. That's a lot of pressure! However, I know that it's how I handle the pressure that makes all the difference. Making deals with companies or losing them all amount to the 10% of what is happening. My reaction is the 90%. I believe that my calm spirit and confidence in striving to make the next deal a winning deal will balance the stress. In my life, the difference is giving my spirit continually to God as a source of comfort, strength, and calmness.

I love the verse in the Old Testament: *"You will keep him in perfect peace, whose mind is stayed on You, because he trusts in You."* Isaiah 26:3

This is an essential part of the formula for living free from the harmful effects of stress. In fact, I utilize prayer and meditation as my top recommended strategies for dealing with the effects of stress. You may call this meditative reflection "mindfulness," a state where you don't ignore the stress but rather think of positive ways to react to it. Simply live in the moment, forgetting what's behind you and not worrying about what lies ahead. Focus on the present. Right here and right now, clearing your mind of everything else. And be thankful. Give thanks to God for every blessing in your life and do this regularly every day.

Notice at the top of the life event test list, among the most stressful events is losing a loved one close to you. In 2005, my beloved grandmother Myrtle died. It was a great loss, but she had lived a long good life and was a great example for all of us. Then in 2007, my mother died just ten days before Christmas. She passed away suddenly in her sleep due to a blood clot to her heart. Then in 2010, my grandfather died. In 2011 both my other grandmother and my stepfather died. Finally, my father died in 2015. In just nine years, I lost every family member older than my generation. It's a tragic fact of life that we all must bear with the passing of loved ones.

As you can see on the Life-Event Test list, death is among the most stressful things in life. After my sisters and I attended funeral after funeral, we learned how to handle a lot of adversity. I bet if I took the Life-Event Stress Test then, my score would have been a 300! However, I believe we are all stronger for it; the sadness and the struggle enabled us to grow personally as we trusted God to bring us through. That verse in Isaiah remains my personal *healing* verse for all events, especially the major ones.

How about you? Do you have a healing verse or power statement from someone you admire? Maybe your parent or grandparent shared a pearl of wisdom into your life that you hang on to, just like my mother's 10%/90% rule for handing stress. You may take that one if you can't recall pearls of wisdom for yourself. It works! In fact, anything will work that's positive and has high sentimental value to you. Just remember to pass it on! If you benefit from something, chances are someone else will too!

Stress levels are also kept at a low healthy level when we exercise regularly. Remember I told you before, sitting is the new smoking! Many of us dislike or avoid exercise because it's something we "have to do." No, exercise is an *outlet* for the pent-up stress that has been building in you since you woke up this morning, got the kids ready for school, fought traffic to work and back, and struggled to meet work deadlines—all while wondering what to make for dinner. Many mistakenly think, "I'll hit the gym for five hours this weekend to make-up for all my gym-time missed this week." My friends, the body doesn't work like that! That's like saying, "I haven't eaten all week, so I'll hit the buffet on Saturday!"

Everyone has 20 minutes every day that otherwise would have been devoted to the evening news or even *Netflix*! Instead, go for a brisk walk. Yes, it can be as simple as just walking! Just do it, and your body will thank you by rewarding you with low-stress levels and amazing sleep!

• BREAKING IT DOWN •

Remember, the ergonomics of stress is not in how we ACT, but it is all in how we REACT.

What is one stress-related event in which you know you could have REACTED differently?

_____

_____

_____

_____

_____

What is one physical activity that you can begin today (and everyday) that you enjoy?

_____

_____

_____

_____

_____

When you face trials and tribulations, what is one source you turn to for comfort in handling that stress?

_____

_____

_____

_____

_____

CHAPTER TWO

Ergonomics of Body Improvement

FIRST, I'D LIKE to apologize to all of you reading this book. I lied. I didn't mean to, and it was not intentional. Every chapter is supposed to be independent of each other. It's great when you are short on time, find a chapter heading that interests you, and tackle it. However, the last chapter was about stress and its impact on your body, and this one is about body improvement.

So, therefore, you should really read chapter 1 before reading this one. I'll be making references to chemicals in your body that are well explained in the previous chapter, and I want to be sure *everyone* is on the same track with me on this one.

In short, if you don't read any other chapter in this book but this one, and the one previous, it will be enough to be a *game-changer* in your life.

We all have stress. Cortisol reigns in America and the world today, especially in recent times with the Coronavirus pandemic. If we had a contest to determine the winner of the number one chemical in our lives today, it's cortisol by a wide margin. We have choices to make, and the right choices should lead to a healthy balance of stress chemicals, but today we have too many choices and too much pressure placed on our success, that the balance is out of whack with detrimental consequences. As a result, the chemical imbalance causes degenerative diseases that kill us at earlier stages in life.

The goal for all of us here is to create more balance of these stress chemicals. Therefore, we need to focus on and hopefully change four facets in our lives:

1) Our *attitudes*
2) What we *eat*
3) Our level of *fitness*
4) The *numbers* that we must consider to gauge and follow our bodies' health.

Let's examine each one of these as it relates to chemical exchange in our bodies:

Our Attitude

Remember in the last chapter where my mom (via Chuck Swindoll, *Focus on the Family* taught us the 10%/90% rule: that life (and stress) is 10% what happens to you and 90% how you respond? Well, what determines your "altitude?" How high do you want to go up? Your attitude will determine that every time. I've never really been a big believer in energy. I'm referring to the energy you can "feel" from someone else, not the endless supply your

4-year-old displays. It's supposed to be like this "sixth sense" that you have when you are alone in the elevator with a stranger, and somehow you either feel safe or unsafe in those few moments. Just in case, though, I propose having a good "elevator speech" in either case. Try saying something so that you and the stranger are not, well, strangers. Both you and the former stranger are picking up each other's attitudes, affecting your whole interaction.

That's a minor example, but what if it's your spouse, co-worker, or boss you are dealing with? Then it's something entirely different! I know it is difficult to "leave your problems at home," but so many of us don't. We bring our work problems home and our home problems to work and expend energy and build up stress in talking to co-workers (or employees) about our problems with the spouse or our teenager (*who, of course, knows everything*).

My challenge to you is to commit to never bring your problems to work. Why? Because it affects your attitude and that of those around you. You, as a leader, never intend to have a negative impact around the office. I believe leaders consistently want the best for and expect the best performance from everyone. However, your body language talks much more than what our mouths say, and that sends ripple effects to everyone around you.

Make a new commitment: Smile. Your attitude is *always* a choice, even if your circumstances reflect otherwise. One benefit is that your positive attitude will uplift both you and those around you. In physiologic terms, both the act of smiling and seeing a smile has been shown to increase the serotonin in the bloodstream. Since higher serotonin decreases levels of cortisol and adrenaline, you will have less body stress. A negative attitude will have the opposite effect, raising cortisol, lowering serotonin, and bringing everyone down both in mood and body function. Leaders are winners! Make sure your attitude reflects a winning attitude and watch your productivity soar!

In this area, I honestly didn't smile enough. I used to hold my head up high and try to maintain good eye contact with everyone I met as a show of confidence. I always used to think, just hold your head up, stand tall, and your confidence in yourself and others will spread. That's not what happened. Instead, folks who didn't know me well would ask if I was arrogant and self-centered. When I discovered this about myself, the change was immediate. Now I smile more each time I encounter others, and while they are looking or not, I always strive to make that conscious effort. Here's what made the big change, not just the smile but also my *attitude* behind the smile. Too often, I brought my problems and anxious thoughts with me and rarely smiled. I couldn't. It's literally impossible to do! Now instead, I focus on my blessings, my hope in God and others, and making someone else feel uplifted. That shift in my thinking has led to an improved attitude and an authentic smile, not a "faked" one (*which anyone can see right through*).

Speaking of smiling, I must reveal a pet-peeve of mine. Raise your hands if you have ever had someone take your picture and say, "Okay, on the count of three, *smile!* One, Two, Three, snap!" Now keep your hands up if you had a terrific smile, and the picture was simply perfect! I have two things to say. First, why are you raising your hands? I can't see them, so put them down. You probably look silly if you are anywhere in public. Second, if you are the one taking the picture, stop counting and start joking! Say anything that would be humorous, and you will get an authentic smile (*I think laughing pictures come out better— my opinion*). I have one friend whose pictures always come out with a genuine smile. His secret? He pictures in his mind everyone naked. Hey, it works! Try it!

Awe laughter. What a great word! *Laughter.* The act of laughing because of something seen or heard. We don't laugh enough, but we all should! If there is one word that consistently elevates the spirit and gives us a positive attitude, it's laughter. Here's why: Laughter releases endorphins, which are natural painkillers. You simply cannot think about things that cause you anxiety and laugh at the same time. But the flip side is also true too. When you are laughing, you cannot still be anxious. Here's another simple fact: the brain cannot process your anxious thoughts while you read out loud. Therefore, if laughing makes you forget your pain and reading aloud makes you forget your pain, why aren't we reading comic strips out loud or joke books? I believe this is why funny sitcoms are so popular, especially at night. It's the end of the day, and most Americans want to forget about their long day at work, so they tune in the *"The Big Bang Theory"* or classics like *"I Love Lucy."* Hey, it works! However, we should also be laughing at 7:30 a.m., 10:23 a.m., 12:17 p.m., 1:33 p.m., 3:56 p.m., and 5:06 p.m. too! If you are like most people, you work with other people and people are an endless humor source. Therefore, share some clean jokes (*dirty jokes work too, but we aren't in the third grade anymore!*) or tell a funny story about something that happened to you. This is where laughter helps create positive, meaningful relationships, and we all need more of that!

Frequently when I do a workshop for a group of people, I start with something funny and light-hearted, such as *any* YouTube video featuring cats. It doesn't matter what cat video you show. It *will* be funny. This strategy simply puts everyone's minds at ease, and I believe it gives me an instant bond with my audience. Joel Osteen is an accomplished practitioner of this strategy. The first few words of every one of his sermons start, "I like to start with something funny" followed by a good positive joke.

We all have stressful moments in our lives that become hilarious true stories that we can share with others. Here's a funny story that happened to me, but it was not amusing at the time! Today I love public speaking. The larger the crowd, the more excited I become! However, if you ask folks what their greatest fear is, it is almost always public speaking. Well, that *used* to be me. When I was in college, I became a youth pastor for a small church in Austin, Texas. After I'd been there a couple of years, the pastor asked me to deliver the sermon on a Sunday evening. The church was small, but on this particular evening, the place was packed. It seems that every member decided to invite their friends, their friend's kids, their friend's aunt, uncle, and Cousin Ed! I remember seeing faces I've never seen before. This was my very first time to speak to such a large crowd—or any crowd! Was I nervous? Understatement!

If you asked me to put on a cow suit and jump into a pool of piranhas, I would not have been more nervous than that night. I studied hard but could not get a good flow to my sermon from memory. Then someone suggested I write notes and tape them on the back of my Bible. That way, I can easily reference my notes from the podium without anyone noticing. It was a brilliant and simple solution, but guess what? No podium! No problem, I thought, I'm resourceful and still hold the Bible and turn it over and to see the taped notes without making it obvious. So, I regained my confidence.

Just as the service was about to start, one of the deacons asked me to help move a heavy table out of the room to allow for more chairs. Since I was a young, strong man, I always got asked to move heavy objects. This particular table had a jagged edge that caught the zipper to my trousers and ripped it open. I remember the deacon saw what happened and said to me, "You better take care of that!" So, I ran into the restroom to fix the zipper, but the zipper's teeth were now misaligned and would not zip back up. Right then, I heard my name announced to go up on stage with my zipper very open! Remember, no podium! Nothing to hide behind except for one thing—my Bible with my taped notes! You should have seen me up there. I was standing like a frozen statue with my Bible covering my open zipper for 25 long, long minutes. I could not open the book or even look on the back to see my notes because the issue would have exposed itself! The feedback I received was even more funny. "Gunnar, you seemed so stiff up there! You should relax and move around more." Here's my favorite one, "What's the use of having your Bible up there if you never open the thing?" I thought to myself *if you only knew*. Well, no one ever knew except the deacon, who stood in the back, holding back his laughter. I will never forget seeing his face in the back of the room, which was so beat red because there were times he almost couldn't contain himself.

It's a funny story now, and I thank God for it! Why? Because that event totally eradicated any fear of public speaking that I had or will ever have! Also, I discovered even under those odd circumstances that I could speak. Since that day, I have had the honor of speaking to hundreds of audiences with boldness, confidence, charisma, and a good zipper! Hooray!

I had an attitude of gratitude for the potentially embarrassing event. It is easy to be grateful and possess a positive attitude when things are going great, but that's not reality. Times will get tough. They will get rough. They will seem to overwhelm you. Here is the choice we all got to make: how will we handle it? One of my favorite authors John Tesh, the well-known for his radio broadcast *"Intelligence for Your Life,"* has said, "There's one thing that all researchers agree upon on my show when it comes to sustainable happiness without money: gratitude. They all recommend keeping a gratitude journal. It's a powerful tool. And it's simple. You take five minutes each day to write down things that lifted you, the things you took for granted, or just the fact your wife held that welcome home kiss for a second longer than usual."[5]

Therefore, keep an attitude journal. You will reflect on more of the things that matter and remember the ones that can create entertaining stories later!

What We Eat

Nutrition. We love that word, right? My sister has a six-year-old and a four-year-old at the time I'm writing this book. They love their vegetables. They love broccoli, especially! They would usually say, "Mom, skip the cheese; we love it raw!" They also love eating raw cauliflower and all those green leaves like kale and spinach. Then the moment she wants to reward them with a dessert like ice cream, they cry and pout, usually shoving the ice cream onto the floor and running far away from the table.

Yes, today is "opposite day," and the above story is true exchange the references to veggies with dessert, and you get the picture.

Are we as adults any different than my little toddlers?

According to the USDA, typical American diets exceed the recommended intake levels or limits in four categories: calories from solid fats, refined grains, sodium, and saturated fats. Furthermore, nearly 1000 calories per day we consume are added fats and sweeteners!

Americans eat less than the recommended amounts of vegetables, fruits, whole-grains, dairy products, and oils. Plus, Americans consume 90% more sodium than is recommended for a healthy diet. By reducing sodium we eat by 1200 mg per day, we could save up to $20 billion per year in medical costs! Fast food is a huge culprit! Since the 1970's number of fast-food restaurants has more than doubled. Fast food tends to be over-fried, over-salted and lacks fresh vegetables and grains necessary for proper nutrition. But we eat there anyway because, well, it's fast.[6]

If you must go to a fast-food restaurant for lunch or any meal, here are some healthier options that will reduce your waist-size and stress-level:

- Salad Bar Restaurants (like Salida) – One of the healthiest fast serve alternatives to cheeseburgers and fries. You can eat here every day and lose weight! You are in complete control of what you put it, which is important, so you know what you are eating.
- Wendy's – Wendy's has far more healthy salad options today than they did a few years ago. Avoid the temptation for the burger and shake.
- Chick-fil-A – You can have skinless chicken tenders here but skip the sauce!
- In-and-Out Burger – If you are craving a burger, go for one wrapped in lettuce, and you just skipped the most fat-producing part of the meal—the bread!

Obesity

According to NIH, National Institute of Diabetes and Digestive and Kidney Diseases, data from 2014 indicates that over 78 million adults in the United States are overweight or obese. That's nearly 2 in 3 adults! Our kids are not far behind that scary statistic, with 12.5 million considered overweight or obese, or 1 in 6 children.[7]

The Center for Disease Control (CDC) predicts that by 2030, half of all adults (115 million) in the US will be obese. Obesity-related illness, including chronic disease, disability, and death, is estimated to carry an annual cost of $190.2 billion. The annual cost for merely being overweight is $524 for women and $432 for men; annual costs for being obese is $4,879 for women and $2,646 for men.[8]

Scary stuff, right? Can we change all of this? Yes, one family at a time, we can teach our kids to eat right by leading as examples! Here are some quality recommendations:

For dinners, prepare a one-skillet meal. All you need are fresh veggies and a protein, and your body will thank you for it! In fact, with the right seasonings, even your kids will be gobbling up this nutritious meal! Mix in green peppers, onions, spinach, mushrooms with a protein like chicken, steak, fish, and voila! That's a fantastic dinner that cost you very little. You served a healthy dish to your family, and as a parent, you feel like a gold medalist!

Also, take your vitamins! All vitamins are welcome, but the B Vitamin family especially are the key to stress relief. The B Vitamins include pantothenic acid, niacin, folic acid, B-6, and B-12. As a group, these are the "stress-relief vitamins" since they support adrenal hormones production. The most effective way to take B vitamins is in the form of B Complex, and when supplemented together, they offer the greatest benefits.

You can always supplement your body with a Vitamin cocktail in the pill form, but don't skimp on the foods that are nutrient-rich in Vitamin B. Here are just a few of the foods we should be eating daily, unless you have a food allergy: salmon, dairy, eggs, grains, and lots of vegetables, lentils, lima beans, bananas avocados.

Here's another great idea; drink your vitamins! Many health stores now carry the vitamin-packed protein powder mixes that I've been making for years. Just add 1-2 scoops of the powder mix with a banana, avocado, and blueberries, and mix it in with almond milk. It's so delicious that you may develop a new habit! I call it my Stress Shake.

Remember that diet is only half of the equation. To lose or maintain an ideal weight, you have to burn more calories than you consume each day. It's that ergonomic balance again. So, walk the dog an extra mile, take the stairs (walking up is much better exercise than walking down), and do whatever it takes to stop sitting! As I told you before (*and will again, you can count on it!*), sitting is the new smoking today, and it's killing us! That leads us into another favorite word—Fitness!

Our Fitness

If you are like so many folks I come across in conversation, then you imagine gyms and fitness centers as terrifying places full of "meat-heads" walking around, flexing their biceps, while you are looking at your biceps and wondering if the muscle is even there. For those in the "obese" category, it's even more the fear of judgment from the other gym-goers. What will they think when they see me?

Let me share with you what the other gym-goers are probably thinking. More often than not, they probably think, "I've been there" and "Glad to see them here and make the right steps to improve their lives." This isn't the playground when we were all kids where the local "bullies" would stand around and make fun of others they didn't like. We are all adults now with a more mature mindset, so dismiss the old thinking of "What will others think?" and change it to "I believe everyone is rooting for me!"

Also, guess what? You don't have to go to a gym to become fit! Just do something you enjoy! I love racquetball and weight-lifting. Some love swimming, walking their dogs. Whatever it is you do, do it! Regular exercise gets your heart rate up to help cardiac fitness (remember the heart is a muscle and needs exercise too!)

Most importantly, when you exercise, you give your built-up stress of the day an outlet! Notice I said, "stress of the day" and not "stress of the week, month, year, etc." Do something involving activity every day! Not only will you become more fit, but you will also find yourself sleeping better at night!

While we're on the subject, a quick word about sleep is important here. Proper sleep is one of the keys to fitness. Deep sleep (called REM, or Rapid Eye Movement) produces the same endorphins as smiling or laughing (see above in ATTITUDE). These endorphins, in turn, reset the cortisol/serotonin balance back to healthy levels. If you are not getting enough sleep—trying to finish that last report or binge-watching that the last episode of *Game of Thrones*—then you are not allowing the body to clear the day's build of stress hormones. But even if you are too busy, the good news is you don't need eight unbroken hours of sleep a night (although that's ideal!). A "power nap" of as little as twenty minutes during the day will go a long way toward balancing stress too.

But back to exercise! The lack of physical activity in our health-conscious nation is dismal. In fact, less than 5% of adults participate in 30 minutes of physical activity each day. That means if we have over 300 million Americans, only 15 million of us are physically active. Yet, we have more fitness center choices than ever before. Just to name a few.

- YMCA – Every city (almost), large and small, has a Y. The name has been around for nearly 100 years, and it's an American staple. One of the most familiar songs of this nation is Y-M-C-A. You just started singing or humming the song. I heard you! I also noticed some of your arms waving back and forth. Go ahead, spread the news! Somewhere, close to you, is a YMCA fully equipped with weights, a swimming pool, a basketball court, and maybe even a racquetball room. And the price? Less than what you probably spend at Starbucks in a single week!

- Formal gym and fitness centers – Some are designed and upscale, such as LA Fitness and Life Time Fitness. Although these tend to be more expensive, there is a range of costs and packages that should suit your style and budget. Find a fitness center that "fits" you and commit to going at least three times a week. Most of these gyms are even open 24 hours, so just go for it! And take your kids! Just don't forget to get your sleep.

- Stationary bicycle gyms – Biking is a healthy and popular alternative. Cycling outdoors can be dangerous, but more gyms are popping up that offer stationary cycling programs. Beware, though, these tend to be scheduled classes (no self-paced cycling), and some of them can be grueling for a new exerciser.

- Dance and combined dance/exercise programs – The most popular classes in this category are Zumba, Pilates, and Tae Bo. There are free-standing schools all over the community, and the YMCA (and most other gyms) also offers a range of classes. These are a great and fun way to start moving those ossified muscles!

- Yoga Studios/Classes – I hope this isn't a stretch for you, but if you wake up at night with muscle cramps or always feeling "tight" in your legs, then Yoga is an excellent choice for increasing your flexibility. For many years I was a practicing massage therapist, and I can tell you that when I stretched my clients, the most flexible were those involved in a regular Yoga class. If you are worried about what others may think of you, start in the back of the class, and watch what everyone else is doing. Then you will gain more confidence and eventually be a yoga leader for others to follow. That statement isn't a "stretch" at all!

Get your kids started in the exercise routine, so it becomes a way of life as they get older. Otherwise, your kids will be sitting in their room, playing video games, and not getting any physical activity. Statistically, children now spend on average seven hours or more in front of the screen (TV or computer), and only six states require physical education in every grade. Therefore, it is up to you, the parent, to take them to a place to fulfill their need for physical activity.

Are you ready for a little fitness test? Go ahead; it will reassure you that you can probably do more than you think you can!

- Can I walk a mile in 15 minutes or less?
- Can I carry a couple of grocery bags from the grocery store to my car without difficulty?
- Can I climb a flight of stairs without heavy breathing?
- Can I perform the plank for at least 45 seconds? It's a core strength exercise that requires you to lie face down, mounted up on your elbows, and push up on your toes, so your body is stiff as a board.

If you can perform these tasks, you can also perform any physical requirements at the gym or fitness center. Furthermore, if you picture gyms full of muscle-bound meatheads walking around and showing off their muscles every 5 minutes in the mirror, think again. People just like you, regardless of what shape you are in, can be found at the gym. Once you walk into one of these fitness centers, you will be glad to be there!

Our Numbers

When you go to the doctor, without fail they always want to talk about your numbers. For many that is a terrifying encounter! In fact, I know many friends and family members who can't remember the last time they had a wellness check-up. Why? They don't want to hear any bad news, and they are sure the bad news comes from the numbers that the doctor will inevitably want to see.

So, what are these numbers? Well, stay tuned! One of the best ways to encounter stress in our lives is with facts. Knowing the truth is always the best medicine to relieve the stress of not knowing!

Therefore, know these numbers and formulas. Memorize them and then go ahead and make an appointment with your doctor. I know it's nerve-racking, but you will have that steady stream of unnecessary stress keeping you awake at night until you do this. Here's the good news: once you know where you are physically, you can make the right decisions to make some important changes. That, my friends, will prolong your life, give you a more positive attitude, and make you smile more!

The main numbers that the doctor will focus on are 1) Heart Rate, 2) Blood Pressure, 3) Cholesterol, 4) Blood Sugar (or Glucose), and 5) Testosterone.

Notice that weight is not on the list. Your doc will certainly weigh you and give you a lecture if you are overweight or obese. But the absolute number of pounds is not a great indicator of health, nor is Body Mass Index, or BMI. Remember that the basketball icon Michael Jordan was considered overweight based on his BMI. That is because the scale cannot factor in things like lean muscle mass, body fat percentage, or even the size of your skeleton (yes, some people really are "big-boned"). And people tend to obsess over the weight numbers. Look at the diet and exercise commercials on television. "I lost 15 pounds! I lost 60 pounds! etc. etc." But what happened to your fitness? Or your blood sugars? And is there a difference in fitness between 150 and 155 pounds?

(Spoiler, the answer is *not necessarily.*)

Now onto the numbers you really need to know:

Ergonomics of Body Numbers

Heart Rate

According to the American Council of Exercise, you need at least 150 minutes per week of moderate exercise. That's the key to having a healthy heart.

How many times per minute does your heartbeat? This is the single most important question in fitness because ultimately, your heart is the most critical organ in keeping your body functioning. Its job is to get oxygen-rich blood out to the tissue and the brain. If it beats too fast (tachycardia), then the red blood cells do not have enough time to get their full share of oxygen to deliver. Also, since the heart is just a muscle, beating too fast can lead to tiredness or even muscle injury. If it beats too slow (bradycardia), the blood may not be getting to the muscles fast enough to give them the oxygen they need to do their work. Your heart rate should change according to what you are doing. At rest, it should be somewhere between sixty to ninety beats per minute. So roughly one beat per second is considered a normal rate at rest. When you are exercising, the rate will typically go up. It has to because your muscles and other organs need more oxygen to have the energy to do their work. The range for exercise heart rates will vary by age, but in general, the heart should not go up above 120 beats per minute for more than a short time. Part of a more effective cardio workout is to keep your heart rate above 100 beats/minute for about twenty minutes.

The resting heart rate is the most sensitive indicator of your level of fitness. A better heart rate means your heart is in better shape. Like any muscle, it can be trained to do the work more effectively, so it doesn't have to beat rapidly. The more you work it out, the stronger it gets. The stronger your heart is then the less effort it will take to pump the blood around the body. Your goals should always be a heart rate of fewer than 75 beats/minute.

Blood Pressure

Your blood pressure indicates the force of circulating blood against the walls of your blood vessels. In simple terms, where the resting heart rate is a measure of the heart's fitness, the blood pressure is a measure of the rest of the body's fitness to circulate the all-important blood. The readings here are similar to a fraction, with one number on top and the other on the bottom. The top number represents Systolic pressure, representing the pressure against the arterial walls when the heart muscle contracts. This number is a gauge of how hard the heart itself is working on getting the blood out. The bottom number is the Diastolic pressure, which measures pressure in-between heartbeats. It measures the function of the blood vessels in the arms, legs, and trunk in simple terms. Higher systolic pressure means that the heart has to push harder to circulate (maybe because the muscle is damaged and ineffective or there is a blockage close to the heart). A higher systolic means that the distant blood vessels can't function properly to move the blood along the pipeline, possibly due to a clot or calcification of the vessels ("hardening of the arteries").

A normal individual will have a reading of 120/80 or less. In general, the lower each of those numbers, respectively, the better shape you are in. On the flip side, the higher those numbers, the worse shape you are in. If left untreated, high blood pressure can lead to a heart attack or even a stroke. Blood pressure is normally elevated in times of stress and can be elevated temporarily by eating large amounts of salt. But the longer the blood pressure stays high, the worse the risk that it cannot return to normal. The good news is that blood pressure can be very responsive to diet changes and especially fitness and exercise.

Cholesterol

The blood cholesterol level is roughly a gauge of how much fat (lipid) is in the bloodstream. Everybody has some and needs some, so be careful about fat-depleting diets that claim to bring your cholesterol level down to nothing. That's impossible. Normal cholesterol should be less than about 200 at fasting (no eating for 24 hours). High cholesterol levels are associated with heart disease, possibly by creating clots or thickening blood in the heart's arteries.

We now all know that two types of lipids circulate in the bloodstream. There are Low-Density Lipids (LDLs) and High-Density ones (HDLs). There are also complex fatty sugars called triglycerides, which may be associated with types of Diabetes (see next section).

When you visit your doctor, ask for a blood lipid test, or even a full blood panel. The LDLs are the bad lipids, and the HDLs are the good lipids. When you eat an excess of bad calories from complex sugars or corn syrups or high contents of animal fats or drink alcohol, your body turns these into LDLs. On the other hand, HDLs come from simple sugars, carbohydrates like pasta or bread or vegetable oils. The HDLs are processed into useful energy for the body (this is why you need both HDLs and cholesterol), but the LDLs cannot be processed as efficiently and so are stored as fat.

When tested, you want to see triglycerides less than 150, and your LDL under 100mg. Your HDL should be at least 40ml or higher. If you see your HDL under 35 and your LDL count over 250, you will need to make some nutrition changes right away!

Diabetes (DM)

In simple terms, diabetes is the inability of the body to process sugar effectively. There are two types of diabetes. Type 1 ("childhood" or "insulin-dependent") tends to be due to a problem with the genes. Type 2 ("adult" or "insulin-dependent") is acquired by years of bad diet and poor fitness, although there may be a family or a genetic tendency towards it. Type 2 is positively associated with obesity and is an epidemic in America these days. According to Bill Phillips, a leading expert in the fitness industry, millions of Americans have Diabetes, and many of us have it undiagnosed! That's not good because Diabetes is the leading cause of blindness, kidney problems, heart disease, and stroke.

The detection of DM is very easy. Your doctor simply orders a fasting blood sugar (or glucose). Like the cholesterol above, it must be done before you have eaten anything because the blood level sugar is so sensitive to sugar intake. Even if you sneak a coffee with cream before the test, it can throw the values out of whack. A normal fasting sugar should be 100 mg/dl. These numbers are always being evaluated, and there is some push to define sugars between 80 and 100 mg/dl as "pre-diabetes" – a condition that may turn into type 2 DM without treatment.

I think it is best to consider yourself as always "pre-diabetic" in terms of your fitness and eating habits. There is no reason to wait until the diagnosis to start being more active, fit, and have better eating habits in terms of sugar, bread, fat, and alcohol intake. In fact, I've already given you a lot of good reasons to start right away. And remember that prevention is always cheaper and easier than treatment.

You may have seen the television ads talking about A1C or hemoglobin A1C. You do watch a lot of TV, don't you? Anyway, HgA1C is a test used if you are diagnosed with DM. It measures how "sugar-coated" your blood cells are and is an indirect reflection of how well your blood sugar is managed over a long period (it may take more than a month to change during treatment.) The level of HgA1C should be well below 5.7 percent, but there is nothing magical about the value. Unlike high cholesterol, triglycerides, LDLs, etc., the A1C doesn't cause the problem; it reflects it. So, stop watching the TV ads and start getting outside more! Start walking your dog and/or jogging to get that fitness in your life more before you have the problem.

Testosterone

We quite rightly associate the male sex hormone with men's health, but it's worth remembering that even women have levels of testosterone as it's important for normal function. Not only is this hormone related to maturation (and aging), but it most likely has an important effect on stress management in both sexes.

For men, the testosterone level is an important number. Low T is a condition for millions of men, and the signs and symptoms are usually the same: low sex-drive, possible erectile dysfunction, decreased muscle size, and fatigue. What numbers do you want to see here? Anything over 300 to 1000 mcg is good. Note that these numbers go down as you age, which the numbers high in your 20's and lower in your 40's. Testosterone is easy to supplement with options of gels, injections, and pill forms. You just need to check with your doctor to ask what's best for you.

These are the top five numbers you should know when you see your doctor. Knowing these numbers will give you peace of mind and could save your life. Now I know many of you have pre-existing conditions of high blood pressure, diabetes, etc. Therefore, your doctor will know what's best for you. Remember this. I've yet to encounter someone who decided to see their doctor for the first time in a long time who did not come out with more knowledge or hope of improving their bodies and numbers. They are usually glad they went and hopeful that they can make any necessary changes.

Excuses, Excuses

Are you still hesitant to start doing something physically active? Find a friend and make a commitment! The excuse I usually hear is "no one wants to walk their dogs with me" or "I have no one to work out with me." Have you asked anyone? You may be surprised to find your neighbor or someone who was using the same excuse! Here's another excuse I typically hear, "I don't have time! I have kids to feed, a 40-hour workweek, traffic to fight, and a dog and cat always fighting!" Here's my response, "No, you don't have the time *not* to work-out!" Then after they say, "Huh?" I reply to them that with just twenty minutes of cardio per day, you will be more productive in all the other things.

Here's why exercise is so important. When you become physically active, your serotonin, epinephrine, and acetylcholine spike up. These are the same chemicals needed for extra brain power and memory retention. A research study conducted by East Carolina University found that when kids performed 10-minute bursts of exercise throughout the day, such as jump rope, they were better at focusing on their homework. As a bonus discovery, the kids also behaved better in class! This, of course, translates the same for adults, who discover they can focus easier on important tasks and become more productive.

This all boils down to how you manage yourself throughout the day. Stay tuned; in Chapter 6, we tackle the Ergonomics of Time with a sound plan for you to maximize your day!

A Prime Example

In the final part of this chapter, I would like to share some facts I've recently learned about the longest-living people on Earth. Japan-ians are people who live in Japan. Yes, I know they are Japanese, not Japan-ians, but the word is fun to say! The Japanese are outliving everyone else in the world, especially those who live on the small island of Okinawa. There, the highest number of centurions are living and still working (might I add). What is their secret?

Well, they follow the Ergonomics of a Healthy Body! They maintain healthy attitudes, diets, and they continuously exercise. Their medical numbers are fantastic and many of them live to see years after their 100th birthday. These centenarians have healthy habits that they have practiced all their lives, and I'm sharing these secrets with you right now.

They Eat well. Very well. Our American diet consists of vegetables, only occasionally. Their diet is seven portions of vegetables, daily! Many of us do not even consume that much in a week, and we should! I know the thought of broccoli is not very appetizing, so be creative! Raw is always best when it comes to eating veggies, but you can boil them and add a sodium substitute. I believe one of our biggest struggles when it comes to eating is not during meals but when we sit in front of the TV. Potato chips are evil, so throw them out and replace them with cauliflower instead! Mix them up with some grapes, and you've got a nutritious snack that will never, ever, cause weight gain.

It's interesting that in Okinawa, the vegetable of choice is the sweet potato! They eat this more than any other food item, and benefit from it! However, they do not smother it with butter and brown sugar like we Americans. They eat sweet potatoes lightly baked or fried in vegetable oils with either no dressing or a soy-based sauce. They even eat them raw in slices, which preserves all the good vitamins (_remember the B complex? They are all there!_)

In America, we over-consume everything. But in Okinawa, no one eats until they are full. In fact, they eat until they are about 80% full, then they make it a point to stop right there. They take their time to eat. Remember, the experts tell us that it takes approximately 20 minutes after you start eating for the stomach to tell the brain, "I'm full." No wonder most of us are overweight! Most people "woof" down their meals in two minutes, much less 20 minutes. The bottom line? Eat slower and stop eating when you feel *almost* full.

They exercise, and they don't call it exercise. They call it "climbing the stairs to deliver some goods" since there are no elevators. Okinawans are constantly moving, constantly walking, and never sitting for long durations of time. A stationary body stays stationary, and a body in motion stays in motion. So, keep moving! Take the stairs, take walking breaks. And find a fun activity! Your body will thank you, and you will live longer for it!

They hug. I have never seen someone with a bad attitude go around hugging others. There is always a sincere smile and a sincere embrace when it comes to hugging, and it's probably the main reason people live so long in Okinawa. Rarely are the elderly feeling lonely and depressed there! They are so close to their families that they know they are loved.

> *"Age doesn't matter, unless you're cheese."* Billie Burke

There is always more to it than that, right? I'd love to fly all of my friends to Okinawa and ask the inhabitants a million questions. However, since many Okinawans are not fluent in English, find a centurion right here in good ole' USA! You will discover so much wisdom, and usually, these old folks are more than willing to share their secrets for long living. That's what John Tesh did at a dinner party. He sat down with Sadie, who was 102 years old at the time. Here's their conversation:

JT: What's the secret to long life?
Sadie: Be kind and forgive people.

JT: Do you have any special healthy diet and exercise routine?

Sadie: I eat when I'm hungry. I walk, and I go to sleep when I'm sleepy.

JT: You said you were married for sixty years. What's the secret to a great marriage?

Sadie: Marry a good one.

Amazing. So simple, isn't it? And that's the point of this chapter, well this whole book. Maybe its title should have been "The Ergonomics of Simplification" because the purpose is to help others live with less stress and more joy!

So, let's review Sadie's advice for living a long healthy life: Be kind and forgive people. Don't hold grudges, try to get even, or try to take revenge. Just let go of the offense and forgive. Be kind to others, and they will be kind to you. So simple. So healing. So Godly.

What else did Sadie say she does? She eats when she is hungry and sleeps when she is sleepy. In short, she listens to her body! Researchers tell us that we should eat once every three hours, and these should not be large meals, but smaller ones. That keeps are blood numbers where they should be and keeps our minds sharp.

Regarding sleeping, there's also more research coming out in favor of power naps. Just 20 minutes naptime in the middle of the day (when your body is feeling sleepy) is much better than drinking a Coke or a shot of caffeine. Sadie has learned an important lesson that perfectly fits body ergonomics, *the art of listening to your body!*

I once worked with a group fitness instructor who had the opposite body-philosophy. Her belief was, "just fight through it." One day she led a group of guys and girls through a very aggressive body workout. Everyone was sweat'n to the oldies! There was lots of hopping, jogging in place, jumping, and constant movement. What was wrong with the picture? The instructor was sick. She had a fever and should have been lying in bed and allowing her body to recover. Some of her close friends encouraged her to go home, it's just a fitness class, and someone else can lead it. Her reply? "No, I will be fine as long as I just fight through it!" Result? She died the next week. Her flu developed into pneumonia that proved untreatable. It's a dramatic example of what happens when we ignore what our bodies tell us.

•BREAKING IT DOWN•

1. When was the last time you had a wellness checkup? What were your numbers?

_____

_____

_____

_____

_____

2. Start a Gratitude Journal today. What will be your first entry?

_____

_____

_____

_____

_____

3. Find someone twice your age (or multiple times your age if you are a teenager) and talk to them! Listen closely, and you will learn timeless wisdom too! What is their secret to long life?

_____

_____

_____

_____

_____

CHAPTER THREE

Ergonomics of Work

EMPLOYEES HAVE IT made in today's world, and they don't even know it.

Let's rewind. About 80 years ago, even before the Great Depression, chairs were made of wood, un-sturdy, and did not recline. The working hours were long, and the pay was pennies, not dollars, by the hour.

You could get a massage, but it was unregulated in those days and mostly performed by untrained individuals. It wasn't until the 1970s that massage's influence started to grow, particularly among sports athletes. Besides, who could afford a massage even if you found a good therapist? According to Maslow's Hierarchy of Needs, basic needs always supersede luxury, and food on the table is more important than a good massage.

There existed the hard labor of employees for industrialists like Andrew Carnegie and his steel mill and John D. Rockefeller's oil derricks. Many movies and documentaries have been made on the extreme working conditions of that era's labor force. Today a good day's pay would be in the hundreds of dollars compared to a good day's pay back then of about 15 cents. Workers would get a break just long enough to smoke a cigarette. There was no bottled water back then. The labor force, hundreds of men, would be forced to drink from a single garden hose. The working world back then was a world absent of any ergonomics. Back then, the word wasn't even invented yet. It wasn't until after World War II that the real application of ergonomics started in efforts to improve aircraft design as it applies to limitations of the human body.

In the 1960s, ergonomics began to evaluate computer equipment and how we, as humans, interact with machines while sitting at a desk. In the USA, our focus has always been on the behavioral aspects of such interaction, while in Europe, the focus has been much more on human physiology. Today, the word "*Ergonomics*" ties in all three: engineering, psychology, and physiology. This is all to reduce the risk of health problems at the workplace. Yet our problems not only persist but are ever-growing![10]

According to the American Institute of Stress, medical issues tied to stress today are more evident than in the past. On an average workday, more than a million workers miss work due to stress-related complaints. Upwards of 75% of workers claim to be more stressed out than previous generations. Shockingly, work-related stress causes 120,000 deaths and costs in healthcare results in $190 billion every year! Work-place stress results from two leading causes: The first is leadership, which is covered in chapter 5 of this book. The second cause is the actual ergonomics of the office environment, the topic of this chapter. The type of questions that all leaders should be asking their workers are the following:

1. How many of you are experiencing neck and back pain resulting from sitting in your current chairs?

2. How many of you would prefer better nutritional sources through-out the workday?
3. How many of you would take part in some active exercise breaks if it was available?
4. What recommendations and suggestions do you have to make your day more enjoyable?

Employees must have a voice. They want to be heard and understood. They want to make sure that when they speak, someone is listening. The result? Their suggestions may cost an organization a little bit upfront and save a lot on the back end! Absenteeism costs our country billions and billions every year, with depression leading the cause of it![11]

I was recently talking to a lady who works at a major department store who spends most of her workday on her feet. She asked what I do for a living, and I mentioned I was writing this book. She then stopped me mid-sentence and said, "Oh my goodness! That's great! Thank you!" and she went on to start complaining about how tired her feet were by the end of the day and that most of her co-workers have had to "fake" a sickness day to get some needed FOB relief (*that means Feet On Bed, y'all*). Then she made an exaggerated comment, "I'd say that 99% of all injuries are predictable and preventable!" I simply disagree with this statement. Yes, I agree that most work-related injuries are preventable, but it's just not that high. I'm more comfortable with a 97% statistic. *That was funny, right?!*

According to Medical News Today, here's the ergonomic breakdown of well ... ergonomics at work for those who sit and stand all day.

Ergonomics of Prolonged Sitting

Sitting is normal. Too much sitting wreaks havoc on our backs. Edward Laskowski from the Mayo Clinic reports "too much sitting overall and prolonged periods of sitting also seem to increase the risk of death from cardiovascular disease and cancer."[12]

So here is how you should sit while working at your desk:

- Your computer monitor should be kept at arm's length
- Line up your head over your shoulders, shoulders over your hips.
- Rest comfortably on your hip bones *(the two you got in your tush)*
- Feet flat on the floor, with your knees and forearms parallel with the floor.
- Sit for a maximum of 40 minutes and take a standing/walking break to prevent strain.
- Use a sit/stand desk to help you alternate the two positions without work interruption.[13]

Sounds easy, right? It is very easy, but you have to consciously sit while being fully aware of your shoulders, chest, and feet. Practicing the correct standing and sitting postures will benefit your back in the long run!

- Your computer screen: Think about how unnatural a computer screen is for our eyes. You focused on two colors in the older days of computers: black background with lime green letters. Does anyone remember that? Today our computers contain over 16,777,216 colors![14]

Our eyeballs are sensitive organs that require proper care. I am very fortunate. All my life, I've been called "eagle eyes" because my vision was 20/10. Normal vision is 20/20, which means that you can see objects very clearly at 20 feet away.

My vision was even better, in which objects that most people could see at 10 feet, I could see at 20 feet. I loved showing off with my friends challenging them to read the list of ingredients on a label of soup from a distance of 20 feet away. They could read the name "Campbell's Soup," but I could read the contents' fine print!

Sadly, those days are gone as I'm now in my 40's. My sight has been reduced to 20/20, which really sucks! It's true, I've always been told that once you hit that age, your vision goes bye-bye!

I know everyone feels sorry for me about my fading vision, and I thank you for your empathy!! It does mean a lot! *Do I hear a violin serenading in the background?*

Here's the best way to prevent office eyestrain. Occupational Health & Safety tells us that it's best for your sitting posture and eye strain prevention if your screen is approximately two inches above your eye-level at the center of the screen. Plus, every 20 minutes or so, take your eyes off the screen and focus on an object at least 20 feet away. This allows your eyes to relax and reduces the possibility of headaches.[15]

One of the most ergonomically designed office environments I've ever seen is the NOC room at Southwest Airlines headquarters in Dallas, Texas. They called in a chair massage company I helped operate to come in and give some much-kneaded relief (*there I go again*) to their hard-working crew. This group of folks is responsible for scheduling all the pilots and flight attendants for all their planes daily, managing around 8,500 crew members. That's a lot of managing! Not to mention that number nearly doubles around the holiday season!

What made this place so ergonomically friendly? It was the entire ambiance of the room. If you ever get the chance, find a friend who works there to show you around. The room is huge, maybe the size of a small Walmart. The lighting is very subdued with dimly lit flat screens that are at least 50 inches each in diameter. Each workstation had its screen or set of screens that angled at 45 degrees towards the worker. Even the data on the screens is very eye friendly. Astonishingly, I don't remember seeing one scrap of paper *anywhere*! This area is in operation 24 hours every day, and the workers are there for 8-10-hour shifts.

That's one example of an organization that puts ergonomics to work so that employee-productivity is at its best. According to a study conducted by CBRE in an article called, "The Snowball Effect of Healthy Offices," when an organization gets the ergonomics of the office right, employees thrive. They conducted a study to measure the effectiveness of employee wellness and productivity by implementing five changes to their environment. These changes involved both environmental and health-related aspects. In the list below, the first two changes were environmental, followed by three health-related changes, and the percentage of performance improvement:

1. Natural Space – Placing plants around the office, increased 10%
2. Right Lighting -- Circadian lighting vs. old lighting, increased 12%
3. Healthy Nutrition – Avocado and spinach smoothie vs. donuts, increased 45%
4. Mental Balance – Mindfulness meditation and chair massage vs. stress tests increased 30%
5. Physical Exercise – Activity vs. no activity, increased 12%

Let's examine a little more closely why these small changes, which cost an organization very little, have such a powerful impact. After all, this is ergonomics at its core meaning, correct? *You are supposed to be nodding your head YES here!*

Plants are vital to our existence and have proven to have numerous health benefits and proven to ease headaches and stress. When I walk into an office environment with plants strategically placed, the first thing I think of is the word "inviting." Plants have a non-verbal ambiance that says, "You belong here! Welcome!" In fact, task performance went up 12%, and more than 70% of the workers felt happier and more energized! Indeed, plants are powerful messengers in home and office. I strongly encourage it, even though I failed Botany class. *I prefer plant-based meals, not plant-based courses!*

Having the right amount of lighting in your office makes all the difference. Does anyone remember the old days of office lighting? Envision a large space of cubicles with flickering fluorescent lights everywhere, accompanied by that annoying low hum or buzzing sound. Hell is much worse than that picture, but not by very much! Today, most office lighting utilizes either LED or circadian lighting, which are both better alternatives that lessen eye strain and tension headaches. Circadian lighting is designed to support the human circadian rhythm. If you break up the word "circadian," in Latin "circa" means "around" and "diem" means "day." Therefore, this lighting falls in sync with your body's clock, so to speak. In CBRE's group study, task performance increased by 12%, and over 70% felt happier and more energized.

Typically, companies will provide vending machines filled with chips and candy bars, or supply donuts for employees. Why? It's cheap, easy, and seemingly what workers want to help them fulfill breakfast or snack attacks. However, it's harmful and leads to obesity and poor performance. CBRE gave two control groups bad snack versus good snack, and here's what happened: The group with the donut-type foods and bottomless coffee performed poorly, and the ones with the healthy smoothie did better big time! Elizabeth C. Nelson, Head of the Healthy Offices research team, said, "with these kinds of results, it's amazing that water is not 'incentivized' more often, using fruit like berries or oranges, herbs like mint or lavender, and vegetables like cucumber."

As a result of better nutrition choices, the workers increased their performance by 45%. Nearly 80% felt more energized throughout the day, without experiencing a sugar-crash in the middle of the afternoon.

I have already referenced how positive a 15-minute chair massage can be for mental relaxation and mental balance. Mindfulness has boomed in the workplace in the past decade. It comes in many forms. Some companies choose to implement "mindful breaks" in which anyone can de-stress in a separate room or go for an outdoor walk. For a more structured approach, yoga is offered regularly, as well as mindfulness sessions and chair massage. These choices only require a few minutes of the workday, and remember, you do not want to sit a full hour at a time. Standing and walking breaks are *highly* encouraged for your physical and mental health. At CBRE, their workers discovered that their ability to be productive was up 30%, and more than 60% felt happier and more relaxed as a result of mindfulness breaks.

As for the breakdown of what was more popular among employees, regular chair massages ranked 68%, 32% ranked meditation, and 29% ranked yoga.

Yes, I'm going to repeat it. *Sitting is the new smoking!* CBRE confirmed the mounting evidence that the more you get up from your chair and move around, the better. Even as much as 32 times in the workday! In the next chapter, I offer some great stretches and simple exercises that anyone can do to get the blood moving but not the sweat pouring. In their study, CBRE went further by replacing regular chairs with medicine balls, stationary bikes, and even treadmills! They found that interaction increased, but productivity decreased. Medicine balls are fun to sit on and to bounce up and down but offer no back support. Treadmills are noisy and impossible to type on a keyboard and run at the same time. *However, it would make a great video on YouTube!* Everything has its place, and so does exercise equipment. I recommend offices to purchase a volume of these choices that's fitting to the size of your employee base, but in a separate room to encourage active movement. When CBRE implemented such active places, more than 75% of the employees used them through-out the day. Plus, productivity rose by 12%, and over 70% of employees felt healthier as a result.

What was the overall consensus? By making these changes over seven months, involving over a hundred participants, employees feel healthier, happier, and more productive. They loved coming to work (*surprise*) and feel a sense of accomplishment at the end of the day. Elizabeth Nelson stated that the costs associated with sickness and burnouts and employee turnover are significant expenses that could be drastically reduced or eliminated by introducing healthier offices.

Even more surprising is that participants were inspired to make similar changes in their personal lives following the study. They became more active and ate healthier at home. They called this "The Snowball Effect." Remember, it takes 21 days to start a new habit and to break old ones. This study was much longer than that, with unexpectedly positive results!

CBRE conducted this survey in collaboration with the University of Twente in Amsterdam. The results are groundbreaking, to say the least.[16]

Let's round all this practical information into GunnarT's top ten list. These are my daily top ten principles that you can do every day at work or at home. Here's the good news, most of these changes cost nothing—not even a dime. Only a change in office furniture will cost the organization money, such as switching out regular office furniture for sit-stand desks that allow the worker to sit or stand at the workstation and still be productive. Other expense-related changes include switching out the computer screens, keyboards, and the office chairs themselves. All of this is well and good and encouraged if the company can afford the upfront cost of designing an ergonomically friendly office environment. Still, the following *free* practices will go a long way if implemented and encouraged daily by peers and leadership.

GunnarT's Top Ten List

1. Stand during phone calls.
2. Sit for a maximum of 40 minutes, then take a standing break.
3. Take a break from your computer every 30 minutes, such as read something in print, make a phone call, or talk to a colleague.
4. Take your eyes off the computer screen every 20 minutes and focus on an object 20 feet away.
5. Get moving! Skip the elevator, take the stairs.
6. Conduct standing or walking meetings.
7. Eat your lunch away from your desk.
8. Periodically walk around the office, or even outside-Movement Motivators are explained later.
9. Add some plant life to your life.
10. Practice mindfulness through mental relaxation and prayer.

Standing/Walking Meetings

A note on conducting a standing meeting: Several years ago, I was an administrator at a small high school in San Marcos, Texas. Every Thursday, we had a meeting in the boardroom with about twenty chairs around this long rectangular table. The meetings were supposed to be approximately 30 minutes long, held after all the students had left, and when most of us were tired and ready to get home. The meetings *never* lasted 30 minutes. Some meetings lasted over an hour because several teachers loved to hear themselves talk on and on. One thing all organizations have in common is meetings. Some have them every day, and others have multiple meetings every day. Then the head admin guy implemented a new meeting policy. All meetings were conducted with no chairs, and everyone would stand the entire meeting. Guess how long those meetings lasted now? Surprise, not one meeting lasted as much as 30 minutes. One meeting lasted about 12 minutes, another one for almost 20 minutes, but you get the point. Standing meetings are great if you have long-winded participants! Plus, standing for one hour burns 48 calories!

Walking meetings are also great if you have good weather outside. You may also have a designated tree that grants large shade and plush grass. Just beware of little critters like ants that can interrupt your meeting. They can really bug you! (*eye-roll here*)

Are there any benefits to walking around at work? Yes! According to a study by two psychologists Oppezzo & Schwartz. In 2014 they asked several participants to walk after sitting for 30 minutes and then sit after walking. Here is what they found:

- Creativity went up 81% when walking.

- When seated after walking, participants exhibited a creative boost.
- Outdoor walking resulted in the greatest amount of problem-solving solutions.

Oppezzo & Schwartz concluded that walking "opens up the free flow of ideas and increases productivity and physical activity in real-time and shortly after."[17]

Therefore, if you are a leader in an organization, remember that an organization that moves is an organization that thinks better.

Sitting Kills, Moving Heals by Dr. Joan Vernikos, Former Director of the NASA Life Science Division, urges all of her workers to take standing breaks. She compares sedentary workers who sit all the time to weightless astronauts in outer space. Over time, astronauts will begin losing muscle and bone because there is no resistance to gravity. Similarly, out-of-shape individuals also start losing muscle and become highly susceptible to many health-related problems.[18]

Here's a great idea: Let's trade our seats for our feets! One of the most requested workshops that I conduct for companies is one titled *"In-Office Exercises & Stretches to Reduce Chronic Stress."* It's easy to understand why everyone loves this workshop. It gets everyone moving! There is very little sitting in this particular workshop. Instead, everyone is stretching their legs, torsos, necks, arms, and bodies to encourage better blood flow. We also do exercises that get the heart pumping but not the sweat dripping. All of these stretches and exercises are illustrated for you in the next chapter. Do them! You will find that afterward, you feel better and even become more productive at work.

Ergonomics of Prolonged Standing

What if your job requires you just the opposite? How about those who stand all day? Well, if you are a hairstylist, doctor, pharmacist, flight attendant, or work in the foodservice industry, you are in this boat. You stand between 4-8 hours per day, and your feet are aching by the end of the day. According to Healthline.com, in a 2014 survey, over 2.4 million workers complained or missed work due to foot pain and discomfort, and the large number who missed work with back and hip pain related to their feet. Holland and Higuera wrote some sound advice on practical tips our standing workforce can start doing today.

1. *Wear the right shoes for you.* Good arch support helps reduce soreness in the legs and feet. And the heal should not be elevated beyond two inches. Ensure the shoes fit and are not too small, or else you may experience reduced circulation and even blisters on your feet. Here's a fact most people don't realize when it comes to standing all day: your feet actually get bigger by the end of the day.

   Therefore, it's recommended to buy work shoes that are up to a half-size bigger than your normal shoe size.[19]

I don't have a position where I stand all day, except when I give keynote speeches requiring me to stand for an hour or more. Then I'll easily spend another hour or two greeting participants and having nice casual conversations. I have <u>huge</u> feet; I wear a size 14, and when

I stand for long periods, I sometimes will wear a size 15 shoe. I know it's a bit off-topic, but it's really hard to shop for good shoes when you have big feet. Most shoe stores have shoe sizes no larger than a size 12 or 13 in men's sizes, and although online shopping offers a broader selection, I like to try on shoes and walk around in them for a few minutes before purchasing them. I encourage you to do the same. Decide to purchase your "working" shoes at a physical store versus online, so you are confident you have shoes that feel great and offer your toes some "wiggle-room."

I have a small bragging point to make here: When you have feet like mine, you can save on renting those skis for waterskiing! Go barefoot!

2. *Stretch often.* Your body will always tell you when it's time to stretch. Listen to it! Forget what anyone around you may think, and just do it! For good stretches, see the exercises in the next chapter.

3. *Ice your feet.* Yes, I know that ice is cold. It's uncomfortable, and you might even get "cold-feet" when you think of even doing it! However, pediatrists recommend that by immersing the foot in ice-cold water for 20 minutes works to combat inflammation that prolonged standing creates on the foot. It's effective in healing any swelling that comes with standing or walking for long periods.

4. *Massage your feet.* Ah, now you are talking! I love my foot massages! You can always massage your feet with your hands, but it's more beneficial to roll a tennis ball or baseball under your feet from toe to heal several

times. This exercise will stretch those tight foot muscles and help foot recovery.

5. *Elevate your feet.* I know this is a lot to ask here, but you <u>must</u> do this. Grab your favorite pillows and stack them under your feet while watching the evening news. This will help decrease the day's swelling and even help you sleep better. Plus, with all the good news you always hear on television, you will go to sleep with constructive happy thoughts!

Do any or all of these foot-pampering tricks, and you will feel much better by the next morning! Repetition is key, so do this daily to reduce the consequences of too much prolonged standing.

Standing is better than sitting for long periods, but there should be a balance. Everyone who stands for a long time eventually will have aching feet and tightening of the hamstrings (*the muscles behind the knee and into the back of the leg*). But those of us who sit for too long will have neck and back issues. Often, I will see people standing with incorrect postures that will also result in upper and lower body stress. Therefore, here is how you stand:

- Stand like a relaxed soldier, with your shoulders square and down.
- Hold your head held high but keep your neck muscles relaxed.
- Lightly draw in your core stomach muscles, without tilting your pelvis forward.

- Avoid locking your knees and allow a slight bend that feels most natural.

- Do your best not to continually shift your standing posture to one side and then the other. You may be reducing stress on one side but doubling it on the other!

- Never hold your phone up to your ear for more than a few minutes. If that phone conversation will be a long one, use the speakerphone option or purchase some earbuds.[20]

When you picture this in your mind and correct yourself throughout the day, you will feel better and even look taller!

A True Model

One very famous person we all know has a very stressful job and always on her feet. She has been doing the same job for thirty-five years now, and yet she is always smiling. That's why I admire her so much. She never complains or has a bad day. She is also constantly moving, having to turn the letters every time they light up. Do you know who this person is yet?

If you guessed the beautiful, ageless blond on Wheel of Fortune, you are correct!

Just think about how hard her life must be! She has to be up, and out of bed by 3:00 p.m., put on her make-up and choose a wardrobe specifically made for her, get to the studio before 6:00 p.m., and stand for a full thirty minutes as contestants yell out letters from the alphabet. Wait! Today's letters just need to be touched, not turned, so Vanna now has to simply touch the lit-up squares to reveal the letter. In her tough five-hour workweek, she is constantly standing, smiling, and moving. Wait! That show is only thirty minutes long, so let me re-phrase what I just said. In her rigorous two-and-a-half-hour workweek, she performs. I can honestly say that she deserves the $8 million annual salary compared to the famous game show's host, with a well-earned $12 million annual salary.[21]

I can just hear you now saying, "Wait a minute Gunnar, my job is much tougher than her job! I have to work 40-60 hours per week, and I have to *think* at my job! I don't make anything near $8 million per year." Now before I hear you next say, "Life's not fair!" First, it would be utterly ridiculous for anyone to compare your life to Vanna's life. Be instead the person God intended you to be! Think about this little ergonomic principle:

We must believe that we are gifted for something, and that this thing, at whatever cost, must be attained. Marie Curie

What is your gift? What are you good at and enjoy doing more than anyone you know? Vanna discovered her gift, which is turning letters. What is your gift?

Also, ask yourself this, what difference are most celebrities making in the world? If you are a school teacher, I believe your impact is a thousand times more influential than most celebs. If you are a leader in any organization, the same is true for you. And for a little peace of mind, game show hosts have problems too.

Now before I conclude this section on standing/walking meetings, I have a very important point to make here. While writing this chapter, I went for a nice walk since the weather was sunny and warm, amongst green trees and nicely cut grass. I was walking alongside a colleague of mine when she said, "I wish my life were as easy as Vanna's" (*referring to the stress of her job and kids at home*). That was the spark that led me to write that piece, and I would never have thought of it if I didn't take that stroll through the grass. Therefore, take more walking breaks or meetings, and you might come up with the one idea that will make you the hero in your organization!

Based on a recent study from Stanford, "a person's creative output increased by an average of 60% when walking and many people anecdotally claim they do their <u>best thinking</u> while walking."[22]

Not Taking the Easy Way Up

Take the Stairs

Unless you work on the 88th Floor, here's what some daily stair-climbing can do for you, according to Cornell University:

1 flight of stairs, 3x per day = 15 calories
2 flights of stairs, 3x per day = 30 calories
3 flights of stairs, 3x per day = 45 calories
4 flights of stairs, 3x per day = 60 calories
5 flights of stairs, 3x per day = 75 calories
6 flights of stairs, 3x per day = 90 calories
7 flights of stairs, 3x per day = 105 calories

There are also several brands of smartwatches and Fitbits today that can track your steps to keep you motivated. Remember this: it takes 3,500 calories to burn a pound of fat. That's the equivalent of taking those seven flights of stairs every day for a year!

Here are some *stair-y* facts on stairs:

- Stair climbing uses three times more energy than stair descent.
- Stair climbing for 3 minutes burns 30-40 calories.
- Stair climbing requires between 8-10 times more energy expenditure than resting (*like in an elevator*).
- The exercise equivalent to 7 minutes a day of stair climbing reduces coronary heart disease incidents by nearly two-thirds.

Therefore, take the stairs. They are good for your heart and keep you moving up!

Movement Motivators

What's a movement motivator? It simply a lure that gets workers away from their desks for brief periods of time. These short breaks have been shown to help brain function. These motivators are mostly small changes that leadership can do around the office, and I guarantee that something so simple can be incredibly effective at boosting office productivity.

- Movement motivator #1: Copiers and Water Coolers. Place the copiers in a separate area from the water cooler and coffee/tea areas. This encourages more walking and movement. If these three are in the same area, someone making copies can easily get some water while making copies. It's efficient, but that requires less movement than if that water cooler is even twenty paces away from the copy machines! Also, keep the coffee/tea area in its own area away from the copier and the water cooler. More movement makes the brain happy!

- Movement motivator #2: Communal Trash Bins. Remove the trash bins from worker's desks and have larger trash bins in designated areas. This increases the frequency of movement and also creates more spontaneous interactions. These interactions can lead to many positive outcomes, such as productive conversations and deeper meaningful relationships. One word of caution, no trash-talk allowed!

- Movement motivator #3: Establish a Stretching Zone. Every office typically has one or two rooms that are sitting empty. Place some yoga mats and foam rollers in there and encourage stretching breaks for your staff. I cannot emphasize enough how beneficial this is for stiff and tired muscles! If all of your team spends at least 10 minutes stretching and breathing, they will feel calmer throughout the day and find themselves more productive!

This is the perfect lead-in for the next chapter. Let me show you movement of all kinds to loosen you up, keep your posture better than ever, and keep you healthier throughout the workday. You might want to take a minute now to change out of your expensive suits and dresses, and put on something sporty, loose, and casual before we move on.

• BREAKING IT DOWN •

Remember sitting kills, moving heals. Therefore, let's brainstorm how we can all incorporate more movement.

In what ways have you been sitting and standing improperly? What can you do today to change?

_____

_____

_____

_____

_____

What Movement Motivators would work in your office?

_____

_____

_____

_____

_____

Can you think of a Movement Motivator that was not mentioned that you and your team could implement?

_____

_____

_____

_____

_____

61

What other ideas can you think of that will work for your team?

_____

_____

_____

_____

_____

CHAPTER FOUR

In-Office Exercises and Stretches

THERE IS NOT a subject in which I have been asked to speak more frequently than exercises and stretches that can be done in a normal office day. Everyone knows that too much sitting in bad for you, and many people struggle to fit in any exercise at the gym before or after work. What's more, even if you hit the gym and work out every day, you *still* need to incorporate some easy stretches and exercises to keep you moving throughout the day.

First, we will review and analyze some good stretches, followed by some easy and effective exercises.

Stretches for Prolonged Sitting

1. Head Tilt

2. Curtsy Lean

3. Standing Side

4. Door Post

5. Arms Behind Chair

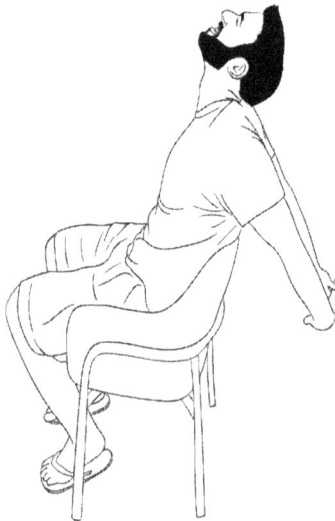

6. Arm rolls

7. Arms Across Body Shoulder Stretch

8. Triceps stretch behind the head

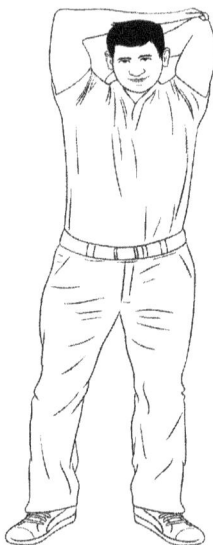

9. Inner leg side to side stretch

9b. Inner leg side to side stretch

10. Pull head forward into lap stretch

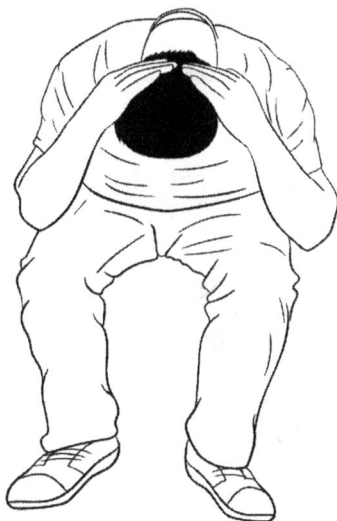

Exercises for Prolonged Sitting

11. Jumping Jacks

12. High Knee

13. One-legged hops

14. Push-ups

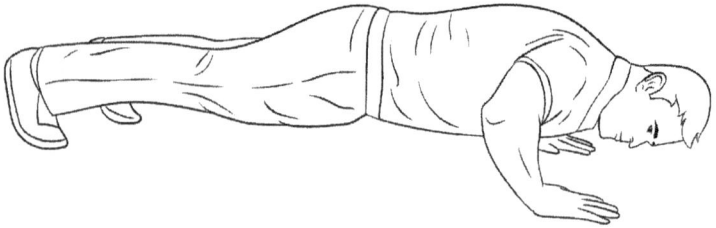

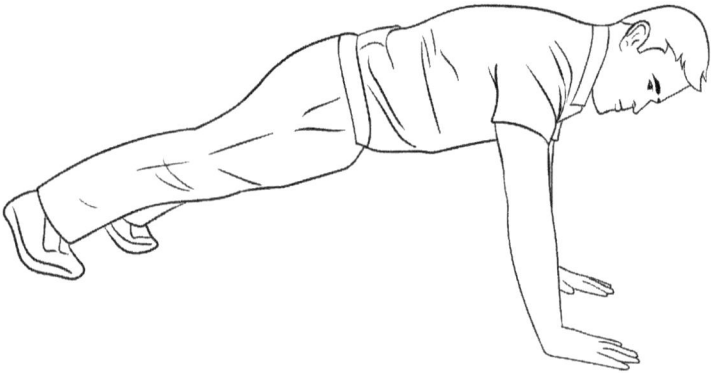

15. Just dance

Stretches for Prolonged Standing

1. Calf raises help pump blood out of the foot where it pools through the day and back into the body where it belongs.

    - Stand tall on the edge of a step, tighten your abdominals (stomach muscles).
    - Secure the balls of your feet firmly on the step with heels hanging over the edge.
    - Raise your heels a few inches above the step as you stand on your tiptoes, hold for two seconds.
    - Lower your heels two inches below the platform, then raise up again.
    - Repeat ten times

2. The runner's stretch
    - Face a wall and place hands against it.
    - Extend one leg behind your body.
    - Push your heal to the floor as far as it will go.
    - Hold for a moment until you feel the stretch and then switch sides.
    - Repeat three times on each leg.

Now I want to encourage you to pull out a blank piece of paper. Do it right now while I wait. Oh, also grab a pen. I'll even play music while I wait for you to get these things.

(Music here...nice elevator music) Ahhhh.

Ho-Hum

Ho-Hum

Are you back yet? Geez, you take forever.

No worries, I'll wait a little longer.

I'll just watch an episode of Wheel of Fortune. Gosh, you take a long time!

Okay, sorry, but I just can't wait on you any longer. Let's move on, and hopefully, you found your pen and paper.

I call this little exercise, "Your Sit-Stand Day."

Your Sit-Stand Day

Ask yourself, what activities do you do in a workday? Here are the answers I often get in my workshops:

Drive to work	
Take the elevator up	
Check email	
Answer phone calls	
Talk to co-workers	
Work on project	
Eat lunch	
Get water/drinks/snacks	
Organize the workroom	

You probably have many more activities you perform while at work, but these are the most common activities if you work at a desk all day.

Next to each activity, place a (stick-figure man), either standing, sitting, or walking. Which one are you doing the most? At work in an eight-hour day, are you sitting all day or standing all day? It's all about balance here. Remember, you don't want to be sitting more than how long?

The answer is 40 minutes. Therefore, for which activities listed above, are you sitting that you can change to either standing or walking? Also, don't wait until the 40 minutes are up before you stand and move around. Move around as much as possible!

Here are some helpful hints for the examples above.

1. Take the elevator up can be switched out with stairs instead.

2. Checking your email can take a while, so limit yourself to answering a half-dozen before talking a short walking break to the water cooler.

3. Answer the phone (if it's a cell phone) while standing or walking, but *not* while sitting. Remember the added benefit that you can become more creative while moving vs. sitting. Pace the floors! Even if it drives your co-workers nuts. Just do it.

4. Talk to co-workers. Above all things, I *highly* encourage you to do this not just for the exercise but also for the important interaction. Stand and/or walk when talking to those you spend most of your day with and foster those relationships. Our younger generations lack meaningful relationships. In his book, *Leaders Eat Last,* Simon Sinek makes some strong points here that Millennials are so attached to their mobile devices that they not only lack human interaction but actually crave it. Now more than ever, take a break—productively. Especially if you are a Gen X person or even a Baby Boomer, give your Millennial co-workers the attention they need, and ask them how their day is going. Be a listener before you are a talker. One more thing, in a world of superheroes like Superman and Wonder Woman, the real hero is <u>you</u>. Talk to your co-workers and stand or walk while doing it. It just might be the best part of your day, and theirs too!

5. Eat lunch, but never at your desk. Here lies another opportunity to connect with those around you in your circles. Also, why sit while eating? Take advantage of any high-rise

tabletops around the office. That's at least thirty minutes of *less* sitting you can do, which is always a good thing!

P.S. on #5, *please* eat with your mouths closed. The Bible says, "Thou shalt eat with thy mouths closed, not open." II Opinions 4:17

Okay, so I made that verse up. I admit it! But still, please don't chew your food in a manner for the entire world to see. No one wants to see your food post-chewed before swallowing. I can promise you that!

My dad was *very good* at marriage. He must have been since he was married five times! One of his wives was of Asian-descent, and she claimed that they have a culture where it's polite to chew with your mouth wide open to show appreciation for your food. Well, I was just a teenager at the time, but I swear I will never forget this. While she was talking to us in a mall food court, and while chewing her food, I watched a fly buzzing around her head and then right into her mouth. She never knew she just ate a bug, but I sure did. My dad was wondering why I was laughing so hard. I was literally on the floor, laughing until my sides hurt.

Wow! I believe I just cured the entire world from ever eating with their mouths wide open. It's disgusting, and you never know what may *fly* in there!

6. Stretching and Exercise Breaks. I have a question to ask you. What stretches and exercises did you enjoy doing the most? You can list them at the end of this chapter, as I have laid out several blanks you can fill in. Do them—every day. Switch them up hourly, daily, weekly. The more you do them, the more your co-workers will do them too!

On your "Your Sit-Stand Day" exercise, in between all those activities you listed, list the exercises and stretches *by name* that you plan to do and do them!!

You will feel better after you do any combination of these stretches and exercises throughout your day, and I guarantee you will sleep better too!

That leads me to my last activity, which I bet *nobody* listed—sleep. Yes, you would probably be fired if you slept at work. So, to prevent this from happening, sleep at night, on your bed, for a minimum of 6 hours. Why? Well, think about everything you put your body through! Just like your cell phone needs to be recharged when the battery gets low, so does your body! Bill Phillips, *"The Better Man Project,"* shows plenty of research on the importance of sleep, but I'll share the one that stuck with me from my college studies.

During the first 3-4 hours of sleep, the brain repairs the body. In the second 3-4 hours, the brain repairs itself. Have you ever wondered why you feel "groggy" when you don't get enough sleep? Now you know! The brain simply has not fully repaired itself yet. Therefore, do your best to get the sleep you need so you can perform with a full battery tomorrow. You are welcome!

THE ERGONOMICS OF PLANTAR FACIITIS

I tend to stand a lot when I'm working with clients as a wellness coach, speaking or performing massage therapy. Often I will feel a sore tightness in the bottoms of my feet. This is known as Plantar Faciitis and it is the most common standing injury of workers today. It's painful and seems like it never goes away once you get it because not standing often is not an option, especially if you are a doctor, pharmacist, hair stylist, massage therapist, dancer, and so on.

What is it exactly? There is a thick band of tissue known as the plantar fascia that runs across the bottom of your foot from your toes to your heel bone. When you do not stretch this area enough and overuse it, you can get inflammation.

You know you have it when you wake up in the morning and walk barefoot across your hardwood floors. It feels like walking on a thousand nails at once. I have encouraged my clients to do the following four steps to treat it, and I have a 100% success rate in helping others get their feet back into a healthy state.

The Four Steps In Treating Plantar Fasciitis:

1. Buy shoe soles that are made specifically to treat the inflammation. Dr. Scholl's Heel Pain Relief Orthotic is an excellent choice and I used their soles in my shoes to help standing and walking much more tolerable.

2. Avoid artificial sweeteners! These are often cause inflammation in your body to get worse. If you must sweeten that cup of coffee or iced tea, then reach for raw sugar or Stevia. Stevia comes from a natural root and it's a more natural alternative to the artificial stuff.

3. Buy Zyflamend. This is an herbal remedy that is the best of anti-inflammatory alternatives out there ... in my humble opinion. The ingredients are full of antioxidants including turmeric, green tea, ginger and rosemary. It's for your whole body, not just your feet, but it really does accelerate the heeling for this condition.

4. Stretching your calves, Achilles Tendon, and the foot facia is absolute key to healing Plantar Fasciitis and preventing it. The best stretch is a yoga pose called Downward Dog.

This works 100% of the time in plantar relief. It only takes two minutes, and sometimes it's sufficient in healing Plantar Fasciitis in this one step alone! I recommend doing the following exercise three times per day; first thing in the morning and right before bedtime. How do you spell R-E-L-I-E-F?

Downward Dog: Start by getting in push-up position. Have your hands and feet shoulder width apart and bring your hands a little closer to your feet by bending at the waist (butt up) and keeping your legs straight. Press your heels to the floor and hold for one minute. Relax and repeat 2-4 more times.

• BREAKING IT DOWN •

When you feel strong and healthy, you will be more confident about your work. Bill Phillips, Better Man Project

Name your favorite stretches that you can do at work.

_____

_____

_____

_____

_____

Name your favorite exercises you can do at work.

_____

_____

_____

_____

_____

Name three people at work you can start connecting with more while standing.

_____

_____

_____

_____

_____

CHAPTER FIVE

Ergonomics of Leadership

*"Success is not final; failure is not fatal; it is the courage
to continue that counts."*
Winston Churchill

THERE IS NOT a more important topic than this one as it applies to the workplace. Real workplace ergonomics involves the comfort level of the chair you sit in all day and your desk's height. There's a real science to *ergonomics*. So how do we use the same ergonomic approach to define and improve the leaders of today?

Let's look at some of the best, and worst, leadership examples during our darkest hours in history.

In 2017, Christopher Nolan directed a movie called *Dunkirk* that told the story of Britain's rescue mission to save over 400,000 of their own soldiers from the tight grip of the German invasion in the port of Dunkirk, France, in May 1940. To me, this is one of the finest examples of leadership that I have ever read, and the story encompasses the very essence of leadership itself for company leaders today to follow.

First, a lesson from history: As a result of the attack on Pearl Harbor in December 1941, the United States was thrust into WWII. The small nation of England had already been in the thick of the war for seventeen months, beginning with the Battle of Britain in July 1940, and the British Isles needed stronger leadership more than ever before. Then there was a new threat to the UK called *Operation Sea Lion*, with Adolf Hitler. The enemy Axis Power's forceful leader created a massive air and sea invasion to take down the UK and take it over.

The people of Britain were fearful of the impending air and sea attacks from the Germany armies and were rapidly losing all hope in fighting back at all. Then, however, they witnessed a successful mission that gave them a glimmer of hope in their leader, Prime Minister Winston Churchill. The mission was codenamed "Operation Dynamo," and encompassed the evacuation of Dunkirk. The British forces had been sent to aid the French Army against the Germans invasion of France but were overcome themselves and forced to retreat. They all gathered at the port of Dunkirk, waiting to be rescued.

Imagine, here gathered at the coast of the English Channel almost half a million men waiting for their country to save them, seemingly helpless against the inevitable attack by the approaching German Army. For several days the massive attack never happened. Although they were sitting ducks, the German tiger never pounced. Instead there was a long lull of silence. Little did they know that the Germans needed time to repair thousands of tanks that were out of service, and they needed to protect their flanks that they assumed were vulnerable, according to a diary from the German Commander at the time, Gerd von Rundstedt.[23]

Churchill knew he had to rescue his troops and the French from an impending attack and thought he had little time to act. Although the German tanks were out of service, the Germans persisted, and all large floating vessels from the nation of Britain were easy targets. His solution? Send out small vessels instead. As crazy and bold a plan as it was, it worked!

Coined as *The Miracle of Dunkirk*, Churchill ordered hundreds of small ships and vessels to sail to the port and collect the stranded soldiers. It took over 900 vessels to collect the 338,226 soldiers, both English and French. It was indeed a miracle, and miracles can happen when you have strong, courageous leaders.

Further research reveals something fascinating to learn about this heroic leader: Winston Churchill started out with a lisp and horrible stuttering problem. According to an article dating back to February 6th, 1941, in the Kansas City Star, a story headlined *"Churchill Has Mastered a Stutter and a Lisp to Become an Orator,"*

> *Winston Churchill grew up with a lisp and a stutter, the result of a defect in his palate. It is characteristic of the man's perseverance that, despite his handicap, he has made himself one of the greatest orators of all time.*[24]

Ronald Reagan is another person who inspired an entire nation when he spoke. Reagan has been recognized as "The Great Communicator." When he spoke, Americans had a sense of peace and trust in him to be an effective leader. John F. Kennedy was also considered a great orator and therefore had a tremendous following for his leadership.

So, leaders are born, right? If you believe that, you bought into the same lie that sides with the statement that great orators are born. Leaders are communicators. Leaders are developed.

Leaders have followers. Are you a great leader? That depends on what you are communicating to those who follow you.

Why did the people of Britain come to trust the judgment of their Prime Minister so quickly? For one, he had no fear, and just as fear is contagious, so is courage. Second, he had vision, and his vision was that of a nation with no German influence whatsoever. Third, he knew how to communicate the reassurance and security of his most important message: that together, the people of Great Britain could accomplish great things. Together, they could overcome the German threat and be victorious.

This type of leadership is what I call *Persuasional Leadership*. He persuaded his people that there was hope, and to embrace hope in moving forward. Churchill also had *positional leadership* because of the office he held. But even greater was his *persuasional leadership*. Let me explain the two leadership definitions in greater detail.

Positional leadership is limited as it's just a title for the person in power or a supervisory role. You may be in a position of power now, such as a school principal or CEO of a company, but only for a period of time. Always keep in mind that a leadership title does not guarantee positive leadership on followers. I'm sure you are thinking of a leader you didn't like for one reason or another. I'll expand on the negative effects of these types of leaders shortly.

Persuasive leadership is more effective in the long-run and outlasts a leader's term of power. If you were to break down the word "persuasion," the Latin meaning is a powerful force for a leader. *Per* means "through," and *suasio* means "sweetness." Therefore, being *persuasive* means using sweetness to get people to do what you want. But being a *persuasive leader* means relating to those who follow you, and not forcing them to follow you. There are essentially five elements to persuasional leadership:

Confidence, Adaptability, Vision, Passion and Compassion.

I'd like to give an example of each of these five elements with leadership legends whom we can all relate to in one way or another, then put it all together at the end.

Persuasive Leaders have Confidence

Courage. It takes courage to take steps in the right direction. It takes courage to move forward when everyone else retreats the opposite direction. It takes courage to step onto a sinking ship to save it. This is the stuff superheroes are made of in Hollywood, and it's what real heroes are made of in leadership. Churchill's persuasive leadership still lasts in all the history books, with the ripple effects of freedom throughout all of England, Europe, and even the United States. On the flip side, persuasive leadership can also be negative. Think about Hitler's persuasiveness on his own people. He basically "brainwashed" them to believe that the persecution of over 6 million Jews, was somehow a good thing. In fact, if I was alive and living in central Europe in that time, I too might have been persecuted as I'm one-quarter Jewish. It's interesting to note that Hitler himself may have had Jewish and African roots, according to a study involving saliva samples from 39 of his relatives, noted by Heidi Blake of *The Telegraph*.[25]

Just think about how courageous Winston Churchill really was at the time. You have a superpower coming at you in full force (Nazi Germany), and you inspire your followers to run *towards* the enemy, not away from them. It happened at

Dunkirk, and it happened throughout the war because Germany was never able to penetrate Great Britain. Even though Winston himself had failed in his past leadership endeavors, he was now leading a nation, which was operating in fear, into war by persuading them to face those very fears. Many experts say that Churchill's courageous leadership saved not just all of Britain, but the entire world.

Can anyone possess persuasive leadership, without having a leadership title? Now that's a great question! We understand the reverse is true, that the title doesn't make the leader persuasive; but can anyone, with or without a title, influentially persuade another? Or a better question to ask would be, do you consider yourself a leader, right now?

Let's stop here and take two steps backward. What is leadership? John C. Maxwell is probably the world's greatest guru on leadership, by expert opinion. He is widely known as a leadership expert, speaker, and author. He has studied this subject for over 40 years. Here is how he defines it, "Leadership is influence. Nothing more, nothing less." It's an amazing truth that to lead, you start simply by *influencing others*. If you just have one person who looks to you for direction and follows your example, you are a leader!

Persuasive Leaders Empower Others

Another successful Who's Who we all know is none other than Bill Gates, the founder of Microsoft. Here's his forecast of Leadership: "As we look into the next century, leaders will be those who *empower others*." Notice his first words were, "*As we look into the next century...*" This was written before the year 2000, and this is now the next century. Therefore, the time is *now* to start empowering others in leadership!

Let's measure the influence level of just these two individuals. John C. Maxwell is just a normal kid from Michigan. He saw from a young age how much influence he had learned from the great leaders of his day, and he decided to write a book about it. Then he wrote another book, and another, and another. Altogether over four decades of writing, he has sold over 20 million copies, and much of his work has been translated to over 50 languages. He is number five on the all-time *New York Times* bestseller list.

When I ask people if they know who John C. Maxwell is and they respond, "No clue," I then ask that person, "What do you do?" Suppose that person's response is a positional leadership title such as manager, supervisor, human resources, or even CEO. In that case, I respond to them with another question, "You aren't interested in growing as a leader, are you?" I'm not trying to be mean, but I believe very strongly that knowledge is power, and you can't empower others if they think you are a dummy. Leaders need to be credible sources of information, and when you educate others, you empower them too!

My friends, if you are not reading at least one book a month, you are not growing as a leader. Some avid readers read as many as 5-10 books each month. As I'm doing this research, I'm reading about 20 books this month alone. I can understand if you didn't think you were bearing the title of *leader*, that you might not be reading a book on leadership. Let me remind you of the definition of *leadership*: Influence. I believe *everyone* is a leader. If you want to start feeling and acting like a leader right away, you can start today by complimenting someone on their recent performance or the fact that they always chew their food with their mouth closed. What are you doing? You are elevating their spirits, making them feel good about themselves. You *are* influencing them! Do you want to go the extra mile in learning lessons in leadership? Mentor someone else. Volunteer to mentor a co-worker or even a young student. Teenagers, now more than ever, are seeking genuine people as role models. Find one and be their mentor. If you are an influencer, you are a leader.

John C. Maxwell's name is the first name you see when you google "leadership books" and the first books you see on the shelves of "Personal Development" at any bookstore worldwide. If you bear the title of leader, or you are a positional leader, there are hundreds and hundreds of books on this subject. Read them! I've discovered that many cities offer book clubs where you get the executive summary versions of leadership books. I think that's an excellent choice if you don't have time to read. My point is this: *Never stop learning.* For the sake of repeating myself, I'm going to repeat myself but differently, *strive to learn every day that you are living and breathing on this planet.* If one day you lose your eyesight and can no longer read, learn braille, then start reading in braille.

> *"When you stop learning, you stop growing. When you stop learning, you stop leading."* Ken Blanchard

One thing you should read every day is the newspaper. Why? Because it's the best way to stay current with everything that's happening in the world. That brings me to the third element of the ergonomics of persuasive leadership.

Persuasive Leaders Have Vision and Adaptability

I think all of us have heard the following phrase: "There are two things certain in life: Death and Taxes." True, but there's a third one to add: Change.

Change is inevitable. Think about Blockbuster Video. In the 1990's they were the #1 retailer of video rentals. For anyone born after, let's say circa 2,000, here's how we used to watch movies at home. First, we got in our car. Second, we drove to a store called Blockbuster. Third, we selected all the movies we wanted and rented them from the store, usually for up to seven days. Fourth, we would drive back home, insert the DVD (in the '80s and early '90s, these were VHS tapes), and watch the movies. It's apparent that online streaming (Netflix) has taken over the movie and TV show market. Blockbuster simply failed to change with the changing times and went belly-up. Blockbuster is gone!

Here is another fact about the fast-changing times of today. What platforms today are the most popular forms of social media? As of 2018, the most utilized are Facebook, LinkedIn, Instagram, Twitter, Snapchat, and YouTube. How many existed just ten years ago? Only Facebook, LinkedIn, Twitter, and YouTube. How many platforms existed 15 years ago? Only one of these. LinkedIn was started in 2002, then Facebook started in 2004, then YouTube started in 2005, and then Twitter started in 2006. But do you remember Myspace and Friendster? Here's what is interesting about Myspace and Friendster: they thought they were just in competition and never saw Facebook coming. Reading the newspaper or receiving daily newsfeeds is the best way to stay current in these rapidly changing times.

Change is everywhere, and if you are alive right now, which I can safely assume, you are alive in some exciting times! One of those areas experiencing change is the way leadership is in their organizations and thank God for that!

Everyone on this planet may not know who John C. Maxwell is, but I'm sure everyone knows who Bill Gates is and what he has accomplished. Some say that Bill Gates changed the world with the invention of the Internet. Well, that statement is false. Bill Gates did not invent the Internet (neither did Al Gore or

George W. Bush), but he certainly forecasted it well. In his book, released in 1995 titled *"The Road Ahead,"* Bill Gates painted the reality that we all live in today. He predicted as a result of the Internet, everyone will have a personal computer in their homes, and the entire world of capitalism is about to change.

We'll find ourselves in a new world of friction, overhead capitalism, in which the market information will be plentiful and transaction costs low. It will be a shopper's heaven![26]

Around that exact time in 1995, eBay was launched, from the sale of a single PEZ dispenser! (If you don't know what that is, it's a candy dispenser for kids and obsessed collectors). Today, eBay is a multibillion-dollar business selling millions of PEZ dispensers daily, and many other items of value! Another retail giant starting up around that same time was Amazon, which has made online shopping the norm for millions of consumers. Even when Gates updated his book in 1996, both of these companies and the entire dot-com bubble were in its infancy. Bill Gates is what is known as a *visionary leader*. When he started Microsoft in 1975, it became the largest PC software company ever. His entire vision for Microsoft's future changed when he noticed the Internet was gaining "critical mass," and it was then that he redirected Microsoft to become an Internet-focused company from a software company. As a result, Microsoft is nearly a trillion-dollar company today, and Bill Gates is one of the wealthiest individuals who has ever lived.

Bill Gates sees the new generation of leaders as those who empower others, which is easy when you have a motivated visionary leader. This is especially true with our youngest generation in the workplace today, the Millennials. They may have a bad reputation in the workplace, but I'll tell you that they also have a common ground that is a wonderful thing: *they want to work in a place that has a purpose.* They want to make an impact and to have a purpose of their own. In my expert opinion, Bill Gates is again correct—*empowerment is key.*

"Without vision, the people perish." Proverbs 29:18

Persuasive Leaders are Compassionate

Webster has the be the smartest guy I know. Here's how IT defines Compassion: *sympathetic consciousness of others' distress together with a desire to alleviate it.*

Do you notice the words "consciousness of others' distress?" That's what I think of when I hear the words "disgruntled employees." Who wants to work around people who bring you down all day? A lack of passionate leadership results in the opposite, which is apathy. An apathetic employee is a *pathetic* employee. Obviously not a happy camper!

Dave Ramsey, in one of his talks said, "bosses push, persuasive leaders pull." When times are good, and when times get difficult, followers will look to their fearless leaders for guidance and safety. Visionary leaders see more than others do. They see the bigger picture. They persuade their followers to stay strong and keep moving forward. They pull their followers in the best direction for both the company's betterment and the work culture itself. Ken Blanchard, in his book, *The Heart of a Leader,* says, "Vision gives meaning to our lives and provides direction. It helps us get focused, remain energized, and produce great results."[27]

Another tech guru we all know is Steve Jobs, who was indeed a visionary leader who could see way beyond what anyone else could for electronics' future. Everyone wanted to be on Team Apple because of his vision and the company's seemingly limitless possibilities. However, Steve Jobs was not a compassionate leader. He was the type of leader who did not make his employees feel safe because he was very intimidating in his leadership. In an article written in *Study.com*, Steve Jobs was fired from Apple, despite being its founder and CEO, for being such a difficult leader. He was noted for "being a difficult boss, with little care or empathy for his employees. That was the big reason for his termination." Yet his vision was so strong that workers stayed in the game. When Jobs returned to Apple a few years later *(to save the company from its intermediary's failed leadership)*, he resurrected the company to be the enormous success that it is today. That's the power of a visionary leader.[28]

When you combine the power of positive influence from leadership qualities, *vision* plus *persuasiveness*, you will have an unstoppable work culture.

Here's an example of the power of influence from a compassionate leader. Let's say you have a worker who made a mistake or didn't get a project done on time. You bring that employee in your office, and you ask them, "What's going on? How are you doing? I noticed you did not get the project done on time, so do you want to talk about it?" Then comes reassurance. Reassure them that you are there for them and that you are sure that they will have everything done as expected by the end of the day.

That's compassionate leadership. But to display empathy towards difficult employees, it takes humility. Remember, persuasive leaders, pull, *not push*. Just like that trickle-down theory, leaders learn from other leaders, and all leadership is contagious. That worker in the example will likely display that same compassion towards others, and his or her feedback most likely will be more constructive than destructive, and thus more inspirational for greater performance. The empathetic influence displayed upon one worker will be passed on to another, and the result will be an entire workforce persuading another that anything is possible. That's the power of compassionate leadership from a persuasive leader in action!

Leadership styles need to change from what they used to be. I believe most of us have had a pushy boss or someone with a formal title that says, "I'm the leader, now do what I say!" Like many ego-centric positional leaders, he did all he could do create the illusion that he could do anything. The "my-way-or-the-highway" leader will always have employees that believe they are just expendable and of little value to the organization. This undervalued worker will do as much as he/she can to be satisfiable and never tap into their potential to be productive employees or leaders themselves. All the worker knows to do is clock in, do the job, clock out, and then do it again the next day. And don't tell the big boss, CEO, manager, any bad news. It's as if the leadership mentality says to its workforce, "Make a mistake, and you will be easily replaced with someone else. You exist to make *my life* easier by making our company money, and if I perceive you as a threat or liability, adios!" Or it says, "Although you may get a promotion, your big boss, CEO, supervisor is still above you and will always be above you." Well, that's the classic ego-centric positional leader, and the employee simply does what is asked, *without question.*

My friends, that's not leadership, that's dictatorship. That's the exact type of leader Stalin and Hitler was when they led their countries into warfare. Their motivation (other than hatred for inferior races) was power and profit. Their missions were as self-centered and egocentric as one could even imagine: to take over countries, acquire more citizens, and make them pay heavy taxes to the government. How is this different than the motivation of the typical self-exulted leader? It's the same— power and profit. All workers are hired to make *me* money, make *me* receive recognition, make *me* a big star. It's all about *me, me, me,* the leader!

Ken Blanchard, another one of my favorite authors on leadership, had his take on this type of leadership:

Focusing on the negative often creates situations that demoralize people. When a positive response follows good performance, people naturally want to follow that behavior.[29]

One of my all-time favorite movies, *National Lampoon's Christmas Vacation* (1989), illustrates this type of leader. The movie features Chevy Chase (Clark W Griswold) as the hapless employee and Brian Doyle (Murray) as his tyrannical boss. In several scenes, Clark's boss is this grinding leader focused on the money, not the employees, so he removes all the Christmas bonuses to make the company even more money. Also, every worker is forced to "brown-nose" to appease him in hopes of getting the next promotion. As a result, everyone functions as robots, doing whatever he said *without question.* The movie has a good ending, though. After a series of funny events, including the kidnapping of the boss by dumb cousin Ed, Clark confronts his ego-centric leader about his disdainful attitude and actions and reminds him that without people, there is no company. I bet after being kidnapped by one of his employees the boss learned a real lesson in compassionate leadership!

For all pushy bosses, "If you are leading, and no one is following, you are simply taking a walk!" John C. Maxwell

Do you know what else made Winston Churchill so effective in his leadership? It was never about *him.* It was about the people of Great Britain and their allies, and he empowered them! That's compassionate leadership. I love his story because here's this speech-impaired kid who grew up to overcome his impediments, to rise a vastly powerful position in leadership, and to help Great Britain to win the war, and even the United States! Amazing!

Remember, no obstacle or limitation is too big for a God with no limits!

There's another great story about the persuasive wisdom of Winston Churchill. Following the war, he was asked to speak on numerous occasions. For the boys at the famous Harrow School, he was asked to speak and was given a full hour for his presentation. Altogether he spoke for only 5-10 minutes, but he ended it with this command to all the boys, and all the free world: "Never give in, never give in, never, never, never, never!" Then he proudly walked off the stage. I doubt anyone in the audience forgot his words since they were so few, yet so unforgettable! Sometimes, less is more.

Always remember that real leadership is not only for those at the top. Real leadership is not a title, and no leaders are born. Real leadership is learned! And everyone can learn how to become a persuasive leader!

Did you know that even the most reclusive individual can influence up to 10,000 others in her or his lifetime?[30] That's a lot of people! Ask yourself of all the people you encounter day in and day out, especially with the wide reach of social media these days, how many are influenced by your words and actions?

Here comes the answer.

All of them!

We all become known for our words and actions. Think about how many "friends" follow you on all of your social media. I'm not handing out any guilt trips here, but everything you write and do on social media *defines you* to the entire world. Some of my friends have literally ruined their lives by posting stupid stuff, and they all knew better! Realize this: *you* are a leader! Regardless of your title or position at work, people follow you. People are watching you. People want to be influenced by you. So, become a persuasional leader yourself, and influence them! Just do so wisely!

Persuasive Leaders are Passionate

Wikipedia is another friend of mine. Here's how IT defines passion: *intense, driving, or overmastering feeling or conviction; a strong liking or desire for or <u>devotion</u> to some activity, object, or concept.*

I used to be a high school basketball team coach when I was fresh out of college. It's ironic because I was never a good basketball player. Yes, I am tall at 6'1, and I have that "I'm an awesome bad*#* player" look, but when I start playing, I would rarely be passed the ball. I wish we got points for air-balls because when I was under pressure, the guys didn't know if I was shooting or passing the ball. I believe I shot the ball one time, and it successfully hit the backboard, but that's about the limit of my success as a basketball player. However, as a basketball coach, I did exceptionally well. In my first year of coaching, my team finished in first place in our small town of Pleasanton, Texas. For the longest time, I believed I was just given "a good hand" of players, but the players' parents let me know that it was my leadership, not the players themselves, that led the team to victory. That really persuaded me to become the best empowering leader that I could be for my players, and the example I followed was none other than John Wooden.

If you don't know of John Wooden, he was the basketball coach at UCLA from 1948-1975, winning ten NCAA National Championships. It's interesting to note that UCLA had no formal basketball program when he arrived on campus. In fact, Coach Wooden was the first official UCLA coach as before then the program was run by student interns! He built something from scratch and developed a masterpiece through his empowering leadership style.

Bill Walsh, the legendary former Head Football Coach of the San Francisco 49ers, said this about Coach Wooden:

> *John Wooden is a 'philosopher-coach' in the truest sense: a man whose beliefs, teachings, and wisdom go far beyond sports, and ultimately address how to bring out the very best in yourself and others in all areas of life.*
>
> *He is a master teacher who understands motivation, organization, and psychology. Coach Wooden is able to successfully share his wisdom because he has a gift for expressing his philosophy directly and simply, in a manner accessible and applicable to everyone.*
>
> *Coach Wooden's own life is the embodiment of enduring American values. His priorities are, and always have been, correct – family, faith, and friends—and he has never veered from them in spite of professional success and celebrity of the highest magnitude.*
>
> *John Wooden is an American legend welcomed and respected by today's citizens and leaders. He is a very special American.* [31]

To me, John Wooden is about as opposite as can be of the egocentric leader. He exemplifies how leaders today should be, and he lived those qualities! I honestly believe that he would have laid down his life for his players. How many leaders today would do the same for their workers?

Wooden exemplified a passion for his players and held them to a very high standard, exactly how leaders of any organization should be with their employees. Coach Wooden's players all followed him and succeeded, winning ten national championships and more than 660 games, including an incredible 88 consecutive victories from 1971-1974. He was an awesome leader!

Enjoy some of my favorite insights from the wisdom of John Wooden:

> *Try your hardest in all ways and you are a success. Period. Do less than that and you have failed to one degree or another.*

> *Your journey is the important thing. A score, a trophy, a ribbon is simply the inn.*

> *Are you going to make mistakes? Of course. But it is not failure if you make the full effort.*

> *Did I win? Did I lose? Those are the wrong questions. The correct question is: Did I make the best effort? That's what matters. The rest of it just gets in the way.*

> *I have never gone into a game thinking we were going to lose. Never.*

> *Do not be too concerned about what others think of you. Be very concerned about what you think of yourself. Be true to yourself first, then comes the opinions of others.*

> *Goals should be difficult to achieve because those achieved with little effort are seldom appreciated, give little personal satisfaction, and are often not worthwhile.*

> *You can make the biggest difference of all. You can change yourself.[32]*

How did Coach Wooden start each season? How did he pave the road to success? He started with the absolute basics.

Every pre-season, he would sit down with his collegiate athletes and teach them how to put on their socks. Here is the greatest basketball coach in history (according to many sports fans) teaching accomplished and highly recruited stars the little details that can have huge impacting results. Literally! Why? Well, if you have any wrinkles in the socks you are wearing, it could cause a blister, and blisters will slow down performance every time.

That's my exact intent with you, the reader, in this chapter. I want to teach you the Ergonomics of Leadership from the experts who know this subject well enough to preach it. Also, I don't want you to get any blisters either.

John Wooden also lists his "Eight Suggestions for Succeeding," which I think are essential for every leader. His observations are in *italicized bold*. I have followed each with leadership applications which I feel emphasize his observations:

1. ***Fear no opponent.*** Respect every opponent. Your opponents are your competitors in this big game called Corporate America. Keep your focus on your players, not their players. You can't control anyone else's players other than your own, and to focus on your own professional growth and performance will lead to victory.

   "Your game is only as good as your practice." Ken Blanchard, *Everyone's a Coach*

2. ***Remember, it's the perfection of the smallest details that make big things happen.*** Change is in the small details. Positive feedback is essential. Keep it constructive and you will keep moving forward. It literally can make the difference between keeping a good employee or losing them to another company. Our words are always free, so give them away wisely!

   "The key to developing people to catch them doing something right." Ken Blanchard, *The One Minute Manager*

3. ***Keep in mind that hustle makes up for many a mistake.*** Hard work is rewarding mentally, physically, and physiologically! You get a shot of serotonin (the feel-good chemical) when

you hustle and do a job well done. If you are a leader, always keep your eye for positive hustle with your workers, and you can expect more hustle!

"Don't wait until people do things exactly right before you praise them." Ken Blanchard, The One Minute Manager

4. **Be more interested in character than reputation**. Always follow through with your words and actions consistent with what you promise. A good reputation is what's on the outside, which is always a reflection of what's on the inside, your character. And it's what's on the inside that counts!
   "Let your Yes be Yes and your No be No." Matthew 5:37

   "Character is following through on your decisions." Ken Blanchard, Consumer Mania!

5. **Be quick, but don't hurry**. Enjoy what you do. Being passionate about something means carefully planning out your day before it even begins and doing things diligently and quickly. Hurrying means you put it off until the last minute. Changing your habits means changing your performance. In all the world, there is just one you!

   "The trouble with being in a rat race is that even if you win the race, you're still a rat." Lily Tomlin, actress and comedian

6. **Understand that the harder you work, the more luck you will have**. I've never been a believer in "luck," but I believe in divine blessing and guidance. Some people believe "God helps those who help themselves." I don't believe in this statement, and it's not a statement from the Bible. I do believe God helps those who *can't* help themselves. Plus, God

rewards hard work with His blessings. All that's required is faith and hard work!

"Think Big! Act Big! Be Big!" Norman Vincent Peale

7. **Know that valid self-analysis is crucial for improvement.** We are always our own worst enemy in this department. We judge ourselves way too harshly. That's why managers and leaders must be empathetic when it comes to constructive criticism and positive reinforcement![33]

"Feedback is the breakfast of champions" Rick Tate, Leadership expert and author

"Real communication happens when people feel safe." Ken Blanchard, The Heart of a Leader

8. **Remember that there is no substitute for hard work and careful planning. Failing to prepare is preparing to fail.** I make frequent trips all over the country. If I want to go to Houston from Dallas, I have to take I-45. If I want to drive to Austin from Dallas, I have to take I-35. If I have no idea where those two cities are on the map, I can't just take any road I want and hope to arrive at my destination. It seems silly, but that's how many leaders run their organizations. When you ask, what is your goal? They reply to make money. That's not a destination; that's a result of driving to your destination. Knowing your destination is to know your purpose. The exciting part of reaching your destination is the journey itself.

I read all sorts of material out there every day. My father passed years ago, but he taught me to read the newspaper every morning. He also taught me to read a lot and to study my Bible. He was a good man and a good father, and thanks to him, I do my best to read as much as possible daily. As a result, I was fortunate enough to stumble upon a great issue of *Fast Company* titled, *"How to Lead with Optimism."*

Here is why I'm excited to share some gold nuggets from this publication. I find it impossible for an optimistic leader to lead without passion. In my organization, everyone who works with me will tell you that I'm a passionate leader. I love the team, and the feeling is definitely mutual, without question. We have fun and make the most of every day, bringing our brand of stress relief and our empowering workshops to every company we touch. Below are some examples of other leaders who are leading with optimism and passion, harvested from the pages of that informative magazine: *Little Ergonomical Principles of Leadership from Successful Leaders - Fast Company, Issue 222*

1. ***Don't be a perfectionist***. You can't think about being perfect; you just have to keep moving forward. Perfection is the enemy of progress. -Elizabeth Gore, Dell Technologies

2. ***Be forgiving***. The most empowering thing a leader can do is acknowledge a (employee) mistake and move ahead. Example: In my first job, I showed up to a meeting thirty minutes late, and my boss said, "I know you will never sleep through a meeting again" - Eric Kinariwala, Founder of Capsule, Capsule.com *(That's persuasional leadership!)*

3. ***Be personal***. People are craving human interaction. That's going to move the needle more than any technology you could ever dream up. - Tina Sharkey, Entrepreneur and Operator of Brandless

4. *Let your guard down.* When people feel like they can talk freely and really be themselves, it makes it easier to collaborate. – Maelle Gavet, COO Compass

5. *Get a groove on.* We have an open office culture that's really fun we play cool music. It bothers me when it's too quiet. – John Foley, CEO Peloton

6. *Be passionate.* John Collison, Cofounder of Stripe, talks about how he creates a culture that thrives. The bottom line is the values that keep a company moving in the right direction. The values are the foundation, such as communication, integrity, excellence, and respect. He states, "Those were actually Enron's values. It's easy (to devise and live by a set of values) when you are starting out. But as an organization grows, you have all these competing priorities. Culture is what happens when the CEO isn't in the room. The values we developed were instrumental in gaining a competitive advantage."[34]

Ken Blanchard puts this another way, "Leadership in not just what happens when you are there; it's what happens when you are not there."[35]

Just like the passion that Winston Churchill had for his country, and Coach Wooden had for his players, these leaders have for their organizations. Do you see it in their own words? They love the company they lead, and they exhibit compassion for their employees.

The passion here is like that of a mother of the bride on her wedding day. This is what is evident in the observation made by John Collison: When the leader is passionate, so are the employees. Can it be that simple? *Yes,* because all leadership is contagious! Highly contagious. A passionate leader will have passionate employees, and passionate employees stay with their leaders.

When I was growing up, our President was Ronald Reagan. As a teenager, I looked forward to hearing him speak to the nation more than seeing a new episode of *Three's Company* (Yes, the roaring 80's!) The popular President had a passion for the people of the United States of America that was unquestionable. I remember the sense of security I had knowing his leadership was like a rock, unshakeable. He was not just our President and our leader, but also our best friend. One of Reagan's ideas was to implement a plan to reduce taxes on businesses and the upper class to stimulate economic investments, which would have benefited society as a whole in the long-term. It was deemed as "Reagan-omics" or better yet known as "The Trickle-Down Theory." As a result of reducing taxes on the rich, more of the wealthy would invest in other US companies and allow greater payouts for employees, creating a "trickle-down" effect. But that didn't happen, entirely. Instead, more investments were established offshore in the attractive returns offered by Swedish bank accounts.

Proponents of Reagan's plan claim that it would have worked if more of the wealthy invested in America. However, he still had a "trickle-down" effect, just not what was expected. His passionate leadership trickled down to all of us, and as a result, the 1980s was one of the best decades for us as a country. It was a time of "strength through peace," ending the Cold War, strengthening relations with the Soviet Union, and a robust economic policy with a considerable decrease in unemployment and inflation.[36]

Companies thrived in this time, and as a result, homeownership increased, and unemployment decreased significantly. Reagan was one of the few presidents that everyone actually wanted to run a third term. That's how much he was loved as a leader. He is a strong example of persuasive leadership at it's very best. Why did most Americans follow him? Because they wanted to follow him! That's how good our organizations *can be* with persuasive leadership.

All leadership regimens will spill over to its followers, every time. You can be passionate about a movie, and you will have others who agree with you simply because they want to follow you. That's leadership. You can let a driver who is in a hurry cut in front of you on the road, even when you are in a hurry. That's leadership. You can give to the poor, and others will follow your example. That's leadership again. The ergonomics of leadership is simply this *be influential with passion!* And watch how passionate your followers will become!

I once heard a leadership expert say, "Real leaders are ordinary people with extraordinary determination." At the end of the day, you are already a leader if you interact with other human beings on this planet. Be a good one. Be a happy one. And let your passion spill over and infect your entire workforce. As a result, when people feel valued and loved will be passionate themselves, and more work will get done. The mission is clear, their jobs are secure, and their future is bright. Those are nice results of the passionate leadership of a persuasive leader!

Let's stop here and do an ergonomic assessment of what we have learned about persuasive leadership. A leader is a good leader if he or she is:

- Confident and Driven
- Adaptable to Change
- A Visionary
- Compassionate
- Passionate

- Humble
- Happy and Fun (*Actually, I threw this quality in there, which demonstrates the results of a persuasive leader in action*)

All these qualities add up to people following you because of the law of attraction. This type of leader needs to emerge in every organization that desires to grow. Our hard-working employee force needs to be rescued by good, caring leaders in one way or another.

Years ago, I was a speaker at a week-long Christian youth camp in the summer of 2002, known as Still Water Sports Camp in the beautiful Texas Hill Country That summer week was very, very rain stricken. We had a lot of campers and a lot of rain. The fields first were just muddy, but eventually, rainwater had risen to such a high level that the nearby river flooded, and water spilled over into all the cabins. I remember that everyone had to sleep with their luggage on their bunk beds, and some lower bunk beds were literally underwater, so only the top bunks could be used.

The camp's purpose was to train the youth in multiple sports, but eventually, only swimming made sense. The youth really got creative, and everyone had a good experience, but the rain never stopped. It was like God was flooding the Earth *again!*

There was only one small bridge that vehicles could travel on to get in and out of the camp. It was the only way out of the camp, with the river flowing powerfully at dangerous levels. This became a huge problem as the food trucks were unable to get to the camp, and we were running out of food for almost 100 counselors and campers. Furthermore, the bus to take all the kids back home also could not get across the bridge. The news teams from the area sent helicopters to cover the situation, and as a result, panic started to emerge.

However, we had a mission. We were passionate about these kids, and we had to get these kids home, no matter the cost. The camp had several canoes, and several of the adults volunteered to take the kids across the river. Two-by-two, we paddled each camper across the river, without a single fatality or injury. We created a system in which one canoe would be supported by another to cross the river on a diagonal, and it worked. It took hours, and all of us were physically worn out, but we were excited that we accomplished a task that seemed impossible as a team.

We were passionate about getting the task done efficiently and effectively. Lives depended on it.

Take that same passion, mission, and determination, and apply it to everyday leadership. Imagine how much more employees could accomplish if they operated the way we did in saving those campers! The employees want this, but it flows down from the leader. When we get leadership practices right, employees will be able to do amazing things!

There you have it, the very principles that make leaders *extraordinary.*

If you are a compassionate leader, you will naturally practice empathy for your employees. When I talk to organizations, I emphasize *passionate leadership.* The opposite is apathetic leadership, and if that's you, I promise no one wants to work for you. All forms of leadership are contagious, even apathy. Here's a taste of what you can expect under this type of leadership.

Today there are several apps and review platforms: namely Google, Glassdoor, and Angie's List. I recently researched a small organization of 50-70 employees since I heard about their high employee turn-over rate. So, what are the past employees saying? What I found was disturbing, and it was all about the leadership, not the salary or long hours. Here is just one review that I found:

> *Respect is a major issue here. Expectations are unclear and not communicated. People are afraid to voice their grievances or you will probably be let go. No one listens to the younger employees who are in the trenches day in and day out. This place is better suited for complacent workers than anyone with a brain. There's a high turn-over rate because nobody wants to stay. No loyalty here. Glassdoor, Company undisclosed*

Does this remind you of the company you work for or even one that you run? As you can see, this is *not* indicative of compassionate leadership. If this organization wants to attract good talent and keep the good talent they do have then changes need to take place fast!

The result of apathetic leadership is a workplace culture littered with apathetic employees and a high turnover rate! Who can work productively in such an environment? I'd rather work for a happy leader who is humble enough to change as needed to make their employees feel happier themselves, and safer as a result.

I'm going to challenge leaders who have no passion for what they are doing: get out of leadership or humble yourself and make some changes!

Now for a more positive example of someone who changed his entire organization around by simply making changes to himself and his employees' policies.

Simon Sinek shares a story about a company called *Next Jump*. The CEO, Charlie Kim, had the common practice, as most companies do, of letting people go based on the year-end performance of the company. As a result, he could sense the fear of his people worrying about their job security. He said,

"We want Next Jump to be a company that our mothers and fathers would be proud of us building." Therefore, he implemented a Lifetime Employment policy, which meant that no one would be fired to balance the books, or even for poor performance. Those whose performance was low would receive coaching, but now they are part of the family. You would only be gone from the company if you chose to leave, or intentionally tried to sabotage the company in some way or violations of moral turpitude. With this policy, they tightened up on hiring new employees, only allowing one in a hundred applicants in the organization. The results?

(1) Everyone communicated with each other more openly
(2) Team cooperation increased
(3) Mistakes and problems were fixed more quickly, long before they escalated.
(4) Performance enhanced greatly!
(5) Revenue growth by more than 60% since the policy was implemented.
(6) Turnover decreased from 40% to 1%
(7) Everyone was loyal to each other and operated like one big happy family.

This results from a leader who chose to renew his passion for his company and compassion for his people. Find your passion and lead or get out of the way!

I can promise you that the corporate culture at *Next Jump* jumped! When corporate culture is elevated, business performance is elevated as well. According to Kevin Hodes, Founder, and CEO of *Swypit*, he has witnessed that strong corporate cultures are affiliated with strong financial results for the organization. In short, a strong corporate culture happens when the employees of the organization are in line with the company's values, traditions, and behaviors.[37]

Here's the good news. A majority of corporate executives want a strong culture to exist in their organizations. They care about their employees and really want the best for them because it affects everything the leader wants to achieve. Hodes indicates that, "Over half of senior executives believe that corporate cultures are a top-three driver firm value, and 92% believe that improving their culture would increase their firm's value. Surprisingly, only 16% believe their culture is where it should be."[38]

What is the remedy then? What can be done to create a stronger culture? The answer requires two elements: The corporate leader has to want a better culture for his/her employees, and it must be acted upon "deliberately and with transparency."

As an organizational consultant, I propose a strategy for leaders and employees to list all the things about their culture in which they are *grateful*. Why? Stale cultures thrive on negativity. So much so that everyone forgets how good things really are in their environment. Then ask for an anonymous survey titled "Top 5 Things I'd Like to See Changed." Follow it all up with a meeting of leaders and employees like "Meet in the Middle." A message for all leaders is this: Do you remember the third thing that never changes? CHANGE. You will have to compromise to strengthen your organizational culture. What is it worth to you to sacrifice some benefits and even part of your salary for the benefit of those who follow you? Are you willing to do all that you can to make your organization healthier and *happier*? Will the trade-off be worth it? I can answer that with a resounding Yes! I firmly believe that gratitude is contagious. Consider the Meeting of the Middle a "jump-start" for all corporate leaders who want a better world for their employees.

How passionate can a leader truly be? How passionate is a mother on her daughter's wedding day? It should be that high, and it can be when you joyfully lead others in the five elements of Persuasive Leadership.

I love crashing weddings, always great food, and almost everyone knows someone named "John." Then I blend in with the crowd and cry at the wedding. I'm just kidding, but you can't ignore such a lively culture! Have you seen the movie, *My Big Fat Greek Wedding?* Take that same love and passion and apply it to leadership in our companies, but hopefully without all the craziness of trying to get everything perfect. I've never been to a wedding event with everyone mopping around, breathing heavy sighs, rubbing their temples to ease a headache, and looking at the clock every five minutes. Other than keeping to the schedule, no one cares about the clock, and ironically time flies! Why?

Everyone is having so much fun and is filled with joy! Everyone looks forward to getting to the next bite of food, interacting with the others, and helping guys like me find my friend "John." In short, if everyone enjoyed coming to work every day, even Mondays, it's hard to imagine anything but a boost in employee performance. If you want to be an effective persuasive leader, you need to add value to your employees every day. Inspire them with your words and actions, be a leader who is fun to follow! Now imagine what would the outcome be for your organization? That's the ergonomics of leadership:

- The *courage* of Winston Churchill
- The *vision* of Bill Gates
- The *passion* of a mother on her daughter's wedding day
- The *compassion* of an empathetic leader
- Then you have *momentum*

The Result of Persuasive Leadership: Momentum

"Momentum is not the result of one push. It is the result of many continual pushes over time." John C. Maxwell

Your people will always buy into you because they buy into things bigger than themselves. Never let the fire die. I can see a leader might read this chapter and make some changes the next day, but then over a short time, let things drift back to the way they used to be. We are all "creatures of habit," and if we do not invest the time it takes to make changes and sustain those changes, we will all change back.

You can't display compassion towards employees one day, then scold them in front of their peers the next day. Just like a car continually needs gas, so do all of us when it comes to encouragement. We have all heard the term "At the end of the day," probably thanks to the Kardashians. It's a common term that we all use now, just like we all used the term, "That's awesome!" in the '80s and '90s. Well, I believe it's "at the beginning of the day" that matters. How do you start your day? I sincerely believe that reading the newspaper to stay current is great for being up to date, but the news is often very negative and may not be the best way to start a good day. I prefer to start the day by reading something positive and inspirational before reaching for the newspaper. I have a little booklet filled with inspirational scriptures that motive and inspire me each morning. I want to encourage you to do the same. Being first inspired by your Creator through His words of encouragement will inspire you to "trickle" the encouragement and positivity down to others. Stay away from the fire, and you will grow cold every time. Instead, decide to grow—every day.

The experts say it takes 21 days to either break a habit or develop a new one. I'm giving you, the reader, five elements of persuasive leadership to implement in your work environment over the next three weeks. It's not even realistic to think as an HR person or any one of the decision-making responsibility that bringing in a talented speaker for a single employee workshop will change everything for the better. Sure, everyone can learn something great, but it takes the leadership to decide to change first before expecting employees to change.

With momentum, everyone is excited about the changes and wants to contribute to the overall success! Momentum encourages creativity with no bounds. Creativity says, "There's always a way, always an answer!" Inspire your people to take breaks, lots of them. Encourage them to move around and converse with their co-workers. This is how great ideas can flourish. In doing so, employees will love where they work, they will love you as their positional leader, and look forward to Mondays.

• BREAKING IT DOWN •

Little things make big things happen. John Wooden

In what ways have you influenced those around you?

_____

_____

_____

_____

_____

What brought you to your current position of leadership? Why did you choose it?

_____

_____

_____

_____

_____

How can you implement change in your office environment that can boost interaction?

_____

_____

_____

_____

_____

What makes you passionate about what you do?

_____

_____

_____

_____

_____

CHAPTER SIX

Ergonomics of Time

IN 1989, CHER came out with the smash hit song, *If I Could Turn Back Time*, which was #1 on the Music Billboards for many months. Even today, it ranks as the #57 on US Billboard 200, and I believe it's a huge hit for more than Cher's incredible voice and melody. It's just something we can all wish we could do, right? I believe we would turn back time for millions of reasons, if only, if only.

Have you at least once in your life asked yourself, "Why did I do that?" or "If I could just go back and change things." Well, you can't go back. Every second that passes by always stamps itself as history, and time only moves in one direction. Forward.

In its truest essence, *time management* would be the ability to manipulate time in which we could go forward or backward, or *time travel*. What would you do if that were possible? Would you jump around history just like in the movie *Time Bandits*, or would you try to change history like in *Back to the Future*? If given the opportunity, maybe some people would try to change major events, such as the Pearl Harbor attack, JFK's assassination, or even 9/11.

However, I can guarantee every one of us would also opt to prevent a mistake we made in the past, change a major career decision, or choose to take better care of ourselves. I know I would have taken the opportunity to at least get a glimpse of alternate career decisions. Like many Millennials today, I remember being a sophomore in college and deciding on a career path, after changing my mind at least four times. One afternoon I was eating lunch with my closest friend Casey, who chose to go the medical route and became a doctor. By this time, I had finally chosen to go into Education and become a teacher in Health and Science. Since many of the preliminary classes in our two fields were aligned, he made me a proposal (*no, not marriage*). He asked me to consider following him into the medical field as well. I wanted to say "yes" but doubted my ability to pass the "weed-out" classes such as Statistics, Chemistry, Advanced Anatomy & Physiology, etc. I was just worried about becoming a statistic by not passing Statistics. After all, statistically, only 56% of those who take Statistics pass the class, and I recently learned that 69% of all statistics are made up on the spot! (*If you did not get that joke, you have been reading too long. Take some time out before reading more about making the most of your time.*) Heck, I may not have even passed Chemistry, but the chemistry I had with Casey as a study partner would have been a real push for me to buckle down and get through medical school successfully. To my good friend Casey, all of these classes came much easier, and his grades were usually much better than mine. But my mother was a teacher, and she encouraged me to stick to the field of education as she saw it as something I could always *fall back on.*

So, I stayed with Education and became a teacher and a coach. I even attained my master's degree in the field and became a Principal. Then I pursued my doctorate in Education and became a teacher-trainer, and eventually a corporate wellness owner. Although I'm happy in what I'm doing now, I've always wondered where I would be if I had become a medical doctor instead? Casey became one, and today is doing very well. Do I have regrets? Not at all! Do I wonder where I would be today as a physician? Yes, all the time. My point is that we all have decision points in how we spend our time and who we become as a result. I rest on the fact that God is in control, and I'm right where He desires me to be.

One very true statement is how much time we all waste. I remember Betty White hosting SNL and making fun of Facebook, saying, "It's such a wonderful waste of time." Isn't it, though? How much time have you spent accumulating "friends" when, at the same time, you are feeling all alone in this world? How much time have you spent in front of your computer today? This week? This year? According to CNN's research, Americans spend more than 10 hours daily on-screen time, including phones and computer screens. That is 50-80 hours per week and 3,640 hours annually, in front of the screen. Is all this a complete waste of time? Well, that depends. If you are connecting with friends on Facebook or Instagram, and actually making true friends in the process, or using these platforms as a tool to plan your days or upcoming events with your friends, that's time utilized effectively. If you are an entrepreneur, business owner, or in any marketing capacity, you *really* need to spend *more* time on all these platforms! That's where everyone's attention is focused these days, and the Internet is very underpriced for what you can get out of it. That's definitely *not* time wasted! However, other than utilizing social media platforms for creating meaningful relationships or marketing a business, I doubt anyone will be on their deathbeds, saying, "I just wish I had spent more screen-time!"

So, if we can't "manage" time, how can we plan our days better, since we can never go back and change it?

I love this topic, *The Ergonomics of Time*, because time is the only thing in all our lives that works completely equal for all of us. We all have the same number of seconds, minutes, and hours in each of our days. Think of "time" as a game, and we are all players in it. There are strict rules for this game. One, as we have already discussed, we can't reverse time or go backwards through it. Two, we all go forward at the same rate as everyone else. Time is constant. Three, nobody gets to "glimpse" at the outcomes of our decisions. So, we all take the same risk. Four, everyone gets to choose how they spend their time and reap the rewards and consequences of actions performed in the present.

It's fascinating to me how so many people make the most of their time and therefore soar, while others settle for less with no direction. In this game of *time*, we have the game of *life*, and we are all here for a *purpose*. I strongly believe that if you find your purpose, you will spend your time more wisely. I think it is the Greeks who have this saying, "Either you find what makes you tick, or what ticks you off!" It's time to get excited about your purpose and begin your journey. How long will it take you to become successful? That's entirely up to you.

Statistically (dang, I love that word!), Millennials will change jobs every two years. Every two years!! Why is that? I believe the reason is that they feel they are not making a difference in their company, and therefore feeling somehow unimportant. I also believe they most likely chose a job that simply didn't line up with their passion. After studying many expert opinions on how to spend our time on Earth effectively, I've come up with five simple rules for making every day count:

1) Discover your Purpose
2) Map out your Time
3) Get Serious
4) Grow
5) Have Fun

I'm going to take a moment and refer back to the Pareto Principle, which contains the 80/20 rule to many things in our lives. In his day, back in 1895, he noted two kinds of people in his society: the "vital few" and the "trivial many." The vital few make up 20% of the society, and the trivial many the remaining 80%. He also discovered that this principle applied to many other applications as well. For instance, 20% of your activities will account for 80% of your results. For the social media giant, Twitter, 80% of its content is created by 20% of its users. Also, 20% of a company's products and services will account for 80% of its profits. I wish I could say that 80% of us work hard and therefore rest comfortably as the top 20% of the richest people in America, but you know that's not true. Why? Far too many of us are wandering around in life, not going in *any* direction, floating from profession to profession. Just as a dog chases its tail going in circles, so do too many of us. You may have a job, but chances are it is not aligned with who you are or what God created you to be.

If this is you, start praying for God to reveal His purpose for you. You are a masterpiece, and *no one* on this planet is like you. As a child (or even recently), you may have been told that you are a mistake, you have no purpose. That is a lie! God doesn't make mistakes, and therefore you were designed with a purpose. How do you find your purpose? That's is where most of your time should be spent in discovery.

Discover Your Purpose

When you were a kid, what did you dream of becoming? When I was five years old, our school went on a field trip to a firehouse, and I wanted to become a fireman. That changed when I was nine years old and stared in a school play, and then I wanted to become an actor. At the time, the movie *The Goonies* was in theaters, and I wanted to be one of those kids on the silver screen. Then I saw the movie *Top Gun*, then I wanted to become a fighter pilot performing stunts in the air. I must have changed my mind more often than a dog sniffs his vomit, but so do almost all of us, right?

My suggestions for making the time to find your purpose is as follows:

1. Pray for God's direction in your life. After all, He is the only being outside of the rules of time because He created it! He is transcendent of time and can see your entire life from beginning to end, so trusting in God is your first step in finding your purpose.
2. Brain dump everything that excites you as a career path. That means to just write everything that catches your imagination down in a list in no particular order.
3. Use the Internet. This is a *must* in obtaining the job you desire since almost every organization these days require online applications to be completed. To get there, you need to discover what is available out there through job search engines. Read blogs too! Many organizations'

blogs discuss future job openings, and you can get to the front of the line this way. This is how you effectively spend your time in front of the computer. Research everything on your brain dump list and then make a separate list of "Pros" and "Cons" for each one of them. Now you can weigh your decision to choose a shortlist of what career path might be right for you.

4. Take an introductory course in your top three choices. I call these 101 classes. You can take classes online or in a traditional setting, but the most important thing is to take the first step and do it. I promise you this will be the best usage of your time if you have not yet discovered your purpose.

Map Out Your Time

Okay. So now you have completed step one and chosen your career path, let's say you chose something in the field of law. Now you need to plan every one of your semesters to the finish, then map out your plan to find your perfect fit in the field. It doesn't matter if you are in the discovery phase of a career or already well into one and trying to accelerate; it all boils down to utilizing your time so effectively that you go to bed at the end of each day feeling fulfilled. That's the whole purpose of this chapter, fulfillment with no regrets; the art of knowing that you are living life to the fullest every single day.

How do you live every day so that when you go to bed, you know that even if you could turn back time and live the day all over again, you wouldn't change a thing? That you *owned* the day! You can live every day, *smarter*, not *harder*. I call this mapping out your time because you have mapped out your day. It is sort of like your daily schedule, but one that maximizes your satisfaction at the end of the day in complete fulfillment. The effort is well worth it if you can lie down in bed with a smile on your face, give a nice long sigh, and then enjoy a good night's sleep.

In 2006, Will Smith played the role of Chris Gardner in a movie called, *The Pursuit of Happyness*. Based on Gardner's actual story, the movie focuses on Gardner's true events to get a job at a prestigious brokerage firm while homeless with a young son. To get the job, he had to compete in an internship that lasted many weeks, enduring many hardships and humiliations to beat out all other applicants. How did he do it? He wasted none of his time but stayed focused and serious about his productivity.

Chris Gardner's efforts are the complete opposite of what I see when I walk into countless organizations. I see many of the employees checking their Facebook feeds, gossiping with co-workers, or watching the clocks to hurry out of work to beat the traffic. These same workers often complain about their salary or whine about their co-workers, and they all claim they feel "stuck" at work with no hope of moving up the ladder. My friends, how can you expect to get a raise or a promotion when you are not bringing value to your organization? It's nonsense to think that you will receive such recognition without working harder and becoming serious about your work and efforts. What made Chris Gardner so unique? He had every excuse not to do well and instead excelled beyond all the others. He went from zero-to-hero, and today he is that rarest of things, a self-made multimillionaire. He had to map out every day and stick to it!

Therefore, let's examine what this would look like. First comes the mornings, then the afternoons, then the evenings. Early mornings are when you want to prioritize what's most important and do that thing first. Today we tend to overschedule our days and push the most important things to the side. It's all about commitment and keeping focused on getting things done with a sense of priority.

In *Today Matters*, John Maxwell tells a story about Charles Schwab, the president of Bethlehem Steele in the early twentieth century. He meets with management consultant, Ivy Lee, in efforts to improve his company's productivity. Schwab explained to the consultant, "We know what we should be doing, but if you could show us a better way of getting it done, I'll listen to you—and pay you anything within reason." Lee's advice was simple but effective. When Schwab implemented Lee's plan, his company became the largest independent steel producer of its day. Schwab saw so much productivity as a result that he wrote Lee a check for $25,000 (an equivalent of a quarter-million dollars today).

Lee's plan is something that I have implemented into my own life, and I do all I can to stick to it. His words of wisdom became the essence of how I plan my time, and hopefully, they will become yours. Here's what Lee told the steel magnate to do:

1. Pull out a blank sheet of paper.
2. Write down the six most important things you have to do tomorrow.
3. Number them in order of importance to you and your company.
4. Fold the paper up, put it in your pocket, and don't look at it until the following morning.
5. Wake up the next day, eat a good breakfast (I recommend eggs; they feed the brain and spark creativity!) Speaking of eggs, I've always wondered why anyone orders eggs-over-easy because you lose all the yolk that

way. Egg yolk runs off the fork every time and drips onto your pants, then you have to run to the restroom with a wet towel and rub out the mess, then you walk out the restroom, and everyone thinks you had an "accident." Make it easier for yourself an order eggs-over-hard or get them scrambled. That way, you won't be scrambling to the restroom and enduring more embarrassing moments!

6. After breakfast, take that paper out of your pocket and look at item #1 on your list. Don't look at the others; just look at that one and start working on it until it's completed. Then once it's done, look at item #2 and get that one done. Then move onto #3 and then #4 and so on. It's alright if you only get #1 and #2 done in a day, says Lee. You would not have gotten more things on your list utilizing any other method.

7. Do this every day and watch how more productive you become![39]

When company leaders ask me about the problems they have with employees not being productive and even "slacking-off," I ask them about the daily agendas set out for the employees. It's a simple and obvious expectation that once workers show up, they know the tasks they need to get done for the day, but that's not always the case. As leaders, we need to show our employees what is expected of them and hold them accountable for the most important tasks. I sincerely believe that if all organizations operated in the fashion outlined by Ivy Lee for Charles Schwab, more employees would stay on task, and more productivity would result.

Get Serious

There is an art to getting focused, and focus is how you get serious about accomplishing anything. I believe in a good work-life balance, but you can only give full attention to one thing at a time. Forget multi-tasking! You can't be 100% focused on one project while checking your Facebook, texting your friends, and watching those hilarious cat videos on YouTube. Gary Keller writes in his book, *The One Thing*, "the question of balance is a question about priority when you act on your priority, you will automatically go out of balance, giving more time to one over the other." To be successful in anything you do, you must learn to push everything else to the side and give that *one thing* your undivided attention. There's always time later to play, check your Facebook, and so on, but work comes first. Always.

A great example of this was Andrew Carnegie, the second most successful businessman of the 19th century, after John D. Rockefeller. In 1885, in Pittsburgh, Pennsylvania, Carnegie addressed the students at Curry Commercial College. His talk entitled *The Road to Business Success*, gave advice that seems very contradictory to what most have us have been told. Here's a section of what he said to those students, and to all of us today:

> And here is the prime condition of success, the great secret—concentrate all of your energy, thought, and capital exclusively upon the business in which you are engaged. 'Don't put all your eggs into one basket' is all wrong. I tell you 'put all your eggs in one basket, and then watch that basket.' Look around you and notice, men who do that often do not fail. [40]

I love learning from the Greats of Old because their principles are timeless. You can't focus on multiple things at once, as you must if you 'put your eggs in different baskets.' I often wonder where the saying came from, don't you? I imagine some goofy kid on the farm was in a hurry, had to gather the eggs for the family, put them all in one basket, and tripped along the way. He scrambled the eggs all over his clothes and the lawn! That brings me to another point—*go slow and take your time!*

You can't rush greatness. You have probably heard stories of songwriters who would write that one big hit in just a few minutes. That's not rushing; that's the power of inspiration! I often get great ideas at red lights. I really hate red lights because they somehow know I'm approaching, and they turn into a fast yellow and then red just as I reach the intersection. However, the number of 'ah-ha!' moments I've had at all those dang lights is countless. You can't rush greatness, because it needs time to build up within you. Once it's built up in your mindset, and it's all you have been focusing on, just like those eggs in the basket, that's when inspiration happens!

I once met a young man at a networking function who was a very chatty fellow. He seemed to know everyone, while he was making the rounds promoting all five of his business. When he circled over to me, he began to tell me about all of his endeavors. He was 19 years old, and already started an iPhone repair company, an eBay company, a landscaping company, a house cleaning business, and a marketing venture through all his followers on his YouTube channel. I asked him this question, and the same question applies to anyone with multiple baskets: "That's all great, but which one do you enjoy doing the most?" That question made him shut up for about twenty seconds, then he replied, "I love doing all of them!" Then I asked him, "Have you ever been to a circus?" He said, "Yes, why?" It was here that I pulled out an important fact I had learned about lion-tamers, which was completely applicable to the situation. I said, "Have you ever noticed how the lion-tamer will sometimes pick up a chair and point the legs towards the lion? Why do you think he does that?" The lad replied, "He uses the stool to defend himself, right?" "Nope," I answered. "The tamer does that to confuse the lion. The chair has four legs, and the lion can only focus on one thing at a time. At first, the lion focuses on the tamer for an attack, but once the chair's legs are pointing toward it, the lion sees four targets. It can't focus on four things at the same time, so the lion backs down and walks away." When I said this, the lad did what the lion does, he was taken back, scratched his head, then replied to me, "So you are saying I should just focus on one of those jobs I'm doing, and forget the others?" I said, "Exactly! Just focus on the one business you enjoy the most. A job will be profitable if only you can give it all you got." I think that changed his life, and I'm not lying!

When you take that one task, that one job, that one business venture, or that one project, you have to put all your eggs into that one basket. Every day. First thing in the morning, until you have either completed it or at least have seen significant progress. Mark Twain once said

> *The secret of getting ahead is getting started. The secret to getting started is breaking your complex overwhelming tasks into small manageable tasks and then starting on the first one.* [41]

Therefore, write out what excites you! What is it that you know you can do better than anyone else? Do that thing. Get started. Jump out of the plane and grow your wings on the way down. Actually, use a parachute. If you jump out of that plane without a parachute, you will squash your dreams and all your organs. But you get my point, right? You may be excited about starting a business, and that's the exciting part. It's often easy to come up with ideas, but it's the follow-through that's tough.

Let's say that my chatty young friend decided to stick with his iPhone repair business. It's very exciting to think about all of his friends out there with broken phone screens and tech issues. But it's not exciting to raise the money needed to start the business and make it profitable. You must undertake many formalities, such as deciding the corporate entity (such as LLC, S Corp, C Corp, or Sole Proprietorship.) You then have to decide how to market it, where you will run your business, whether to include business partners or other investors, and so on. I encourage you first to commit completely, then stick with the process while you figure it out.

Chris Gardner is a prime example to follow in *The Pursuit of Happyness*, which is based on a true real-life story. He discovered his purpose (to become a broker) and make lots of money as a result. That was the exciting part. But once he committed, he had to work for free in a long internship. He had to figure it all out. He figured out little things, like how drinking less water and coffee led to fewer restroom breaks and therefore gave him more time to make phone sales. That was the tough part. He worked hard, remained focused until he got the job. That's the power of focus and persistence. To succeed and achieve your goals, you have to grow and focus on your personal development.

Grow

Warren Buffet spends 80% of his time reading. While not everyone can have that luxury, we should read for at least 2 hours per day. I recommend you do this in the mornings as a ritual! Because if you are not reading, you are not growing! If you have ever been to a Barnes & Noble bookstore, you will see a Personal Development section. Anyone who works there will tell you that one section is where they sell the most books. Non-fiction books sell more volumes than fiction. Why? Simply because we all have room to grow, that doesn't happen after reading Harry Potter novels. There is magic in growing, but no magic wand is required. The only magic needed is time, time that you have carved out to grow.

Let's break this down for you. Each night before going to bed, you need to map out your day to absorb your plan into your subconscious mind. Sigmund Freud, in 1915 figured this out. He said, "The unconscious mind is the primary source of human behavior."[42] This is your responsibility every day.

There is an old saying that says this, "if it is to be, it's up to me." I have even heard a comedian once say, "Wherever you go, there you are!" So true, isn't it? You and you alone are responsible for your thoughts, actions, and how you fill your days and nights. If you are in it to win it, then you must grow. You don't have to read to grow, but you do have to learn new things. I've learned a few things myself when I discovered Craig Ballantyne in his book, *The Perfect Day Formula*. In his book, he encourages his readers to make simple changes to create powerful new growth habits. For example, try to wake up 15 minutes earlier than you usually do, so you are not in a hurry in the mornings to get your day started.

He quotes the philosopher William James, "Only when habits of order are formed can we advance to really interesting fields of action," and only when we set our minds to a daily growth can we get ahead in life. When we follow good habits, like getting up early, we strengthen the rituals that win our mornings and bring on Perfect Days.[43]

I encourage anyone reading this book to pick up *Ballantyne's*. It will help you organize each day into a perfect formula that fits into your life. Here is what I have learned from his book and other books I've read on the subject of personal growth. The following is a simple formula that you can implement. It's not a bunch of rules, but just five actions that will help you grow and stick to the things that really matter at work and home. The goal here is for you to be at your personal best, and that requires growth and listening to your body (as discussed in chapter 2).

1. Try not to eat anything after 8:00 pm and do your best to go to bed before 11:00 pm. You need at least six good hours of sleep to be fully functional the next morning. Why? Research tells us during the first few hours the brain works to repair the body, while in the second few hours, the brain repairs itself. If you are not getting enough sleep and feel "groggy," now you know why your brain hasn't fully repaired itself yet.

2. Write down the six things you have to do tomorrow, then number them in order of importance, as explained earlier. Clear written goals will help stimulate your thinking and motivate you into action!

3. Map out your day the day before. If that number one item on your list requires a couple of hours, plan on eliminating everything that can keep you from doing it the first thing in the morning. If time allows, plan on doing two of those things in the morning or spread them out in the afternoon.

4. Plan on time to check email, make calls, and coordinating all the small tasks you have to do. Most people do this reactively, but I encourage you to do it proactively. Intentionally make time so you will not be thinking about the little things when you are focused on your most important agendas.

5. Listen to your body. We may have the perfect daily agenda set out during the day, but we get tired after eating a big

lunch and tend to procrastinate important items set before us. To avoid this, eat a sensible light lunch. A salad with grilled chicken is a great lunch choice! However, if you tend to get drowsy during the day, and if it's possible for you, take a 20-minute powernap. This is what it means to <u>listen</u> to your body. There's power in a power nap! Then, give yourself a shot of caffeine and get back to your time map. It works! It's just one of the healthy habits of personal growth—controlling your afternoons.

Stick to a strict regimen and stay disciplined every day, and you will reap the rewards! It may be hard, but you can do it once you find your purpose and stay passionate to the very end. Honestly, this task takes very little time each day but can save you hours of wasted time if you can plan accordingly!

There is one quality which one must possess to win, and that is definiteness of purpose, the knowledge of what one wants and a burning desire to achieve it. Napoleon Hill

Have Fun!

Once you develop a habit of mapping out your days, you will actually become "addicted" to success. Brian Tracy is an incredible author and speaker, but his schedule (like all of us) became hectic. In his book, *Eat That Frog!* he put together simple things we can all do to create great success in tackling our days. Here's what he says about preparing your days to tackle the hardest items on your list first (the frog you have to eat in the morning) and thus feeling great as a result.

It makes you feel like a winner. Whenever you complete a task of any size or importance, you feel a surge of energy, enthusiasm, and self-esteem. The completion of an important task triggers the release of endorphins in your brain. These endorphins give you a natural 'high.' The endorphin rush that follows the successful completion of any task makes you feel more positive, personable, creative, and confident.[44]

Therefore, create your daily list, and stick to it. But remember, you must work backward. Determine where you want to be ten years from now. Now create your 10-year list, written down on a sheet of paper. Then break it down into manageable time bites, incrementally. You know where you are going in the long run, but how do you get there? You create another list of each year leading to the 10-year mark. Great, now you have the time map for the first year, *this year*, because it's the first annual step you will be taking. Then create your monthly list for this year, break it down into your weekly list, and then into your daily list.

Sounds simple right? Yes, but you have to have the daily discipline to do it. You must have reward incentives in place along the journey. In 2006, I joined the *Body for Life Challenge*, started by Bill Phillips. He had a contest that still goes on to this day. You have 12 weeks to transform your body. To begin the contest, you take a body pic standing in front of the mirror, holding a newspaper with the day's date. Then you get serious about eating right and exercising. It was tough for most people because it required new habits to replace old habits. It was tough for me too, but I learned back then the power of mapping my day, and I stuck to it. I had an accountability partner and a good friend who was in it with me, named Dominik. Every day we worked out at the gym and ate a lot of meals together that were very healthy.

Never in my life have I seen such a transformation in my body, mind, and self-esteem! It was rewarding to compete every day knowing I did everything as planned, and the endorphin rush was worth it. Now here is what shocked me about the program and will probably shock you too. You must eat and exercise with "no-cheating for six days of the week," and on the seventh day, you may eat anything you want and as much as you want! Basically, on the seventh day, reward yourself! Dom and I chose Sunday to be our reward day. I recall one weekday during the challenge, we were both at a house party where lots of bite-size treats were being passed around, and we dared each other to eat just one of anything (since it was all unhealthy!). But on Sunday, we would have blueberry pancakes for breakfast, lasagna for lunch, and a nice juicy steak for dinner, and of course, dessert.

The results? We both had a total body transformation, but neither of us won any prizes: $50,000 or a new Corvette, as I recall. Our reward was staring back at us in the mirror, in the goals of body weight and muscle mass we had reached, that was rewarding enough for our hard work! So, here's a similar challenge for you:

Have fun with all this planning! You will see the results! I can imagine a mother working two jobs, all the while dreaming of running a business of her own in which she can work from home. I can imagine the Millennial working at her 4th job dreaming of one day making enough money to buy her own house. I can picture the college student with big dreams, and the Baby Boomer desiring a new direction in life. Wherever and whoever you are in the world, you can achieve it if you can dream it! Achievement is found in our daily agenda. But first, you have to figure out if you are more like Simon or more like Garfunkel.

Applications

Let's examine our two characters: Simon and Garfunkel. Simon plans his day perfectly. He writes down his agenda the night before and gets his list entirely crossed out by the end of the day. Everyone admires him because he is a doer and not just a talker. He lives life proactively!

Simon plays the daily game very well because he plans and keeps thinking ahead. He knows where he wants to be ten years from now, five years from now, and one year from now. Remember, to plan effectively, you must plan backward with the end in mind. Everyone has high respect for him because he gets things done and rarely procrastinates. He knows that if something can get done today, he should do it today and not put it off until tomorrow. He sleeps very well and wakes up earlier than everyone else in his household. He tackles the hardest task on his list first, then has time to check off the smaller and easier tasks. He also has enough time, even ample time, to play with his kids, run errands for his wife, and exercise at the gym. Like all of us, he has stress and realizes that he may never have enough time to get everything done, but he manages his stress amazingly well by living proactively.

Garfunkel on the other hand lives life like most of us—reactively. He never plans out his day the night before, but instead just lives moment to moment. He is not the most enjoyable person to be around because he is usually "stressed out." He has a good job and shows up either on-time or mildly late, and basically "goes through the motions" of his work-life. He is full of self-doubt as never getting a promotion or finding a better job, so he just feels "settled and stuck." He heads home in the 5:00 rush hour and decides to eat a big pizza with a gallon of Coca-Cola. He reclines in his Lazy-Boy chair and watches four to five hours of TV, and the day repeats itself. As a result, he feels unmotivated, unimportant, and dreads work. His weight is beginning to take its toll, adding to his stress. He has never written a goal because he doesn't know where he is going in life. He is just happy to have a job.

Remember the Pareto Principle, that the top 20% of people in this world are the top performers, and the rest of us are the trivial many. You get to decide every day which category fits you best.

So, if you are like our friend Garfunkel, you need to do a few things to become more like Simon. It's ironic, but the more structure you put into your day, the more freedom you will have to do the things you enjoy!

First, change your mindset. James Allen wrote a popular book titled, *As a Man Thinketh*, in which he makes some challenging statements.

> *Men are anxious to improve their circumstances, but are unwilling to improve themselves.*
>
> *All that a man achieves and all that he fails to achieve is the direct result of his own thoughts.*
>
> *Man's mind may be likened to a garden, which may be intelligently cultivated or allowed to run wild.* [45]

Second, choose a new direction. If you dread Mondays and are not literally skipping to work, it's time to choose a new path. Work should be what you enjoy, not something you dread or feel like "you have to do." You need to choose now, not later.

> *The time is always right to do what is right. ---Martin Luther King, Jr.*

Think of Thomas Edison. He worked tirelessly to figure out how to make the lightbulb work. It took him over 5,000 attempts until he finally got it right. His mindset and attitude? I didn't fail 4,999 times; it just took that many times to figure out how it doesn't work. I guess you can say on the 5,000th attempt, the light came on. I think if that were anyone else, they would have given up, and today we would still be using gas lanterns to light our living rooms and offices. But Edison enjoyed it. He never gave up. What's your excuse?

> *The greatest glory in living lies not in never failing, but in rising each time we fail. –Ralph W. Emerson*

Third, picture the end goal. Decide where you want to be ten years from now and map it all out. You must chart your journey by the years, months, weeks, and days, and then stick to the plan.

> *You build on failure. You use it as a steppingstone. Close the door to the past. You don't try to forget the mistakes, but you don't dwell on it. You don't let it have any of your energy, or any of your time, or any of your space.*
>
> *Johnny Cash*

Fourth, choose an accountability partner: This can be your spouse, best friend, or mentor. Let someone know that you want to change your daily agenda and start exercising, reading books, eating better, etc. Then report to them so they can hold you on task. This proven technique will take you further than you can go on your own.

> *If you love life, don't waste time, for time is what life is made up of. Bruce Lee*

<u>Fifth, start today!</u> Yes, today and not tomorrow, next week, next month, or next year. The sooner you start walking a path, the sooner you will reach your destination. Life is just too short to waste time in a profession you do not *love*. Do what you love.

Do what you love. – WeWork motto

I love what I once heard a pastor at my church say, and it's always stuck with me. He quoted Philip Ruth, "Life is just a short time in which you are alive." It's true. Rick Warren, another well-known pastor and author of *The Purpose-Driven Life*, says the life is just a preparation for eternity. Let that one sink in.

We will discuss the *Ergonomics of Faith* in chapter 9 but realize God did not put you here on this Earth to go to a job that you hate, be around people that you can't associate, and be stressed out like poor Garfunkel. Simon says, "Get it together!" And so do I. I honestly want you to live the very best life possible, because in this life, we don't know when the finish line comes, but we do know it's coming.

Do what you want to do and enjoy life! I believe an abundant life is a structured one, with a daily agenda that gives you great accomplishments and the freedom to do anything you want to do!

So, what would my best day look like? The perfect day looks like this:

6:15 am	Wake-up 10-15 minutes early, no snoozing, and stretch your legs, arms and back.
6:25 am	Warm up to a cold shower. It shocks your system and purifies your skin. Or visit a cryotherapy center!
7:00 am	Eat breakfast mixed with protein and carbs, such as scrambled

	eggs and steel-cut oatmeal.
8:00 am	Morning commute. Listen to podcasts or some jamming music (what energizes you?) P.S. No love songs!!
9:00 am	Tackle Project #1 on your list. Minimize distractions.
11:00 am	Mid-Morning Jolt – Drink Green Tea
1:00 pm	Lunch – Eat for vitality, not just to get full. High protein and vegetables
1:30 pm	Answer emails and empty junk folder. Make your phone calls, etc.
2:30 pm	Tackle Project #2 (unless Project #1 is unfinished)
3:30 pm	Take a breathing break. Walk around. Make a new friend at the office!
4:45 pm	Make your To-Do List for tomorrow, and number them in order of importance.
6:30 pm	Resistance exercise reduces stress and increases sleep quality!
7:45 pm	Dinner time! Brown rice and protein. Mix in broccoli with chicken strips in one skillet. Delicious!
10:30 pm	Get to bed! Drink a cup of Chamomile Tea. Help your sleep quality and set the temperature between 65-70 degrees

Your best day should be pretty close to this, with a few differences to suit mood and tastes. The take-home messages are simplicity, focus, and the ability to know your goals and achieve them. That's how you can end each day and sleep soundly in bed.

• BREAKING IT DOWN •

Action Steps List

1. Write down where you want to be 10, 5, and 2 years from now. It can include homeownership and what car you drive but must include the value you will be adding to others in a certain occupation or career path.

   1. Ten years from now, I want to _____
      And _____
      And _____

   2. Five years from now, I want to _____
      And _____
      And _____

   3. Two years from now, I want to _____
      And _____
      And _____

2. Write out three annual goals leading to your destination. They should include your income progression and how to increase your productivity leading to a successful year, every year. In the next chapter, we will delve into finances and building a stronger income, but for now, just dream.

   1. Ten years from now, I hope to be making an income of _____ (this should be greater than year 5, hope you know 😊)

2. Five years from now, I hope to be making an income of
    _____ (this should be greater than year 2, hope
    you know 😊)

3. Two years from now, I hope to be making an income of
    _____ (this should be greater than this year,
    hope you know 😊)

3. For this year, write out goals for each month, total of
    twelve goals. Whatever month it is now, this is "Month 1."

    Month 1 Goal: _____

    Month 2 Goal: _____

    Month 3 Goal: _____

    Month 4 Goal: _____

    Month 5 Goal: _____

    Month 6 Goal: _____

    Month 7 Goal: _____

    Month 8 Goal: _____

    Month 9 Goal: _____

    Month 10 Goal: _____

    Month 11 Goal: _____

    Month 12 Goal: _____

4. For this month, write out up to three items for each week, a total of 12 goals again.

Four weeks from now, my three goals are:

Goal #1 _____

Goal #2 _____

Goal #3 _____

Three weeks from now, my three goals are:

Goal #1 _____

Goal #2 _____

Goal #3 _____

Two weeks from now, my three goals are:

Goal #1 _____

Goal #2 _____

Goal #3 _____

This week, my goals are:

Goal #1 _____

Goal #2 _____

Goal #3 _____

5. Now it's time for your daily agenda for tomorrow. Brain dump ten things you must do tomorrow, then number them in order of importance with (1) being most important, and (10) being the least important.

Item 1

Item 2		
Item 3		
Item 4		
Item 5		
Item 6		
Item 7		
Item 8		
Item 9		
Item 10		

6. Now re-write all of them, but in order of importance. Re-member your hardest, toughest task should be your first one. Your second most important task should be next, and so on. Hint: Checking email should be first on your list. That should be number 6 or further from number 1.

Item 1

Item 2		
Item 3		
Item 4		
Item 5		
Item 6		
Item 7		
Item 8		
Item 9		
Item 10		

Congratulations! You now have a time map of your own! Make copies of Action Steps E & F and work on them every day! You will be saving time every day by doing these steps and sticking to them!

So, what is number one and two? That should be the first thing you will do tomorrow morning. Resist the temptation to do the easier items on your list first. You will get more done by following this formula! Just remember two rules:

1. The hardest most difficult thing I have to do tomorrow is:

2. Don't move on to #2 until you finish #1

CHAPTER SEVEN

The Ergonomics of Money

OTHER THAN AIR, food, and water, there's only one thing in this world that you must have to live, and that is money. You may love it or hate it, but you must have it. It divides marriages and separates the classes. It's the determining factor of the haves and the have-nots. All of us know what it is and why we must have it, but very few of us know how to manage it.

Have you ever wondered how much printed money is out there? According to the "money" section of *Howstuffworks.com*, here's a circulation breakdown as of 2017:

12.5 billion $100 bills equal $1 trillion 250 billion
1.7 billion $50 bills equal $85 billion
9.2 billion $20 bills equal $184 billion
2.0 billion $10 bills equals $20 billion
3.0 billion $5 bills equal $15 billion
1.2 billion $2 bills equal $2.4 billion

12.1 billion $1 bills equal $12.1 billion

That means approximately 1.2 trillion notes and coins are floating around!

Yes, my friends, there is lots of money circulating, and that's just in the United States! You are probably asking, how can I get some of that money into *my* bank account??

Well, I have several options for you. First, you can rob a bank. There are tons of movies and books on how to do this effectively. In fact, what many experts call the very first "action film" was *The Great Train Robbery*, back in 1903 and directed by Edwin S. Porter. In just twelve minutes of viewing, folks could learn how to steal money from the safe on board a train crossing the Western prairies.[46] Of course, all the robbers were either caught or shot. Before choosing this option, check to see if "bank robbery" is legal in your state or country. The chances are that it is not legal, so let's rule out this option.

Option two is to marry into it if you are so lucky as to marry a multi-billionaire. But remember, multi-billionaires are hard to find and typically not still single. Plus, the rest of your new rich spouse's potential heirs may not be too kind to you since the money typically is passed on to the spouse before the children, depending on the probate laws of your state.

Option three is to inherit it, which is typically out of your control. I suppose if you are well-liked or loved by a rich relative, you will hear your name spoken out loud at a reading-of-the-will gathering. Then you will inherit your millions from a parent, grandparent, or a rich uncle. Of course, you might be disappointed to discover that instead of inheriting money, you instead inherit membership to the Jolly-of-the-Month club!

The fourth option is a much better one, and even more legal than robbing a bank! Plus, this option will entitle you to a ton of credibility regarding your financial savvy. You can *earn* it. If you live in the United States, you are already in the perfect position to earn an unlimited income. However, earning money is not enough. You must also learn how to save and invest your money to watch it grow in your bank account!

According to a Harvard study titled, *"Will $10 Million Make You Happier?"* earning your millions makes you *happier* than marrying into it or inheriting it. They interviewed 4,000 millionaires, and this was one of their surprising findings.[47]

This chapter focuses on those of us who have to earn our wealth. The information applies to anyone regardless of how they attain their money, such as saving and investing after becoming debt-free. I organized *The Ergonomics of Money* in a progressive manner to help you with understanding personal finance and finding financial freedom. Just as Coach John Wooden *(the most recognized collegiate coach in history, more about him in chapter r on leadership)* sat down with his collegiate athletes and taught them the fundamental skill of how to put on their socks first, that's how I've laid out this chapter for you. It's the basics, or fundamentals, of money management from what may be the simplest of steps.

Now is the time, dear reader, to start making wiser decisions with your money. It's overwhelming to think about how we are supposed to be saving our money and yet still live in an instant-gratification world. Ahhh, first comes the love of money, and then comes the temptation. When the rent and all the other bills have been paid, and there are still extra dollars sitting in the bank account, many of us typically want to go on a shopping spree. We all need to buy new clothes and things for the household, and how about that old clunker car of yours? Don't we deserve a newer car for all those hours of hard work? And who doesn't want to travel?

At the same time, we must save for our kid's college tuition and our own retirement, and there's always emergencies that must be covered by some hidden nest-egg. Many of us get bogged-down and even depressed with that yearning to do all these fun things with money and can't because the money isn't there at the end of the day.

Now I have a very intriguing question for everyone reading this chapter what if? What if you could?

What if you could shop, upgrade your transportation, and go on a vacation, even if you didn't get a raise?

That's why this chapter is so important for you to read and apply! Most of us are not educated enough about money because it's not included in the mandatory high school classes, and even in college, most of us do not take a finance class unless as part of a declared major. But good money management does not require an advanced finance degree. What is the missing piece? All that is needed is a personalized, balanced budget and discipline. Just as a structured schedule provides more freedom with time, a structured budget pie chart can give more freedom with money.

If you can get a well-paying job, you are ahead of the game if you are a good saver. The old joke goes that the word J-O-B stands for "Just Over Broke," which is true if you cannot live below your means. My challenge to you is to live on just half your means and save/invest the other half. My stepfather used to tell me, "If you can figure out how to live on half your income and save the rest, you will be a millionaire."

Most of us live the opposite of this sound advice. There's a cliché out there that identifies seemly wealthy individuals as "plastic rich." In other words, rich in *debt*. Yes, they live in nice expensive houses and drive expensive cars, but don't have enough cash flow to pay their bills each month. When they don't have enough money readily available, they pull out their credit cards. On the outside, they appear filthy rich, but in reality, they are dirt poor. The image of being wealthy is so important to them, and why? To impress others they don't like? It's a losing game with credit cards and unsecured debt. We will get into that further in this chapter.

I agree with financial experts when it comes to becoming fiscally responsible. To change your outcome, you must change your behavior first. Dave Ramsey reminds us, "Winning is 80% behavior and 20% head knowledge." I'm sharing the best advice available today with you, but it's meaningless until you are ready to buckle down, make sacrifices, and change your *mindset* about money.

Before any of this can work for you, you have to start with a growth mindset. Deciding to take any of the steps illustrated by the following experts is great, but it takes perseverance and the right mindset to follow-through.

> You don't get a growth mindset by proclamation. You move toward it by taking a journey. It's based on the belief in change.[48]

The key here is to train your mind to think differently about money. It is about discovering the freedom money can bring you when it is managed well. I'll show you how to do it but remember it's your behavior that must change before seeing the desired change in your financial situation. Spending is fun, and it's exciting to buy new things but spending money to cover credit card fees is a waste. Let's change your behavior, and see amazing things start to happen.

Ready to start the journey? Come on, let's go.

The Ergonomics of the State of the Union

Houston, we have a problem. A big problem. We are buried in debt with no savings of any kind!

We have seen the negative effects of capitalism, at its worse, during the COVID19 pandemic, which affected every person on this planet. Too many people were hit especially hard—people who had no savings or money set aside. As a result, we relied on stimulus checks that never came on time and leaned on friends and relatives for financial support. We simply were not ready for this, and neither were the institutions that hired us.

As a result of the pandemic, we are currently facing the highest unemployment of our generation. It will take years for many organizations to recover, and many will choose to shut down their operations and close their doors. The actual "day of disaster" for those in the United States was January 31, 2020. Before that time, unemployment was at an all-time low at 5%. It has been over ten years since we recovered from the 2008 recession, and unemployment has steadily decreased. Just two months later, since the day of disaster, unemployment drastically rose to the highest it's ever been since the Great Depression, with over 30 million jobless claims filed, and 10% unemployment. Will we ever recover from this? *Yes!* We always do, and I have faith that we will again!

However, we have learned some hard lessons about our spending and saving habits, haven't we? My warning to all my readers is this*: expect emergencies to come!* Expect them to come next month, next week, and even tomorrow. It's a new normal for all of us, isn't it?

I intend to give you a solid "ironclad" financial plan to help you be prepared, even over-prepared, for the next emergency. There are small emergencies, too, that will happen. Your car tires need replacing; you got a speeding ticket; your son needs new basketball shoes today. Small matters like this can cause your checking account to dwindle faster than you expect, but not if you already have money set aside for such matters. The issue lies in our desire to live too large. Just like my stepfather told me, if you find a way to live on half your income, you can be a millionaire. There are four main items required for you to "check-off" to make this a reality for you: Housing, car, credit cards, and savings. If you have these four in order, you will live larger, and the better off you will be before the next crisis comes! First, let's discuss your largest expense—housing.

The Census Bureau reports that the median household income was over $61,900 in 2018, and the median price of homes is just under $250,000.[49] You will pay more if you rent a home or an apartment that will cost you an average of $1,650 per month. Your housing should not be more than 25% of your take-home pay. Therefore, if your salary is the median as indicated, your housing should not cost you more than $1,270 per month, respectively.[50]

Here's the most tempting problem in living too large. Most of us are emotionally drawn to beautiful, spacious living rooms, big back yards with white picket fences, and master bathrooms that are as big as our bedrooms. These big grandiose houses most likely cost us more than the suggested 25% of our gross income and are the reason most of us are living with too much debt and little savings. You will be surprised how many good options you can find in the housing market, for a price well within your means. Yes, that may mean you may need to downsize now, but when you get your finances in great condition, you can always upsize later!

Let's take a look at how much you can save by reducing your housing payment. If you bring in $61,000 per year, that's just over $5,000 each month before taxes. Your home payment is $1,270 per month, leaving you a difference of roughly $3,500. Of that $3,500, you will pay for your car, utilities, food, clothing, taxes, insurance, gas, and all sorts of things. I challenge you to cut as many expenses as possible so you can maximize your savings and money left over to pay off your debts. For example, find the cheapest gas in town versus the nearest station, buy groceries and cook versus eating out, buy your clothes at the thrift stores versus buying them at full retail, etc.

Your mortgage or rent payment is your largest expense, and your automobile is your next largest expense. Imagine no car expense at all! You should aim for that goal, as it could be saved or even invested instead. I'm going to share with you how I have never had a single car payment, and it's easy to do! LendingTree indicates that a typical car payment costs you $550 new and nearly $400 used, so if you invested that amount from age 25 to 65 in a mutual fund averaging 12%, you would have a nice nest-egg of over $5 million![51]

I have yet to meet a money expert who encourages you to spend money you do not have, especially with credit cards! These little plastic rectangles in your pocket are robbing you of your future! I have a challenge for you right now: Add up your interest payments on just one of the credit cards you own in the past 12 months. The total amount your spent will shock you! It can be thousands of dollars depending on your balance, and all that money instead could be in your savings account. *Sidenote:*

Please do not hate me after you do this exercise. Reality bites, but it will also help change those old habits into a new mindset about money!

Now for my second challenge for you to do, which will suck a *little less* than the credit card exercise. Make a list of all those credit card debts, car loans, and student loans that you currently own. You can begin reducing all of these to a *zero* balance, but it really helps to be at a housing cost of 25% of your income or less. You can do it! It starts in the mind—a decision to stop using credit cards and start saving, no matter how sacrificial that may become.

I have uncovered some realistic solutions in this chapter, and all you have to do is practice the Ergonomics of Money daily. But first, one more challenge, much more fun than the previous two.

I'd like you to escape into dream land.

Imagine what your life would be like with no credit card debt, no car payments, and no student loans. "Wait, Gunnar, I owe the IRS too!" Okay, imagine you owe nothing to them, either. The only debt you have is your home mortgage or rent payments. How much could you save now?

What would you do with that money? When you have a fat savings account, would you want to travel endlessly and see the sunny beaches in Florida and go on a cruise? How about that dream car you have always wanted? Imagine having the cash set aside for such luxuries, all the time, and never needing to put anything on credit. Ever!

Sacrifice now, and you will be able to live later! I want this dream to come true for you. The ergonomics of money is about helping you achieve results. These results will work, but you need to make the adjustments necessary to see it all come true.

First Goal: Establish an Emergency Fund: You should have a $1,000 cushion for emergencies, at a minimum! Then aim to grow it to a full six months of savings of what you pay in living expenses after you pay off *all* of your credit cards. These two items are the first to tackle on your list and the hardest to do. Most of us do not have a savings account and carry large credit card debts. Not you. Not anymore. The next economic disaster can come sooner than you think!

Bruce McClary, a spokesman for the *National Foundation for Credit Counseling*, which conducts an annual financial literacy survey, notes:

> In a study conducted in 2019, 69% of respondents said they have less than $1,000 in a savings account compared with 58% in 2018. Even more staggering is 45% said they do not have any kind of savings whatsoever. Top reason claimed to be is not making enough income. This study was conducted in 2019, with a robust economy that was doing well, and yet people were not saving a portion of their income. [52]

Remember, your goal is to reach six months minimum of living expenses in savings. You might ask, "If I make the median household income of just over $60,000 annually, how much is six months of living expenses that I need to save? If your rent or mortgage is also an average of $1,650, plus the utilities, insurance, and eating costs, add an additional $700. Therefore $1,650 plus $700 equals $2,300, multiplied by six months, means you should have at least $13,800 saved up. Yet nearly 70% of us either have no savings or less than $1,000 for emergencies.

As many Americans live paycheck to paycheck, it starts with a determined mindset that says, "My priority is to save, save, save!" If you are of the mindset that says, "Nothing bad will happen to me, it can wait," then you will be soon disappointed! We are now very aware that emergencies will happen, as they always do. Your alternator will go out, there will be cracks in your ceiling, your kid will get sick or have a sports injury, or the next pandemic will happen. Most Americans pull out their credit card for such emergencies—and there lies the problem. My challenge to you is to build that emergency fund *now*. I know $1,000 is a lot of money but do what it takes to build it. I love that afternoon latte as much as everyone does, but that afternoon latte costs nearly $5. That's $60 per month, $720 in a year, that you can put into savings instead of your daily caffeine fix. It's often the little things that can be sacrificed for reaching a goal.

Therefore, place all discretionary spending on hold. That means eating out less and buying less expensive groceries each week. If you love that afternoon coffee, then buy a can of it that can give you 30 servings or more, lasting you an entire month. One can of coffee grounds costs the same as one cup at full retail. Do you need new clothes? Visit the thrift store and spend 80% less than you would at the department store. It's the little things that add up to *huge* amounts of money you can save and not spend. You will reach $1,000 much faster than you would think! It doesn't take a long time, but it does take a lot of discipline!

One of the positive realizations that came out of the COVID19 pandemic was how much money was saved by eating in. I've heard so many stories shared across social media of people who never cooked, learned how to do it, and loved the money they saved. I have one of those stories.

Since I constantly travel around the country speaking at events and meeting with clients, I ate out *a lot!* I rarely skip breakfast, so I would go to a café and order a delicious omelet with crispy bacon and coffee for about $20. Then for lunch, I would buy from Chipotle or eat at Whole Foods for about $15. Dinner is usually a larger meal and a larger price-tag, sometimes around $25. That's $60 per day, $420 per week, $1,680 per month. Then stay-at-home orders took over our nation. Grocery stores became flooded, and restaurants became empty. Therefore, like a majority of us, I started cooking at home. Two silver linings came out of this for me: One, I forgot how much I love to cook. Two, I saved a lot of money! Groceries cost me only about $140 per week or $560 per month, and I saved $1,120 for each month that I cooked at home! That's almost 70% savings by not eating out!

Everyone can save if you are willing to make some cost-cutting decisions. Once you reach this goal of establishing an emergency fund, you are ready for the next one, and it's twice as hard; yet incredibly rewarding!

Goal Two: Pay off those credit card debts! Two debts do not fall into this goal: student loans and housing, which we will get to later in this chapter. However, your credit cards are robbing you of your prosperous future!

Just one little surprising statement: All those credit card companies *love* you! They love it when you buy things, they love you when you reach your max credit line, and they really love you when you just make those minimum payments. Why? Because almost every penny of those minimum payments you are making are pure interest (profit) for them! And it's crippling all of us!

Americans are at $1.1 trillion in credit card debt in 2018, compared to $807 billion in 2007. That means that we have spent over $200 billion more in credit card debt in the past decade![53]

It's not completely your fault. Remember how credit cards make money? Ridiculous interest rates! Most credit cards charge over 20% interest rates, which means if you put $1,000 on your credit card and pay minimum payments, you will pay a total of $1,471.82 over the next four years! I can think of a lot of things I would rather do with that extra $471.82, can't you?

Here's my challenge to you: own only <u>one</u> credit card and destroy the rest and close out your other accounts! If you travel a lot, choose one card that awards you points and pay it off every month. Most hotels and car rental companies charge "incidental fees," which are holds that are placed on your credit card. After you check-out of your room or return the car, these fees are returned to you—fees that you will never see or have to repay. *(Well, unless you destroy the room with holes punched in the wall!)*

Remember, it's the interest fees that cause your credit card debt to grow and grow and grow until you hit the credit card ceiling. Don't let this happen to you! The only answer, my friends, is to pay off any credit card debt consistently every month. Never make minimum payments. Make maximum payments until there's no more debt and put that card away or destroy it!

<u>Goal three: Call your Student Loan Companies.</u> I am proud of all my education, but not proud of my student loan debts. The financial aid system has made it very easy to qualify for a student loan. If you are in school, have a 98.6-degree body temperature, and a functional brain, then congrats, you qualify! It seems like free money too! I remember being 20 years old and filling out the FAFSA forms, and checking the little box that said, "Do you want the maximum loan amount that you qualify?" I was thinking, "Heck, *yes!*" My rationalization at the time was, "I'm a full-time student and need this extra money to avoid having to work and go to school at the same time." What's my wish today? That I went to school and worked full-time, without taking the loan!

It's more than 20 years later, and I am still paying those student loans! I wish I could invent a time machine, as mentioned in my previous chapter, and talk myself out of it! Here's what I can do. I can encourage you _not_ to make the same mistake I did. If you are Generation Z, I'm mainly writing this section for you! Say _no_ to student loan companies! After you graduate and start working, student loans will become a huge financial drain on you for years to come!

According to _credit.com_, student loan debt in early 2019 was over $1.52 trillion, and the average loan per student is $32,731. This will take you between 10-30 years to pay-off, or $393 per month. You can lease a Mercedes Benz for that price! Instead, your hard-earned money is going to an old debt that will _not_ go away until it's completely paid-off.[54]

Now for the rest of us who are in my boat. You are a borrower and rich in student loan debt. Like me, you have been paying for years, and seems like no end in sight for making student loan payments. You can always defer loans or ask for a forbearance; however, that will not keep monthly interest rates from mounting up.

In the order of paying things off, student loans should be your _last_ priority! If you are ever in economic hardship and can't make the student loan payments, call them up and let them know your situation. The good news is they will usually work out a plan that fits your budget or situation. You can ask for a deferment if you can't make your loan payments, and many times the loan company can offer you forbearances up to a year or even longer.

There are only two ways a student loan goes away. One, you pay off the loan in your lifetime _(which it might take that long!)_ or two, you die. Student loans will not disappear in a bankruptcy, but they will if you cease to live. Just like all debts, treat this debt like your credit card debts. Get out of them! However, the student loan game is played differently. You have greater options versus the credit card bandits, namely forbearances. Call your student loan companies and request the absolute minimum that you can pay each month until it's paid off. Keep reminding yourself that you will be free of that nasty student loan debt. You may not see the light at the end of the tunnel but keep pressing forward. Oh, one more thing, if you know anyone who is considering applying for a student loan, encourage them not to do it, and work through school instead! No amount of education is worth the amount of debt that follows. The loan companies want you to make good money so you can give it back to them with all their ridiculous interest rates. It's about them, not you! Student loan companies are *not* your friends, not don't sign on the dotted line.

Goal four: Pay off your car. There's one thing that I have never done that's worth bragging about: In all my life, I've never had a car payment. Never. I have owned at least a dozen cars in my lifetime and always paid for them in cash. My loving parents bought my first car with cash when I was 16 years old. The first car broke down when I was 18, and my loving grandfather bought my second car with cash. I bought my third car and all the rest with my hard-earned money. I have made some really stupid financial decisions in my life, but this one I got right repeatedly. The reason why I had such wisdom is simply by learning from others early on.

I remember when I was in my 20's I bought a great car at an auction. I checked out the auto selection a couple of hours before the auction started and narrowed my choices between a Buick Riviera or a Ford Taurus. I had saved up exactly $3,500 for the auction and really hoped I'd get the Riviera. The car was pearl white and slightly resembled a spaceship. It was sleek and just looked cool! As the auction started, the bidding started at $1,000, then $1,500, then eventually up to $3,000. I was bidding at every $500 increment, but hope was fading when he yelled out, "$3,500!" I raised my hand, and no one else did! I won the bid! It was an exciting way to buy a car, and I had just enough in my pocket to cover it! Guess how much I paid for that car over time? Zero! Outside of a few maintenance repairs, the car lasted me several years, and I never had to pay a dollar more for it, versus if I chose to finance it.

Eventually, most times, when you finance a car, you will be paying for it when its value is less than what you still owe on it. If you have heard the term "upside-down," usually it refers to car-ownership. The moment you drive a brand-new car off the lot, it's lost some of its value. Cars are necessary, depreciating assets that we must have to get around. Therefore, buy them used and look for the word "certified" when car shopping. That word means that the car has passed the necessary inspections and should hold up for a good while before maintenance issues come up.

How much will a used or new car cost me? Remember, the US's average car payment is $550 for new, $393 for used, and $452 if you choose to lease your car instead.[55] There's over $150 difference between a new and used car that you can save every month. That's $1800 savings for the year! Put that money into your emergency fund or towards buying a new car in cash.

I will say a few words about leasing vehicles. The pluses and minuses are as follows:

Pluses: You are covered if your car needs maintenance or oil changes. If it breaks down in the middle of the road, you get to exchange it for a different car. If you use it for business purposes, you usually will get to claim the entire expense on your taxes. Another plus is you can easily exchange your car at the end of your lease for a different one. After all, leasing companies want you to keep leasing their cars forever and ever, which leads me to the cons of car leasing.

Minuses: Car leases are difficult to get out of their contracts. You will never own the car; you are just "borrowing" it. You can't drive as much as you want. It's limited miles to usually 10,000 miles per year. It's almost as if the dealer says, "Here's your new car! Please don't drive it!"

For me leasing a car is never an option. I choose to drive when I want, and as far as I want, never thinking about the miles. If you are like me, you do not want to have your driving freedom limited. Also, it's nice to know you can drive to see friends and relatives in cities far away from you without worrying about such nonsense. My recommendation to you is to find a good used car and pay for it in full upfront. Then you will pay zero more dollars for your car too!

Goal five: Save up to six months, then three years or more. Start saving, but not in the same account as your emergency fund. That stays in its own account, only to be taken out in emergencies. I suggest opening an account at a federal credit union or something similar. These banks usually offer higher interest rates on their savings accounts. Aim for saving between 6-12 months of living expenses. Should you ever get hurt at work or ill, there are numerous insurance plans out there today that can cover almost every expense you might encounter so that you are never in financial straits. These plans will cover your medical expenses and deductibles, as well as all of your living expenses until you can work again. But even with these insurance plans, think of the peace of mind in having a secure and stable savings that will cover you for a whole year! Knowing the money is there can really help in stressful times.

Just imagine how much better off you could have been during COVID19 if you had a minimum of six months of expenses saved up. Many hard-working Americans lost their homes and jobs and went hungry as they lived paycheck-to-paycheck with no savings. Don't let this happen to you! When we face our next crisis, or you face a personal crisis, will you be ready? *(I hope your answer is YES!)*

Goal six: Invest wisely. You do not have to complete the last step before starting this one. Welcome to the world of investing! Here is where the rich become rich and stay rich. Dave Ramsey advises one way is to invest 15% of your "freed-up" money into Roth IRA's. Do keep in mind that not everyone is eligible to invest in a Roth IRA. Eligibility ends at $139,000 for single filers and $206,000 for married. This is your retirement, so you will want this pot to grow as much as possible! If it so happens that your company doesn't offer a retirement plan or match your contributions, then go with the Roth IRA if eligible. You can choose a financial advisor to help guide you in the right direction. Only remember not to put it all in one place but diversify.

Your investment should ideally be spread into four different mutual funds: growth, aggressive growth, growth and income, and international. Here again, is the power of compounding interest: even just by investing $200/month can make you a multi-millionaire over time!

We are all aware of the volatility of the market. Investing in the stock market has a very simple formula that isn't that simple. There's just one rule to investing: *Buy low, sell high.* Most of the time, it's not as risky as gambling at your local casino, but you can still lose everything you invest. It's a long-term game, unlike gambling. I recommend you not make any investments or buy mutual funds until you have paid off your creditors and have established a 3-6-month emergency fund. You can also invest in a strong mutual fund that has had good performance. A mutual fund is a group of stocks bundled together, which is a safer bet for you if one or more of the bundled stocks fail, the others may cushion your investment.

I also recommend educating yourself about investing before buying-in. Several companies can invest on your behalf. However, you will sacrifice some of your investment to their fees, yet you will have greater piece-of-mind when you lean on the experts. One of those experts I've been following is Ray Dalio, the CEO of *Bridewater Associates.* Good luck hiring these guys to manage your portfolio, unless you can grow your net worth to over $5 billion! However, to follow his wisdom in the investment game, you can start with just a few thousand dollars. I recommend following him because he has one of the most successful investment companies in the world that he started in 1975 out of his small apartment. He offers a "recession-proof" solution to all investors that will perform well in good times and hold-steady in the hardest of times. He calls it "The All-Weather Portfolio." [56]I have included the link here for you to look more into this smart choice for putting your investments: https://nine-thrive.com/how-to-create-ray-dalios-all-weather-portfolio/

When you get to this point with your money, congrats!!! You have worked hard to get to this point, so now, let your money work hard for you!

All your life, interest rates have worked against you, with credit cards and car loans. Now it's time for interest to work for you! When compound interest works for you, then you have discovered why the rich *stay* rich!

Goal seven: Pay off your home. The idea of paying off your home early may seem unrealistic, but it only seems that way because of your small savings account and huge bad debt bills such as credit cards and your car. However, with those expenses gone, this step just became very realistic! Money experts recommend that If you currently have an Adjustable Rate Mortgage (ARM), interest-only, or even 30-year mortgage, consider refinancing to a 15-year, fixed-rate mortgage. This can save you upwards of tens of thousands of dollars through the life of your mortgage! For example, you can purchase a home for $150,000 on a 30-year note with a monthly payment of around $700 per month, but you will also pay thousands more over the life of the loan than a 15-year note. Therefore, I recommend you choose the 15-year note instead. Your monthly payments will be closer to $900 or more per month, but you will pay-off your home quicker and pay less over the life of the loan.

Goal eight: Stay the course. Imagine having a fat bank account, zero debts, and a paid-off automobile. Once you determine how much is needed for usual expenses such as utilities, meals, and entertainment, you can determine how much you want to put into your mutual fund account or 401k.

Now imagine no house payment at all. That mortgage payment is your largest monthly expense. With that gone, all you have to pay on your house, other than repairs, are HOA fees and property taxes. With your new mindset about solid money practices and new habits, you are literally on a solid path to seeing over six or even seven figures in your bank account! Dave Ramsey reminds you to max out your 401(k) and Roth IRAs so you can continue to live and give like no one else—even in retirement.

I'm sure you have heard of Dave Ramsey, popular for his books and radio show. He talks about sound money principles that much of this chapter outlines. Nothing in this chapter has not been repeated somewhere else, as there is nothing new under the sun when it comes to sound money management.

I joined Dave Ramsey's *Financial Peace University* almost 15 years ago, and I follow his principles to this day. Today I'm an entrepreneur in leadership, and by working hard and following the materials I learned from Ramsey, I'm financially doing well! I've had some scary times, especially during COVID19, but I've carefully implemented the Dave Ramsey Plan to ride through them and continue to grow.

I'm sure you have heard the golden rule: *It is better to give than to receive.* It is true! It is Godly! Giving away money feels better than spending it on yourself when giving it to a charity or individual you care about. You will not receive any tax credits to give individuals money, but you will if the money is given towards a 501c3 charity. One of the charities I have supported for many years is *Still Water Ministries.* Their ministry is to offer a wonderful and spirit-filled camp experience for kids of all demographic backgrounds. Caring individuals sponsor most of the kids that go to Still Water Sports Camps. I try to sponsor at least two kids each year. I know the money is going to a great cause that I care about, and you can have the same opportunity to do the same.

I included a link below and in my suggested readings section to Dave Ramsey's *Financial Peace University* because I am a member, and so are a few family members. I encourage you to look into it and pray about whether it's for you. I am in no way compensated for promoting him; I just a huge believer in what he offers to those who want to get serious about out of debt and saving money.[57]

As explained earlier, J-O-B stands for "Just Over Broke," because we typically possess a mindset that says, "Okay, I'm making $5,000 per month, so that means I can have a $2,500 house payment, $1,000 car payment, and shop every month." With this type of mindset, the individual has nothing left at the end of the month.

When I was graduating from college, my wealthy grandfather gave me a big hug, shook my hand firmly, looked me straight in the eyes, and said, "Gunnar, you go get a good job. If you have to work two jobs to put food on the table for your family, then you do it!" I've worked hard all my life, but I haven't always had a job. I found that you can work hard or hardly work with a job, and you still get paid the same. However, as an entrepreneur with a big dream, your earning potential is limitless.

It's the risk all entrepreneurs are willing to take. Many people work hard with no income, but their dreams keep them going. You have probably heard the saying, "Follow your passion, and the money will follow," which is true only if people are buying your product or service. This is a big decision that only you can make, yet it's challenging to have both a job and hold on to your entrepreneurial pursuits. Sure, you may have the financial security of a paycheck, but a job will steal away the time you need to grow an idea to the level of surpassing your income. I recommend saving up to a year's worth of your income, or better yet three years' worth, then leaving your job to pursue your passion. Then surround yourself with a team of experts (motivators) who will inspire you and even work with you. Above all, *possess fortitude*! That is what separates those who are successful with those who are not.

> *What is fortitude? It is the strength of mind that enables a person to encounter danger or adversity.* [58]

Generating ideas is the fun part. The hard part is all in the implementation, no matter what you desire to do. It is *hope* that makes it all worth it, but it will take hard work and the *fortitude* to keep moving forward because times will get difficult during which you will want to give up. Don't. Ever. Give. Up.

I once heard a motivating speech given by Les Brown, one of the most inspiring speakers of our day. I want to share this with you because I believe you have a dream. I believe you have had a dream for a while, and you have been letting self-doubt enter in and steal the dream away. Les Brown said in one of his talks,

> *The graveyard is the richest place on earth, because it is here that you will find all the hopes and dreams that were never fulfilled, the books that were never written, the songs that were never sung, the inventions that were never shared, the cures that were never discovered, all because someone was too afraid to take that first step, keep with the problem, or determined to carry out their dream.* [59]

I once heard another golden nugget of truth from my college professor who said, "In every person's life there will be at least two ideas that would make him/her a millionaire." Of course, not everyone is a millionaire because not everyone acts on their dreams. Instead, they settle. They settle on a job they don't want. They settle on a life they don't want either. Why? For a paycheck. My friends, do not settle for a life that is less than what God has planned for you. You may ask, "What does God want for me, then?" I don't know. But God knows, so ask Him!

Then do what God says and become more joyful than you ever would in a job that is not in line with your passion and desires. You should have a career that causes you to skip to work every day! Not skip work (*Ah-Ha moment*)!

Dig deep. What is it that excites you? What makes your heart beat faster every time you think of your dreams, passions, and/or desires? Now ask yourself this—who put that dream, idea, or whatever it is there? Maybe a friend from your childhood or maybe your parent? Ultimately, I believe it was God who put it there via your friend, parent, teacher, etc. Let's use a bit of deductive reasoning here. If there is a God who did put that dream in you, why did He? You MUST have a purpose!

That purpose is inside you. Find it. Nurture it and let it grow. Become who you are intended to become! I once heard it said that life's greatest thrill is tomorrow!

Begin your journey today! And each day henceforth will be one step closer to fulfilling your purpose. Are you surprised I did not say, "Go out and make lots of money!"? Money is not the destination. It's the result of a fulfilled journey! Money should never be your purpose. Your passion and dreams are your purpose. Do you dream of teaching? Then teach. Do you dream of becoming a missionary in a foreign country? Do it! The money will come. God always provides.

Do you love sports and want to be a pro athlete? Go for it! If you don't make it into the big leagues, then go coach some kids with the same dreams and desires as you! Will you make as much money? Maybe not. However, will you be fulfilled by doing so? Absolutely.

Are you inspired yet? I hope so. I'm so disturbed seeing so many folks going to work with their heads down. They are literally *dragging* into work. If you have any passion or desire to be in your present career, you need to rediscover what makes you come alive and thrive at that work. However, if you have *no* passion or desire to be in your career, you will never be happy based on external factors such as increased benefits, more money, bean bags, or free food. Why? You are not living out your purpose.

What is a displaced person to do? Quit. That's right; you just read that four-letter word I rarely write. Quit your job. Find a new one or start a small company that is more in line with your desires. It makes no sense whatsoever for a cubicle worker to stay in his job when he has a *calling* to teach. Remember in the Ergonomics of Leadership chapter that the word "leadership" means *influence*. We will delve deeper into the impact of influence on other people's lives in the next chapter but imagine in this chapter doing what you love (*and would even do for free*) and getting paid for it. What a revelation! I saw you sit a little straighter just now. Is that a smile on your face that just appeared from nowhere??

Stop thinking about it. Start praying about it and take that first step. As one of Gandhi's most famous quotes:

Be the change that you wish to see in the world. [60]

Ergonomics of Life Insurance

Many investment-oriented organizations such as Northwestern Mutual and Edward Jones offer insurance packages to protect your assets and income. Such insurances include Term and Life Insurance, Disability Income Insurance, and Property Casualty Insurance. [61] Here is what they all mean for you and your family:

- Term/Whole Life Insurance: If you are married and have kids, this is necessary as it will help cover your loved ones in the event you die prematurely. It helps with lost income and can be used for emergencies and even retirement. Heck, you can even use insurance to pay off the consumer and mortgage debt of your loved one. Everyone has different needs, so trust your financial advisor for what policy is best for you.

- Disability Income Insurance: Studies show that you are more likely to become disabled than to die during your working years. Heart disease is still the number #1 showstopper for Americans today, but other causes of disability include stroke and accidents. If these happen to you, that's when Disability Income Insurance kicks in to continue to cover your lost earnings. This is good peace-of-mind.

- Property/Casualty Insurance: This is also known as liability insurance, which protects you from legal losses if you are found legally liable for another person's injuries or damages. It will also protect you if someone without this type of insurance somehow injures you. Renters and homeowner's insurance also fall into this category. Accidents are unpredictable and usually unintentional, but they do happen. It's smart to be well protected!

Experiencing a Windfall vs. Creating a Windfall

What if you receive an inheritance or you win that lottery (because you only spent one dollar to do it!)? Windfalls are nice. One day you are broke, the next day, you are super wealthy. However, even if you become mega-wealthy, it will disappear like a magic trick or the sand in an hourglass if you don't manage it properly.

Gunnar's little disclaimer: Do not blow your hard-earned dollars on lottery tickets. It is such a waste! I promise you that you are not going to win big money. You may win $10 or maybe $50 if you are really lucky, but the odds are so heavily against you that winning big money is nearly impossible.

Let's look at the real odds here. Imagine the entire state of Texas, covered with quarters a couple of feet deep. I guess that would require a few hundred million quarters. Now let's say I blindfold you and tell you to walk all over the state of Texas and find the red-colored quarter. You only get one chance. What are the odds that you would stoop down and find that red coin? About the same as you hitting the lottery, so do not waste your money on it. There are some big lottery winners out there, but it won't solve your problems; it will just give you new ones.

Let me share a story about my poor friend Marky. Here's is an example of what *not* to do, especially if you experience a windfall. His mother actually did hit the lottery and gave each of her kids over $1.5 million. Marky had no experience managing money, nor had he ever had more than a few thousand dollars in his bank account. He was one of those poor-money-manager folks who always had the most amount of money at the beginning of each month, then almost nothing left over by the end of each month. He has never saved or invested because he simply never knew how to do it. His inherited fortune all went into a checking account, and just like that hourglass, it all drained away in less than 18 months.

Here's the lesson to learn from Poor Ol' Marky. If you happen to win or inherit, keep the fact to yourself. Just like magic, people you have forgotten about will come out of the woodwork, with their hands held-out for you to give. Money doesn't change you, but it will change the behavior of people *around* you! Second, hire a trustworthy financial advisor who has a solid track record. We all know about Bernie Madoff, who literally "made-off" with billions of dollars of investor money and lived a lavish lifestyle. He will be in prison for the rest of his life, but there are many copy-cats out there. Exercise wisdom and caution, and you will be just fine.

What happened to Marky? The last time I talked with him, approximately three years after inheriting all that money, he lived in a homeless shelter. He was living on weekly meals provided by various homeless charities. He had to trade the Jaguar he bought for a budget-friendly car but couldn't even afford the gas to go anywhere. What about all of his friends? *What friends?* Everyone who flocked to him when he had money had no intention of running to help him. Not one single person he helped offered to help him back. No one even offered a bed for him to sleep on.

Don't be like Marky, even if you earned your wealth. Earning your wealth may give you much more respect and credibility than inheriting or winning it, but you still have to be a responsible steward for it.

Instead, be like Anne. John Maxwell, the author of more than 40 books on leadership, shares a story of a clerical worker at the IRS who lived on a very meager salary. However, by the time she died, she had saved up more than $22 million! Here's John Maxwell's version of the story:

> Anne Scheiber was 101 years old when she died in January 1995. For years she had lived in a tiny, run-down, rent-controlled studio apartment in Manhattan. The paint on the walls was peeling, and the old bookcases that lined the walls were covered in dust. Rent was $400 per month. Scheiber lived on Social Security and a small monthly pension, which she started receiving in 1943 when she retired as an auditor for

the Internal Revenue Service. She hadn't done very well at the IRS. More accurately, the agency hadn't done right by her. Despite having a law degree and doing excellent work, she was never promoted. And when she retired at age fifty-one, she was making only $3,150 a year. "She was treated very, very shabbily," said Benjamin Clark, who knew her as well as anyone did. "She really had to fend for herself in every way. It was really quite a struggle." Scheiber was the model of thrift. She didn't spend money on herself. She didn't buy new furniture as the old pieces she owned became worn out. She didn't even subscribe to a newspaper. About once a week, she used to go to the public library to read the Wall Street Journal. WINDFALL! Imagine the surprise of Norman Lamm, the president of Yeshiva University in New York City, when he found out that Anne Scheiber, a little old lady whose name he had never heard and never attended Yeshiva—left nearly her entire estate to the university worth $22 million!

So how did Anne Scheiber do it? How did she take a meager salary and grow it into such a fortune? She saved and invested for a very long time. By the time she retired from the IRS in 1943, she had managed to save $5,000 and let that grow for a few years. Then she bought 1,000 shares of Schering-Plough Corporation stock, valued at $10,000. By the time she died, those shares had split enough times to grow her fortune into the millions. She spent her entire life growing that fortune, hardly spending any of it.[62]

The money perspectives of Marky and Anne are like night and day. Marky spent. Anne invested. Marky was selfish. Anne was self-less. Marky quit his job. Anne kept her job, despite little respect, recognition, or even a small pay raise. Marky told the whole world about his fortune, and the whole world came running to him with their hands out. Anne never shared knowledge of her fortune with anyone, and as a result, thousands of college students have been impacted through her generosity.

It is a discouraging fact, but most of us today are living like Poor Ol' Marky. As many as two-thirds of Americans think of themselves as savers, but over half have debt equal to or more than their savings.[63]

I sincerely wish for anyone reading this chapter to become smart investors and be financially secure. As promised at the beginning of this book, I wanted to share the wisdom of the top experts in money management with you. But I urge you to read this abbreviated version of each one of them, then go and buy their books. You can never become too "money-smart!" You will make wiser decisions as I truly believe *knowledge is power!* Time to break it all down.

• BREAKING IT DOWN •

I compiled a smart list that anyone can do, but few do it. Here's my "GunnarT's All-Encompassing Money List," which is a collection of over 30 tidbits of sound financial advice that anyone could practice. You will see many gold nuggets that will help you along with your new mindset about money. But remember that all these experts are *not* your money managers. You are your own money manager. You can decide how you want to spend it and save it. Just be wise.

I once heard a professor explain the difference between experience and wisdom. Experience is learning from your own mistakes. Wisdom is better because it allows you to learn from other's mistakes. I implore you to use wisdom from all the advice you have seen in this chapter and use it to fit you and your needs best.

After all, it's only money. Get paid what you are worth. Ask for that raise!

1. Spend less than you earn and live on half if possible.
2. Make a budget and stick to it.
3. Save up a $1,000 emergency fund first.
4. Pay off credit card debt.
5. Contribute to a retirement plan, whether at work or on your own time.
6. Invest!
7. Update your Will. *(more on this in Ch 10)*
8. Focus on your future, not your past.
9. Keep good records, electronically, and paper.
10. Up your contributions to your 401k plan or IRA.
11. Ignore headlines like "Buy this Stock Now!"

12. Take responsibility.
13. Budget about 25% of your income for lifestyle spending.
14. Learn to cook. That way, you won't eat out so frequently.
15. Start paying off the small debts before you conquer the big ones.
16. Spend on experiences, not things.
17. Keep an eye on your credit score every month.
18. It's worth repeating. Start saving ASAP. It's never too late.
19. Keep your credit use below 30% of your total available credit.
20. Get renter's insurance.
21. Keep your savings out of your checking account.
22. Have an emergency fund at three-to-six months' worth of expenses.
23. Track your income and expenses.
24. Read all contracts carefully before signing on the dotted line.
25. Never co-sign anything!
26. Get Disability Insurance. You never know.
27. Review your credit card statements for errors and erroneous charges.
28. Pay bills on time. You will avoid spending money on late fees.
29. Avoid the lottery. You won't win.
30. Comparison shop.
31. Learn to live below your means.
32. Manage your debt to stay out of debt.
33. Give to God first, not last. The order should be God, yourself, then expenses!

34. Focus on living well in the future, and sacrifice now, not later.

I think there are tons of valuable information you can take to create your own values-based principles. Courtesy of *Northwestern Mutual*, I have included a monthly budget sheet (figure 7.1) at the end of this that's ideal for anyone interested in improving their financial status and credit scores. I suggest writing down your cash flow as it is now so that you can see what needs to change to stay in a solid financial state.

Here's is what a healthy budget might look like:

Tithing/Church support: First, 10% of your income. Interestingly, this is the only thing about our money that God says to "test Him" on. Give Him the first fruits of your labor, and He will honor it! Malachi 3:8-9

Saving/Investing: Next, save 20% of your income, and do this *first*, not last—well, after you take care of your tithe! Pay yourself; you deserve it! It takes discipline and fortitude to do this, but there is comfort in seeing this nest-egg grow!

Essentials: 55% of your income should be spent on essentials such as housing, your car, food, insurance, and any debts you may have (credit cards, student loans, etc.)

Discretionary expenses: 15% should be spent on clothing, meals, and entertainment. This pie piece should first be used to pay down unsecured debts first, such as credit cards.

Remember, your priority should be paying off debts. Just like the movies in which people rob banks, your credit cards are robbing you, and it's completely legal! It's called interest, and if you are making minimum credit card payments, I promise you almost all of it is going towards interest, not principle! That's why it takes forever to pay the cards off unless you make bigger payments and stop making new charges!

There is freedom on the other side, with zero credit card debt! It starts with the mindset, and fortitude to be debt-free for the rest of your life. You can then turn interest around to work in your favor, which starts with the next step: Saving and investing!

Just like Dave Ramsey and so many other money experts recommend, get your emergency fund established, then invest every month with the help of a financial advisor, if possible. If you have a 401k, then make contributions each month and ask whether your company can match it. Many will do so, and frequently it's included as one of your employment benefits, but you should ask anyway (*and be like Anne!*).

There you have it, The Ergonomics of Money. I sincerely believe if you take any of the recommendations from the experts in this chapter on money management, you will be in a better financial place tomorrow than you are in now. I encourage you to make a copy of the budget sheet included in this chapter and work on it every quarter or at least four times each year. You can watch your progress as you begin to climb out of debt and accumulate savings. It's a hard journey, but extremely rewarding! You can do it. I'm doing it now. What are you waiting for?[64]

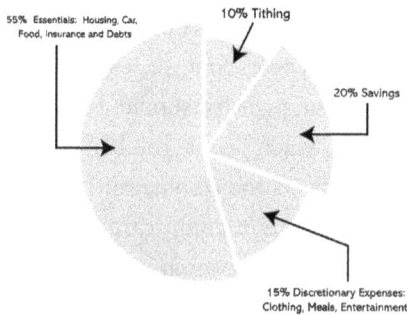

55% Essentials: Housing, Car, Food, Insurance and Debts

10% Tithing

20% Savings

15% Discretionary Expenses: Clothing, Meals, Entertainment

Figure 7.1

CHAPTER EIGHT

The Ergonomics of Relationships

W E ARE BORN for healthy relationships. In fact, we are born into a relationship, beginning with our mother and father. We are meant to be born into a loving family to give love back to others eventually. Love is the opposite of most things: when you give it away, Love grows. And grows. And grows.

However, too many of us feel *unloved* because we lack the necessary relationships to feel good about ourselves and others. I once heard it said that if you just have one true friend, you have more friends than most people. A *true friend* is one who will support you regardless of circumstance. That friend will be there to celebrate your victories and cry with you when you need a shoulder to lean on.

The love between friends is an essential element to have in our lives. The wonderful thing about friendship is that it is completely by choice. You and I have complete freedom in choosing our friends, and our mates as well. But the word "friends" has been watered down in the past decade thanks to social media. We have *friends* on Facebook and Instagram, but how many of them would you call to have lunch or just hang out? How many could you call when tragedy strikes? Outside of family, what friends on social media really care that much about you? Find friends on Facebook, but then attempt to turn them into real friends; one you can enjoy activities together with and really get to know well.

In part, that's a definition of one of the four types of love: *Philia Love.* We'll get into all the types shortly. First, let's define the word *relationship.*

Wikipedia gives us only two definitions regarding relationships between people. One definition is for the kind of relationship found in mathematics, such as statistics between variables or data sets. However, for this chapter's context, let's stick with relationships between human beings and not mathematics. I doubt anyone would have a *problem* with that, right?

In human interaction, the first type is the *interpersonal relationship,* which is the friendship between two or more people. They define it as *close association* or *acquaintance*, but basically, it's your *girlfriends* if you are female and your *buds* if you are male, as a matter of perspective.

The second definition of relationships is the *romantic relationship*, which is in *Eros love* (*see below*). This, of course, is your sexual mate and/or marital partner. Romance is a part of the American dream. We fall in love, get married, and live in a beautiful house to raise our children in a house with walk-in closets and a white picket fence.

The bottom line in the Ergonomics of Relationships is *love*, the love of God, the love between friends, between co-workers, between parents and children, and between spouses. Without love, we are nothing. Without love, the positive influence of others is impossible. Love binds us and heals us. It is even more powerful than the Force in Star Wars. Indeed, it is the most powerful form of influence in the world.

I once heard a story of a puppy raised in complete isolation. The puppy was not allowed to experience human touch or interaction with any other puppies or dogs. The doggy was fed and given water daily, but never given love or affection of any kind. Although the dog wanted it desperately, no one ever petted her or played with her.

Not surprisingly, the dog died at the point when most dogs are healthy and full of life. However, she missed out on the most important thing in life outside of air, food, and water, and that is love.

There's a reason why dogs are given the title of *man's best friend*. A dog wants to give away as much love and affection as it can muster. You can have a bad day at work, and your dog will do all it can do to lift your spirits. Then your dog will expect you to throw that ball for endless hours!

Not to sound silly, but d-o-g spelled backward is g-o-d. No, I'm not declaring your dog is God, but your dog is God-like. Who put all that love and affection in dogs? No dog is ever trained to love humans. It is innate. God is love, and He uses the simple things around us to display His love for us, like our dogs. You may ask, what about cats? Good question. Here is the difference between dogs and cats, as put by comedian Ken Davis:

The dog says, 'You pet me, you feed me and put a roof over my head, you must be God.' The cat says, 'You pet me, you feed me and put a roof over my head, I must be God!'

No joking, there is currently a serious issue with the Transportation Security Administration over people traveling with their pets. All airlines charge a fee to travel with your pet unless they are identified as emotional support pets. Of course, we are all human and figure out ways to save money, so it seems everyone now claims their pet is for *emotional support* so they can avoid the fee. Now the airlines are looking to the TSA to decide how to handle this issue, but it just proves how important relationships are to us. Some people just can't leave their beloved dog or cat at home because their mutual love runs so deep.

However, there needs to be a balance of relationships. Many people live lonely lives, so they buy a pet. That relationship is easy. You feed the dog, and he will love you for life. Human relationships always take more work, but they are what we were created for and are immensely more rewarding. You have the most impactful, difficult, and rewarding form of relationship as a parent to your child, and love is the essential ingredient that will hold your family together. In most marriages I have seen, not only does the spouse leave their former life behind, but often their friends too! In a marriage, it is challenging to form solid friendships with others, but it's also an important part of a healthy balanced life of relationships.

Therefore, I sincerely believe God created us for relationships. He created us to have a relationship with Him, and He created us to have a relationship with others. That's why single people with pets still get lonely at times.

The English language is very limited when it comes to using the word love. We love our shoes, and we love our children.

We love our spouse, and we love experiencing a white Christmas with light snowflakes falling outside our window. Don't we all love this time of year!

Let's instead look at the Greek definitions of love. Here, the word *love* is divided into four different areas that communicate and define this four-letter word's power.

1. Storge or Familiar Love – The love between a parent and their child; teachers with their students
2. Philia or Affectionate Love – Friendships and relations with co-workers
3. Eros love or Erotic Love – Your mate; marital partner
4. Agape or Selfless Love – God's love for you

C.S. Lewis is well-known in the Christian community. You may recognize his name from the books he has written and the movies he inspired, namely *The Lion, Witch and the Wardrobe*. One of his books, The Four Loves, explores the four definitions of love and, therefore, uncovers how our relationships were intended. The book was based in 1958 from a series of radio talks but criticized for its *frankness about sex*. However, the sexual revolution of the 1960s challenged the puritanical and legalistic attitudes towards casual sex, and *Eros love* became more entangled in *Philia love*.

Critics argue that it was in this time that casual sex with others began to shake up the *traditional family*. Divorce rates started to increase, and sexual purity in the marriage began to collapse. The Ergonomics of Relationships is about a healthy balance of relationships, and C.S. Lewis notes that although we are all sexual beings, there is a proper place for it.

Let's examine closely these four Greek words for love, and how they affect the dynamics of all our relationships.

Storge

Storge is the love a parent has for their child and siblings. It's the natural love that family members have that allows them to bond with each other.

Storge love is affection-based and can go bad if needs are not met. One form of Storge is the love of a parent to their child. As you know, there are no instruction manuals when your first child is born, but by the time the second child is born, you can write the instruction manual!

Today there is a lot of confusion as to how to raise your children effectively. Should I let them cry it out? Should I spank them or try to reason it out with them? First, let me say that there is no such thing as the perfect parent, and all parents seek wisdom when it comes to raising a child. Parents and caregivers should always strive for parental improvement. First, a peek at how the previous generations raised their children.

Let's examine the youngest workforce today that has been labeled *the toughest generation* the marketplace has ever inherited—the Millennials. Just as a side note, it's a repeat cycle. I'm a Gen X-er, and the Baby Boomers and Traditionalists labeled us too as *the toughest generation.* Just think of our label. The "X" in Generation X has a rebellious tone to it, and we certainly all challenged the status quo. The word *Millennial* itself mainly just means that if you were in pre-K thru the 12th grade when 1999 turned over to 2000, you are a *Millennial.* Two huge realms of influence hit this generation growing up that had never happened together in history. First, there was a failed-parenting movement, namely the popularized affectionate movement championed by Dr. Benjamin Spock and his followers. Second, the influence of technology led to an addiction-craze for personal devices, such as so-called *smart*phones. Since this section is primarily about the relationship between parent and child, I'd like to focus on raising them in an *ergonomically correct* manner. Yes, it's an official term I just invented to write the rest of my books!

Storge love requires a certain balance when raising a child. Too much discipline and not enough love can lead to a child feeling abused and neglected. Not enough discipline can lead a child to entitlement and the expectation of instant gratification. The correct balance of the two often creates a well-rounded person who knows the reward of hard work and a balanced lifestyle. The Traditionalist generation grew up under rough economic conditions such as The Great Depression of the late 1920s and early 1930s and two world wars. Their parents administered more *tough love* than *affectionate love*. The Traditionalists gave birth to the Baby Boomer generation, who was determined to better balance the two forms of parental love. The Baby Boomer generation gave birth to Generation X. The parental styles began to swing more to the *affectionate* love style but still maintained an equal portion of *tough love*. The *"entitlement movement,"* as often referred, came from Generation X parents as they gave birth to the Millennials. This movement encouraged parents not to remove their babies' umbilical cords until they were at least 18 years of age. The label of a *helicopter parent* became a common norm regarding how parents raised their children.

Once I was sitting in a popular after-hours restaurant *House of Pies* in Houston, Texas. Sitting at the table next to me were three college-age girls and their guy-friend who was late to the gathering. I overheard him tell his friends he was late because his mom didn't want him going out so late. He was frustrated because he was over 18 years old, yet his mother gave him a curfew. One of the girls responding to his embarrassing scenario responded, "I know, I know, I have a helicopter parent too!" The four friends then exchanged stories of their frustrations for several minutes. I can see this from a parental perspective too, "My baby isn't a baby anymore! She has all grown up!" A note to parents: If you want your older teens and young adult children to remain close to you, *set them free!*

As a side note, I want to be very clear that this doesn't apply to every living person who is a Millennial. Every generation has had its share of helicopter parents. Every generation has experienced one extreme or the other of too much affectionate love and not enough tough love, or vice-versa.

For comparison purposes, the Gen Xers were *slightly more entitled* than the Baby Boomer Generation, but they were also a more rebellious bunch. The Generation X group, born 1961-1981 (roughly), was titled latch-key kids because they would typically be home before parents would be back from work, sometimes for many hours. Gen X was also known as the *MTV Generation (after the music video channel of the same name)* and subsequently were labeled as "slackers, cynical, and disaffected." I remember watching MTV with my friends for about as long as Millennials play games online. It was the coolest channel in the world in those days, and yet it was just music videos played over and over again! Oh, and yes, I was called a *slacker* too!

Many of the Gen Xers grew up absent of parental guidance, as divorce rates escalated dramatically in this period, leaving many Gen X youth with single parents who had to work long hours to support them. Therefore, I believe there is a strong tie between Generation Xers who likewise had an upbringing from disadvantaged parental situations (i.e., divorce and latchkey) and a dis-attachment from the affectionate-tough Storge love as parents themselves. As a result, the Millennial generation has been unintentionally misguided by their well-meaning Gen X parents, who bestowed the unbalanced *affectionate* love craze onto them. This has shaped the Millennial generation that we have today. As Simon Sinek coined it in one of his popularized talks, "[*The Millennials*] were told they could have anything they want in life without earning it, and they could be anything they want in life, just by demanding it."[65]

You may be asking at this point, especially if you are a Millennial reading this, "How did the Generation X adults turn out if they were a slacking, parentally-absent bunch as kids?" I believe *all is well that ends well, and all can be well if it didn't begin well*. According to research, Gen X adults "In mid-life, [they are described as] active, happy, and achieving work-life balance. The cohort has been credited with producing notable examples of individuals with entrepreneurial abilities."[66]

For Millennials, that's spells out H-O-P-E for you. I'm a Generation Xer too, and I have seen our *messed-up* generation turn out to be excellent leaders of companies and very successful entrepreneurs. According to Investopedia's research, the Generation X wealth is expected to triple from $11 trillion in 2015 to $37 trillion by 2030 (*also including the transfer of wealth from Baby Boomers*). That means that any human being can be successful through professional development and personal growth, regardless of what generation you come from![67]

Let me also add that I believe the Millennial generation is a smart group of young people, maybe the smartest generation ever. They all want to make a difference in this world, and they have this whole world of technology completely figured out. I always tell people of older generations, "if you have a technological problem, ask a Millennial." The Millennials know that the balance of *affectionate love* and *tough love* was missing when they were growing up, and they want to be better parents. They are tired of the *bad rap* that they have non-intentionally earned in the marketplace, and they want to change that reputation for themselves. If you are a Millennial reading this, you need to know that <u>you are not to blame!</u> Almost every Millennial and Gen Z person I know understands that they really can be anything they want to be, but it only comes through hard work and persistence.

The Ergonomics of a Perfect Parent

My mother and father were, by no means, perfect parents. My folks divorced when I was a young boy, and I would spend weekends traveling from New Braunfels to Houston, Texas, on a Greyhound bus (*about a three-hour trip*). They were both products of traditionalist parenting and were Baby Boomer parents themselves. Therefore, their parenting styles had the balance of tough love and affectionate love perspectives when raising my three sisters and me. They did two things right as parents that I want to pass on to you:

1. My mother and father loved us and showed it through action and constant reminders. Every time we would talk on the phone or leave the house, the conversation ended with the words "I love you!" We did a lot of things together as a family and had good times. I remember lots of laughter and emotional support when things were not going right. That is affectionate love.

2. My mother and father rarely repeated themselves when correcting us. It was (almost) always a command, then consequence. If one of us kids talked back or just did not comply with the request, it was either a spanking or loss of privilege. That is tough love.

Exercising tough love is *tough* to do consistently! Take it from me, a single guy. Give the command, don't repeat the command, and follow-through with the consequence. Every single time! Your kids or teens will never ask for tough love, but they grow up healthier and happier when a good structure is in place, and they know their boundaries.

Trust me on this! Find the balance in your parenting, and you will thrive as a good parent!

Philia

Philia is the love between friends who share common values, interests, and activities. It is freely chosen and, therefore, stronger in the bonding of human relationships. Unlike Storge love, you get to choose your friends. You can't choose your parents, although your parents can choose you if you were adopted. We have all heard, "You are the company you keep," but we rarely consider that principle when we befriend someone. Friendships are vital to a well-rounded individual. If you choose your friends wisely, you will be a better person because of it.

Here is The Golden Rule, founded by Jesus Christ when he taught The Sermon on the Mount. Here is what He said,

> *"Therefore, treat people the same way you want them to treat you."*
> *Matthew 7:12*

Two things to note about His message to us: One, we get to decide how we want to be treated. Two, to receive that treatment, treat others in that same way.

One of the most popular quotes from Zig Ziglar puts it in an even simpler way:

"If you help others get what they want, you will get what you want."
Zig Ziglar

For many years I served on the board of *Rotary International*. This is a global service organization founded by Paul Harris in 1905 to bring together business and professional leaders to provide humanitarian services and advance goodwill and peace around the world. Their motto is "Service Above Self." This is exactly how philia love works! To have a friend, be one to someone else. Consider others better than yourself and remain humble and not prideful. This is what Jesus commanded of His followers, and what Zig Ziglar implied when he said, "If you help others get what they want, you will get what you want."

Friendships are everywhere, and always free of charge. You can forge friendships from your workplace, from your Rotary Club (I really encourage you to join one!), your church, and any other social activity. If you are in the business of selling anything to others or just want to find a group that matches your interests, there is a great app called *MeetUp*, which lists events happening in your area with all sorts of networking opportunities. I love networking events because meeting people there is so easy. I know many people myself who met at some networking event or interest group and forged a relationship. Some people met someone new, found similar interests, and started a new company together. Some just became new friends. Some even found their spouse in marriage! The key is you need to get out there and away from your home. Meeting people in real life is much more effective than meeting them online.

In all relationships, I encourage the Four-Way Test, which is the foundation of *Rotary International*. It was originally for business people, but this test's branches have grown far beyond business because it is psychologically and scripturally sound.

In all we think, say, or do:

1. Is it the truth?
2. Is it fair to all concerned?
3. Will it build goodwill and better friendships?
4. Will it be beneficial to all concerned?

One service among the many projects my club performed for many years was The Dictionary Project. We would meet early in the morning and distribute Webster Dictionaries to the kids at almost 100 elementary schools in Dallas, Texas. Why? Because the prison system knows how many cells to build in their correctional facilities based on how many grade school kids miss school. Fascinating, isn't it? Empty seats in the classroom equal future inmates and lawbreakers. There is overwhelming evidence that points to education as the best way out of the poverty system and a life of crime. A dictionary also helps young kids pass state tests and the SATs when they are in high school and can help lead to a college education.

It was such a great feeling knowing that just by handing these kids dictionaries, their entire future just got a little brighter! We usually took pictures with all the kids and staff while doing this service. One elementary principal heard us teaching the kids the Four-Way Test and told us that she would make that test the normal routine for their kids every morning. I believe every school should be teaching the Four-Way Test and having the kids repeat it every morning as they start their school day.

Imagine if leaders gathered their employees each morning and asked them to repeat the Four-Way Test. Would co-workers treat each other better? I believe the answer is *yes* if the test is then modeled by leadership. Would workers be more productive? Again, I believe the answer is *yes* because the corporate culture would be a safer environment that would allow productivity to thrive. If an organization began every morning with the Four-Way Test, schools would produce more graduates, and companies would retain more employees. Why? As explained in the Leadership chapter, people thrive when they feel safe, supported, and encouraged.

We need to expand the Four-Way Test beyond Rotary International's walls and watch people change for the better. I also believe people will be happier in such a culture where we encourage one another to think less of themselves and more about others.

There is a negative side to philia love, and that's choosing the wrong type of friends. If you have ever heard the ol' saying, "*You are who your friends are,*" well, it is true. As stated earlier, you choose your friends, and you can choose wisely, or you can choose poorly. <u>Attitudes are contagious</u>. Let's assume you are a naturally energetic person and very much an extrovert. You can have a good friend who is just the opposite, someone who is more introverted, and still share that Philia brotherly love for each other. However, I strongly advise not to befriend someone who has a very different attitude and perspective on life than you. If you are a Believer in Christ, the Good Book strongly advises not to be "unequally yoked," which applies to all sorts of relationships, including business relationships, Eros relationships and marriages, and Philia relationships. Why? Because one will affect the other in that relationship, and it will not be you that stands on top of the chair.

Let me explain what I mean. Picture a chair with you standing on top (*playing the optimist on life*) and your friend/spouse/business partner lying flat on the floor on their back, looking up at you *(the pessimist)*. You are keeping full eye contact and are holding hands with each other with both arms extended and locked. You may think that you will be able to pull your partner up off the floor but think otherwise. Every time, it is the one on the floor who will pull you down—not 50% of the time, but 100% of the time.

We all have a close circle of friends. Tons of research indicates that if you want to be positive, surround yourself with positive, happy people! The same goes for money. If you want to be financially successful, surround yourself with friends who understand and apply solid financial principles in their own lives. If you are a Believer in Christ, you should (and must) surround yourself with other Believers as we are all *the Body of Christ.*

> *"As iron sharpens iron, so does one man sharpen another."* Proverbs 27:27

If God is our Father, then the true definition of philia love pours through us, because we are all *brothers and sisters* in Christ! Philia love can be summed up in one verse that Christ told His disciples when he resurrected from the grave:

> *"A new commandment I give to you, that you love one another: just as I have loved you, you are also to love one another. By this all people will know that you are my disciples, if you have love one for another."* John 13: 34-35.

That's philia love, my friends. *Love one another.* Love them at work, love them in the marketplace, and at the grocery stores. Bestow this love on those less fortunate. Give your love away to those who desperately need it, such as the homeless and those who are sick. Bestow this love on the negative and cynical; just don't become their best friend, or you could be pulled into their negative mindsets.

It's challenging at first to have the Philia mindset of loving one another. Still, when your human perspective is changed to a divine perspective, you will see everyone as family, not strangers. That homeless man is your brother, not a person who has a body odor that stinks because he hasn't showered in days, maybe even months. That person you work with whom everyone complains about is your sister, *not the person everyone hates.*

That's the power of philia love, and it is highly contagious. There was a movie titled *Pay It Forward* in which a middle school boy came up with an idea for a class assignment that could change the world. He simply came up with acting with benevolence towards those who were less fortunate, and asking them for no favor in return, but instead to *pay it forward* to someone else in need. It's a fantastic movie and one we should all see because it is Philia Love in action. These simple actions changed people's lives, and we have that same opportunity every day we are alive on this Earth.

I challenge my readers to do two things:

1. Change your perspective of how you see others. See them as brothers and sisters, not strangers.
2. Practice the Four-Way Test in all that you do. Then stand back and watch God move!

Recently I've had the opportunity to put my philia love to the test. I have been posting this incredible story, still in development, with a hugely positive reaction from all my followers. It's the *Pay It Forward* movement, in action.

I was walking to have lunch in Dallas's upscale area and saw a young man who seemed very out of place, homeless, and sitting up on the sidewalk. He was named Augusta. I already knew the question he was preparing to ask me because I had witnessed him ask the same question to two others who did not even acknowledge him. "Sir, can you help me?" he asked. I turned to him and said, "Sure, how can I help?" Let me preface that I do not always hand out money to panhandlers because I never know if they will use it to buy food and water, or cigarettes and beer. His answer impressed me. "I just need $12.50, so I can have a bed to sleep on. You see, I can go to the shelter, and for $12.50, I can get dinner and a bed." His face lit up as I replied, "Done, but tell me how I can really help. What do you really need?" I know, a bold question to someone homeless, but again his answer to that question impressed me even more. "I was in the foster care system, and therefore I have a tuition voucher to go to any state school in Texas. But I'm homeless, who is going to take me?"

I was moved beyond belief. At that moment, not only did I want to help him temporarily, but permanently. I looked at him and said, "You will never sleep on the pavement again. I'm going to take care of you." Let me add another preface, I'm not wealthy or *well-off* by any means, but I had a level of compassion so high for this misplaced individual so high that money would not be an issue or hindrance. I managed to purchase for him several nights at the shelter, and I took him shopping at some thrift stores, as he has only had one change of clothes for the past five years since he left the foster care system.

I told him it was time to find a place to live, somewhere with a low rent that's close to the college he might want to attend. He found one the very next day. The rent was $550 per month, with some money down, all utilities paid. He also found some places nearby that he could work and start making a living. I started a GoFundMe page and shared his story with all my friends and family on Facebook, and within two hours, we met our goal of $1250.00! He had never seen that much money in his life, and now he had enough to start becoming independent and start moving forward.

He calls me his angel. Nope, I'm just a caring individual giving someone else a chance in life. Two things I told him that I want to tell you. To have solid friendships, you need to be a friend first. How do you do that?

> "Above all, my brothers and sisters, do not swear, either by heaven or by earth or with any other oath. But let your YES mean YES, and let your NO mean NO," so that you won't fall under judgement." James 5:12

My translation: *Do as you promise!*

When I showed up the next day to take him shopping, he did not think I would show up. He believed, like others before me, that he would never see or hear from me again. I told him that when I say I'm going to do something, I do it. I do not say one thing and do another. Call it integrity, call it character, call it what you want, but it's the principle I live by.

The second thing I told him, and am telling you now, is to pass it on, pay it forward. I've already heard from my Facebook followers that they have already started seeking out how they can help others in need, and that it's a wonderful feeling knowing that one person is doing better in this world because you cared. Jesus said,

> "If you even so much as to give a cup of cold water to the least of my followers, you will surely be rewarded." Matthew 10:42

Of course, I went way beyond handing Augusta a bottle of cold water, but this is what Jesus meant. He wants us to go the extra mile for everyone we meet in need, and maybe that begins with some cold water, but it doesn't end there.

It's funny, Augusta always tells me that he wants to take me out for a big steak dinner when he makes enough money. I'm thinking, no, you don't need to do that. My reply instead is, "Definitely, and I order my steaks well-done!" It will be a blessing to him to buy me that dinner, and I can't wait for that to happen. He wants to become a child psychologist, helping those in the foster care system. I know he will be a great doctor! His attitude, even in poverty, has been surprisingly positive. I can only imagine that he will become a great leader and impact thousands of lives because he's lived through adversity. All because someone said, "Yes, I'll help you."

Now on to the person you choose to spend the most amount of time with—your spouse.

EROS

Eros is the state of *being in love* between two people. Eros love spans across philia love as friends often may flirt with each other and even start dating. However, for this section's purposes, I want to spend some time just on eros love in marriage. As we all know, usually, physical attraction is the primary attribute that brings two people together. Once the same two people really get to know each other and spend a lot of time with each other, physical attraction is accompanied by attraction to their other qualities, i.e. how smart or organized they are. It would be nice if our drive for sex during the marriage was as high as before the marriage, but in marriage you are *in love* with the whole person beyond their physical beauty.

However, for many reasons, marriages nowadays have a harder time being a classic *happy marriage*. Issues such as infidelity and other pressures seem to be challenging marriages at a whole new higher level than generations before us.

Never in our history has *hooking-up* and having affairs between total strangers been so easy, thanks to technology. It was a long time ago, but I recall an episode of the television sitcom *Three's Company* in which Janet (*the roommate*) introduced the idea of "computer dating" to Jack (*the other roommate*). It was circa 1984 when the episode came out, and I still wonder how the producers absolutely nailed this idea so correctly. Today, technology has made "computer dating" the primary tool in finding someone new. The services are now called "dating apps" and are accessible to everyone with a computer or even a phone.

God wants us to be united, get married, and procreate—or have children. That's His plan for populating the planet, so we all have an important role in marriage! Of course, not all children come out of marriage. There are many single-parent families, and if you were born from a non-marital relationship, I have news for you. You were *not* a mistake! God doesn't make mistakes, ever. Therefore, I sincerely believe that wherever you came from, a single parent or two parents, God has a plan and purpose for your life!

So, love is in the air, as they say! You and your mate are deeply in love with each other, and even believe you were *made* for each other. One proposes to the other for their hand in marriage, and a few months later, you are both saying your wedding vows. At that moment in time, you are both sincerely intending to be married for the rest of your lives. The idea of *divorce* is not something that will ever happen to either of you, yet the divorce rates in 2018 are about 40% to 50% of married couples, and even higher in remarriages, according to the American Psychological Association.[68]

I once heard a comedian say, "When I see people cry at weddings, I simply say to them 'Don't cry, the marriage probably won't last anyway.'"

It's already a climbing trend of people choosing to remain single since the divorce rates are nearly half of married couples. Today a majority of adult Americans are single, based on data from the Bureau of Labor statistics.[69]

The US economy depends on more married couples because that equates with household formation, and statistics show that each new household adds roughly $145,000 to the U.S. economy. Since couples are typically getting married in their 20's and 30's, that represents the Millennial demographic. Several million more Millennials live with older family members than did other generations before them. According to the Federal Reserve Bank of Atlanta:

> *"In 2012, 45% of 18-30-year-olds lived with older family members, compared to 39% in 1990 and 35% in 1980. That increase translates to several million more young adults choosing to live with relatives rather than form a new household."[70]*

Millennials have a tougher time getting stable after college, due to "the millennial trinity of economic despair: not enough jobs, higher housing costs, and much more student debt."

The key here is better preparation for those who choose to get married and start families—to stay married. Therefore, what are the Ergonomics of Marriage?

I recently consulted with my good friend, Steven W. Bruneman, a divorce attorney and published author of the book, *Winning the Marriage Gamble*. He has been married and divorced and knows full well what it's like to be on both sides of the fence. He had facilitated many divorces before going through his own, and now sincerely wants to help married couples avoid the epidemic of divorce today.

As I have mentioned before in this book, my dad was awesome at marriage. He was married at least five times. I don't know I lost count. As a kid, I would travel from New Braunfels, Texas, to visit my dad in Houston, Texas, quite often. As a teenager, I gave my dad a *hard time* asking him, "So Dad, who are you married to now? It's been almost a month since I've seen you last!" I was asked one time by a lady contemplating divorcing her husband, "Gunnar, what was it like having multiple stepmoms and living in a divorced home away from your real father?" My reply? "It was awesome! Double the birthday parties and Christmas celebrations!"

I'd like to take a moment and address every mother and father who have children and have gotten divorced. Just practice storge love the best you can and love the children by spending time with them. To kids, especially "love" is spelled "t-i-m-e." My mother and father both did that well with my siblings and me; they spent time with us. Every time I visited my father, he would take off work and take us to the beach in Galveston or to my favorite hotdog place in the world, James Coney Island.

So, what does my friend, Steven W. Bruneman, have to say about the secret to a happy marriage? Well, a lot!

Here are some of the highlights from his book that I believe every couple, either married or thinking about marriage, should consider.

The Ergonomics of a Good Marriage

Isn't is funny and true that we all plan more for our weddings than we do for our marriages. The wedding is a single event, and the marriage is for the rest of your life (supposedly). For all the newlyweds out there, here is what Steve Bruneman wants to share with you.

> *"Marriage demands sacrifice. Making sacrifices is difficult because we must give up part of what makes us feel good individually. Welcome to marriage!"*

First, you need to **_look less often_**. Steve encourages both the man and the woman in the marriage to minimize how often you look at others you find attractive. I think we have all heard this statement, "It's not the first look that gets you; it's the second look." Men will always notice other beautiful women, and women will always notice other handsome men. Still, it's key to remember that anything further than that first look can literally destroy a relationship.

Second, he encourages both spouses to **_trust each other_**. This sounds easier said than done. This is all about the verse I mentioned earlier in this chapter, "Let your yes be yes and your no be no." You trust that your partner will clean the house when promised to do so, pick up the kids, make reservations for a nice dinner, and so on. However, he goes further than that, and I'm glad he does in his book. He calls it *"talk trust."* In other words, you trust your partner to feel open and comfortable to discuss anything that needs to be discussed. Any topic can be brought up in conversation without an extreme emotional response from the other. Steven says that this is possibly the single most important key to sustaining a long, happy marriage. And it is powerful as it helps man and wife consistently connect in their marriage.

Steven was once asked, "Do you think an atmosphere of free and open communication existed in most of your divorce cases throughout your career?" His response? Never. In fact, in most of his divorce cases, there was literally no communication that allowed openness and honesty. Instead, many couples just choose to live with the emptiness of meaningless conversations until their marriage withers and die.

Third, for the men, ***remain gentlemen***. Open the door for your wife, always let her exit the vehicle or elevator first, and pull the chair out for her at restaurants. So elementary, yet these small gestures have the wonderful effect of making her feel important, showing you to be a gentleman in the public eye, and being a strong example to your children. Yes, just by letting her go first will delight you as well!

Fourth, ***don't let yourselves go*** physically. This affects so many marriages and their sex lives. What brought you two together in the first place? Was it *love at first sight?* This is actually one of those *talk trust* issues when it comes to sex. To all the men out there, finding time to maintain your physique may seem challenging, but spending just 20 minutes in the gym or running around your neighborhood will go a long way in keeping your sex life fruitful. For all the ladies out there, it's even tougher to maintain a sexy figure. Why? Because women naturally carry more body fat than men do (*don't get mad at me, it's God's idea, I promise!*) Plus, if you have children, who in the world has time for the gym? Steve recommends hiring a styling coach or fashion consultant to give your husband just a little more visual pleasure, and your sex life should remain fruitful through the golden years of your marriage. Couples divorce for various reasons, but Steven has found that one of the issues that usually comes up is the loss of physical attraction to the other spouse.

Fifth, **touch your spouse**. Constantly. As simple as it may seem, Steven says couples who hug each other, lovingly rub a shoulder, and hold hands keep their marriage strong and healthy. Eros love demands all of us to be touched in loving and caring ways, without stopping. If you are already touching your mate frequently, you're communicating, "*I still love you.*"

Sixth, **stay educated** on how to keep your marriage a healthy one. Steven calls this "Relationship Education," in which both spouses commit to growing in their marriage. This involves reading and even getting counseling when necessary. It requires sacrifices made one for another through the life of the marriage.

I highly recommend Steven's book, *Winning the Marriage Gamble,* if you are currently in a serious relationship or already married. It's thought-provoking and stimulates couples to catch *red flags* in their relationship that can lead to its destruction. I only included some highlights that I believe can help anyone in a relationship, but Steve delves much, much deeper. Marriage is hard and takes commitment and work.

Steven writes, "This book is a great first step in your relationship education process, and if it's the only relationship book you have read up to now, for gosh sakes, don't let it be the last."[71]

Ergonomics of Millennials and Marriage

It was interesting to discover that Millennials are more serious about monogamous relationships than previous generations before them. Shana Lebowitz of the *Business Insider* writes,

Younger generations of Americans are less likely than older generations to report having extramarital sex.[72]

An analysis by Nicholas Wolfinger, a professor at the University of Utah, published on the conservative-leaning Institute for Family Studies blog, suggests that older Americans (55 and older) are now more likely to have sex outside their marriages than younger Americans (55 and younger).[73]

Here are some other attributes that characterize Millennials and marriage that is worth noting:

- They are more accepting of premarital sex than previous generations
- They are waiting longer to get married. Typically, the late 20s up to mid-'30s are when weddings happen
- They are more willing to live together before getting married (to help prevent divorce)
- They are more open to interfaith and interracial marriage
- Millennial weddings are "more lavish" than their parent's weddings

Here's my take on these facts. I believe it is smart to wait longer before entering into a life-long commitment. Kari Paul of *MarketWatch* writes,

> The millennials who "refuse to get married" trend is not necessarily a bad move, a new study from dating site eHarmony found: It showed the longer people wait to marry, the happier they are in relationships. The survey, conducted by Harris Insights & Analytics, surveyed people on the success of their relationships and found that couples who waited longer after meeting and got to know each other before marrying scored higher on a "happiness index." In fact, the unhappiest group said they got married because "it was time," while the happiest cited "love."[74]

If you are a Millennial, *take your time* in choosing the right mate for you. There is absolutely no reason to rush such a weighty decision. Be selective. If you see warning signs in your dating relationship, such as a bad temper or impatience, it may be a mistake to think you can change them. Often, a mate with a bad attitude or temper will only get worse in the stress of a relationship, and worse of all, you will become the object of his anger. That's just one example, but you can easily detect warning signs through dating, and you don't have to live together to see them.

As far as living together, this idea is very popular with the Millennial generation and the Gen X generation, as much as 64%. It sounds like a great idea, doesn't it? No legal binding contract claiming you as man and wife before you decide to become married. But it rarely prevents divorce. Why? Before marriage, you and your mate are very much in love, and you will probably be blind to potential marital issues. Also, everything you think you need to know before marriage, you can sense in all the time you will both spend with each other in your dating phase. Here's one more thing I'd like to add, living together before the wedding takes the excitement of being together out of the picture. One of the most exciting facts about becoming married is the anticipation of living together. What anticipation is left if you have already been doing so?

Agape

Agape is the love that exists regardless of circumstance or status. This is the self-less love that is the greatest of the four loves. It's amazing to know that regardless of how far we fall or fail God, He will never fail us, give up on us, or just throw in the towel. In fact, His love is literally immovable and never changes. In its real form, agape love is not about our love for God, but His love for us. Agape love serves as the foundation of all the other forms of love: Storge, Philia, and Eros. Imagine you are building a house. You can build that house on a strong foundation or a weak one. The house built on a strong foundation will stand strong permanently, and the house built on a weak foundation will fall. Scripture puts it this way:

> *"Unless the Lord builds the house, the builders labor in vain." Psalm 127:1*

The words "shifting sand" is also used in Matthew 7:24 as one builds their house with a weak foundation.

This is what agape love means for all those who believe in God's unconditional love for us. It means that you can build your house on the foundation He gives you, through His immeasurable love for you. Rachel Dawson, an editor for *Crosswalk.com,* says, "Agape love is love at the highest level. It is so much more than we can ever ask or imagine."[75]

In the Greek, here are the definitions of agape love, mentioned 106 times in the New Testament:

1. Brotherly love, goodwill, benevolence (similar to Philia Love)
2. Love feasts

So, where does this love come from? It sounds amazing because it is amazing. It's literally the best news there is for every man, woman, and child who believes. One of my favorite verses says this:

"God is love. Whoever lives in love lives in God, and God in them." 1 John 4:16

How is Agape love practiced?

"Love is patient, love is kind. It does not envy, it does not boast, it is not proud. It does not dishonor others, it is not self-seeking, it is not easily angered, it keeps no record of wrongs. Love (agape) does not delight in evil but rejoices with the truth. It always protects, always trusts, always hopes, always perseveres." I Corinthians 13

Do you remember how I started this chapter? I started with the very sad story of a puppy that never received love from anyone, yet was full of love to give, but no one received. As a result, the dog died a very early death. God uses the simplest things on earth to communicate His love for us and remind us of His presence. Look at all the amazing qualities of God's love in I Corinthians 13 and picture your dog. There are lots of similarities! Your dog may not always be patient, but she surely always loves you, protects you, and trusts you to feed her and take care of her. On a grander scale, God's (Agape) love naturally expresses itself in "love, joy, peace, patience, kindness, goodness, faithfulness, gentleness, and self-control." Galatians 5:22-23

Therefore, if agape love is our foundation in the Ergonomics of Relationships, let's examine how it affects the other three loves.

One: Storge Love – As a parent, you have the most important responsibility in the entire world in raising your child. Remember, through agape love, God is our Father and serves as our example of being a good, loving parent.

"Train up a child in the way he should go, and when he is old, he will not depart from it." Proverbs 22:6

I'm a huge encourager. I love helping others just feel good about themselves. Why? My mother and father were huge encouragers. They never "belittled" me or told me negative comments. They were supportive of all that I did, and now I pass that on. So will your children, when raised in a Godly environment. Yes, they may sway, as we all do, but Proverbs 22:6 does indicate, "when he is old, he will not depart from it." Just as us Gen Xer's turned out alright, so will the present generation and Generation Z's (*post-Millennial Generation*).

Two: Philia love – I never met my grandfather, Gunnar Eric Thelander, as I was named after him after he passed away, but he lived and breathed philia love to everyone he met. My father always said that my grandfather *never met a stranger*. He saw every person as a *brother or sister* in Christ, and his attitude was so contagious that he consistently *paid it forward*, direct from God Himself (Agape love) onto others. He was never a Rotarian to my knowledge, but you don't have to be a Rotarian to live out the Four-Way Test in all areas of life, and that's what he did with everyone he interacted with.

Three: Eros love -- Through Agape Love, Eros love can be much, much more solid. There is an order to the two loves, and it goes like this: God first, others second, and yourself third. You may have even seen this on a T-shirt or a car bumper sticker, but it is the Agape way to show love to others and your spouse. Where does your mate fit it? Well, he or she is included in "others." I know it seems odd to tell your spouse, you're *second* in my life! However, if you are coming from the Agape love stance, you would want it no other way. Remember, Agape is *unconditional* love. Therefore, in marital vows to one another, "in sickness and in health, for richer or for poorer, to death do us part," this is literally saying one to another, "I love you and will always love you, *unconditionally!*" I believe a lot of divorces can be prevented with an Agape foundation in the marriage. Therefore, do not marry each other for beauty, as outer beauty always fades. Do not marry each other for money, as financial situations will change, often not for the better. Do not marry for any other reason than *unconditional love, Agape love* one for another. This is what it means to have Agape love as your foundation with your mate.

I encourage you to read the next chapter. The Ergonomics of Faith is basically the Ergonomics of Agape Love. This Agape love is amazing, but here is one condition of God's Love. You have to have faith. But faith in what?

It's hard to have faith in what you cannot see, but that is required in *having* faith. You may be asking:

What if I'm an atheist and choose not to believe in any form of a higher power? What evidence is out there to confirm my faith in any god, or the God, at all? Big questions deserve big answers. And you deserve big answers!

• BREAKING IT DOWN •

First, let's put the four loves into practice.

Application for the Ergonomics of Relationships

1. Storge Love

   A. List three ways you practice *affectionate* love with your child.

   _____

   _____

   _____

   _____

   B. List three ways you practice *tough* love with your child.

   _____

   _____

   _____

   _____

   C. List three ways you spend *time* with your child, and the positive memories you want to create.

   _____

   _____

   _____

   _____

2. Philia Love

   A. How many "friends" do you have on your Facebook, Instagram, and other platforms?

      _____

      _____

      _____

      _____

   B. How many true friends do you have that you interact with consistently?

      _____

      _____

      _____

      _____

   C. On a scale of 1-10, with 10 being the strongest, how strongly do you feel that your company and your child's school would benefit by implementing the Four Way-Test daily?

      _____

      _____

      _____

      _____

3. Eros Love

    A. Have you found your mate yet? If so, write here what attracted you to her/him the most? What qualities did you admire the most?

    _____

    _____

    _____

    _____

    B. What excuses are you using today that causes you not to get married or to stay single?

    _____

    _____

    _____

    _____

    C. If you are currently married and struggling in your marriage, what steps are you taking to keep your marriage strong?

    _____

    _____

    _____

    _____

4. Agape Love
   A. Did you know about Agape love before reading this chapter? (Yes/No)

   B. Do you want to know more about God's immeasurable Agape love for you? (Yes/No)

   C. Do you own a dog? (Yes/No)
      (If the answer is NO on the last question, buy yourself a dog first, and get your dog spayed or neutered!) *Side note: Your dog doesn't hold grudges, even if you chopped his ball off! Now that's true love!*

CHAPTER NINE

Ergonomics of Faith

GEORGE MICHAEL HAD a huge hit in the 1980s with his song, *Faith*, in which the chorus sung "you gotta have faith, faith, faith-a." Well, ain't that the truth! We don't think about it too much, but every day we utilize a lot of faith in our world.

When you sit in a chair, you have faith it will hold you up and not crash you down onto the floor. When you sit in your car, you have faith that your engine will start when you push that Start button or turn that key. When you sit on the toilet, you have faith that it will flush. If it doesn't flush, it's best to gather everyone in the house around the toilet to problem solve with their noses pinched, of course!

What is faith exactly? Wikipedia defines it two ways:

Complete trust or confidence in someone or something

Strong belief in God or the doctrines of religion, based on spiritual apprehension rather than proof

I believe many of us desire to put our faith in another human being, such as a mate or a spouse. When you put your faith in another person, it can be a wonderful thing. Many wonderful friendships are formed through faith that they will be *friendly* to one another. Just like the word "love" has several different applications in life, so does the word "faith."

When I attended college at Texas State University, I had to declare a major. Although I was very interested in Aviation and Medicine, my mother encouraged me to go into education to become a teacher. Her reasoning was I would always have a job or something to *fall back on* in the school teaching field. She was right, and so by declaring my major in Education, I was putting my faith in the program that it would carry me to my desired result of school teaching. I taught for twelve years before I moved up into school administration.

I call these "decisions of faith," and we all make them every single day. Parents have faith that their kids will return home from school when the school day ends. Employees have faith that they will be compensated every day for the time they work in the form of a paycheck.

These are the tangibles. These are things we all put our faith into that we can see, feel, touch, and experience. We see the chairs we will sit in, touch the power button on our phones to turn them on, and feel those we love and embrace.

What are the non-tangible decisions of faith? Actually, there is only one non-tangible decision that requires our faith, and that is in God Himself. Who is He? Why do we think about God, even if we do not believe in Him or even consider ourselves religious?

Do you realize that we, as human beings are the only living things that actually *think* about God? Fish don't. Neither do dogs, cats, rattlesnakes, or sea lions. Only we do, for which you actually qualify if you are reading this book. Why is that?

In the Old Testament, the Bible says:

> *He has made everything beautiful in its time. He has <u>set eternity</u> in the human heart; yet no one can fathom what God has done from beginning to end. Ecclesiastes 3:11*

Think about that. And let's use a bit of deductive reasoning here. God purposefully chose to *set eternity* in you and me. That simply means that we were literally *pre-programmed* to ponder eternity and to think about a place where time itself does not exist after we die. We cannot comprehend eternity, but somehow we know it exists.

Therefore, if God chose to plant eternity in our brains, then He has a plan for us to spend eternity with Him. Correct? You might be saying, "Now Gunnar wait, that requires a lot of faith to believe that!" Exactly.

What is the opposite of that belief? Well, I assume nothingness. So, let's use some deductive reasoning for *nothingness*. When we die, we go into blackness, just like before we were born. Our bodies go underground, and our spirit or soul drifts into absolute nothingness if we even have a soul. Therefore, it is safe to deduct that we have no purpose because we have no designer or higher power.

I believe that the above statement rings true to many who follow the headlines of mainstream media. In a recent publication of *Power of Faith*, here is the opening question

"Is Christianity in the US almost dead?"

Here lies the underlying premise of relativism. This is the universal movement in the US that has affected every avenue of mainstream media in the past two decades. It basically removes all forms of absolute truth, and that truth only exists if it is true to you. Therefore, all truth, including morals and ethics, is true as long as *you believe in it.*[76]

We live in the Land of Freedom. Home of the truth and the brave. This land was founded on the grounds that you can believe in anything you want, which is absolute free will. I believe that God would not want that to change in any form. He absolutely wants each one of us to choose to believe in Him or believe in fairy tales. That's the gift God gives to each of us. The freedom to choose.

The publication discovered that the question above is absolutely <u>false</u>. According to a Harvard/Indiana University study released in January 2018, the number of practicing Christians is *growing* each year, not declining.[77]

However, the Protestant and Catholic churches have been declining in attendance. How can this be? This is an entirely new generation of young people, and they are just flocking over into other types of churches, primarily the non-denominational mega churches. Joel Osteen's church is an example of this type, with over 40,000 faithful fans listening each week.

Here's one finding that shocked me in a good way. The number of *church-attending Americans* in ratio terms is four times more than when our nation was founded in 1776. The Millennials are actually leading this group more than the Baby Boomers or Gen Xers. According to this research, podcasts are the preferred method of listening to Bible teachings among the Millennials. Simultaneously, a whopping 78% of Millennials prefer reading the Bible the old-fashioned way, in print.

Across generations, we are gravitating away from traditional churches and leaning towards non-denominational churches that teach good solid Bible-based materials. One of the reasons why these churches are so popular is the message behind them. The message is positive and very *green* for seekers, for those who are new to Christianity and seeking the faith. I use the word "green" to define someone who does not know much about any subject, with a desire to learn more. In this case, it refers to their very own spiritual well-being.

Joel Osteen from *Lakewood Church* in Houston, Texas, is one of America's most popular pastors. He consistently teaches his listeners how to mix faith with God's teachings:

> *Keep following the dream that God put in your heart. Believe. Work hard. There may be some difficult seasons, but you have to keep moving forward. Sometimes we say faith is spelled R-I-S-K.*[78]

Another pastor-giant with a huge following as a part of Christianity's growth today is Rick Warren, from *Saddleback Church* in Lake Forest, California. He wrote the best-selling book, The Purpose-Driven Life, which has sold over 33 million copies in more than 50 languages worldwide. His call to faith in action is very direct, yet embracing:

> *The purpose for your life is far greater than your own personal fulfillment, your family, your career, or even your wildest dreams. If you want to know why you were placed on this planet, you must begin with God.*[79]

The findings are a good sign, yet most Americans are not attending any church at all, nor do they even know what to believe. And who can blame them?

For nearly five decades now, school prayer and Bible-reading has been removed from all our public schools. Also, try finding a plaque holding The Ten Commandments anywhere that's known as a public institution. With God completely removed from our schools, we have embraced Relativism as truth in all we say and do. It's as if the idea of Relativism became absolute truth for all, which beholds the idea that no absolute truth exists. Yet, in all our science classes, Evolution has been taught as a form of absolute truth, without teaching the other side – Creationism, to any of our students. To be true to relativism, we must teach all sides of the spectrum, then let the students decide for themselves what is true, correct?

Still, I'm amazed at those who embrace the Big Bang Theory (*no, not the TV show*) simply because it requires *more faith* to believe that all of life came to be from some massive cosmic burst. Did you know that our Earth is the *only* planet in our galaxy suitable for life of any kind? You might be saying, "Wait, didn't we find water on Mars?" So, what if we did find water? Life doesn't happen if you *just add water*. Any scientist will tell you that water by itself is not sufficient to sustain life, and it takes mass amounts of water to produce enough oxygen for us to breathe. We should not be looking for small puddles of water on other planets, but massive oceans!

The first part of that verse in Ecclesiastes 3:11 says *He has made everything beautiful in its time.*

I choose to believe that we indeed have a Creator who created everything. And I do mean *everything!*

Consider the amount of FAITH it requires to believe the following facts from a Designer vs. Big Bang perspective, according to an exhaustive list of scientifically proven facts from godandscience.org:

> *Uniqueness of the Galaxy-Sun-Earth-Moon system for Life Support:*
>
> *Our planet is perfectly tilted for seasonal weather, in most parts. If tilted any more or less, climatic changes would be too extreme for life.*
>
> *If our Earth were any closer to the Sun, we would burn up.*
>
> *If our Earth were any further from the Sun, we would freeze to death, but all our ice cream would be good!*
>
> *Oxygen quantity: any more or less would destabilize the earth's ecosystem, and make it impossible to breathe.*
>
> *Interaction with the moon: perfect. Any more or less would cause climatic instabilities; including tidal effects of the oceans, magnetic field destabilization, and inadequate nutrients from the ocean to the continents to sustain life.[80]*

There are 63 more facts revealed supporting the improbability that life originated by chance. In fact, the chances that we all came from *random chance* is 1:10 to the 99th power! The chances are better that you play the lottery in every state every time it's offered and hit the jackpot every time.

Albert Einstein, who actually had an IQ higher than mine (*and I'm considered average!*), spent years studying the Universe. His studies not only led him to the Theory of Relativity but also to a "God who reveals Himself in the harmony of all that exists." In his own words, Einstein said this:

The religious inclination lies in the dim consciousness that dwells in humans that all nature, including humans in it, *is in no way an accidental game*, but a work of lawfulness that there *is a fundamental cause of all existence.[81]*

Here is what Albert was saying in today's English language: *It is inconceivable that there was no Intelligent Designer!*

Why are we not teaching this to our students in school? It makes sense that if we live in a relativistic world, we should be teaching both sides and allow our young people to make their own decisions as to whether we were created by an Intelligent Designer or originated from exploding supernovas.

You get to decide where to place your faith. Either you were an accident waiting to drift into nothingness, or you were purposefully designed for eternity. It can't be both.

I lean on the side of *faith* that indicates an Intelligent Designer does exist, and He has a plan for you and me. I have seen many people living like there is no eternity or purpose, and their attitudes reflect it. They *exist*, but they do not *live*. The go through the daily grind of life, clocking in and clocking out of work each day. It's this purposeless cycle of

- Wake Up
- Shower
- Eat breakfast
- Drive to work
- Work
- Eat lunch
- Work
- Clock out
- Drive home
- Eat dinner
- Watch TV
- Go to Sleep
- Repeat, repeat, repeat

Weekends consist of watering my lawn, cleaning my house, seeing a movie, get ready for another week. This is a mundane life of no excitement nor hope for the future and lived selfishly.

What happens to the person who believes in *nothingness* or is atheistic, believing all of life is meaningless? That person lacks joy. You will experience times of happiness, but it will always be circumstantial. You win a golf game, you are happy. You perform well at school or work; you are happy. You receive a compliment, you are happy. Although the two words are often used interchangeably, I believe that there is a distinction between "joy" and "happiness." Why?

Joy is a gift that only God can give to you, through faith, in which you can experience *happiness* in the good times and the bad times. In both the Old and New Testaments of the King James Version of the Bible, you will find the word "joy" mentioned 165 times!

Without faith in God, who do you turn to when adversity happens? Because adversity *will* happen. I can promise you that! Loved ones will hurt you or leave you. Financial pressures will swarm you. Circumstances for every living person on Earth will happen. If things are going well in your life, I'm happy for you! However, that will change, and when tragedy strikes, such as losing your job, who do you turn to?

Here is the point I'm making here. Friends, you can either choose to live *under* your circumstances, or you can choose to live *above* them. But it's not possible on your own strength to live above your circumstances if you leave God out. Only He is sufficient to carry you through every problem and detail of your life, and all it takes on your part is one thing: faith.

Therefore, let me introduce you to my good friend, *faith*. Faith produces hope. And faith in God can move mountains.

I once heard on the radio, "Too blessed to be stressed." When you have faith, you become more hope-filled in your life. You can actually smile through the hard times, knowing that someone much more powerful than you has a wonderful plan through your messes and for your entire life. That's how you can experience true joy through times of adversity.

After all, since God put that little curiosity in our brains about eternity, what if He really does want us to live with Him forever? Don't we all want that peace about it if we found it the answer to it all?

First, let's explore the choices of faith ergonomically.

Dr. K.P. Yohannan is the founder and international director of Gospel for Asia. He has written more than 185 books published in India, five books published in the United States, including a national best-seller with over 1 million copies sold. He builds a solid case for the meaning of faith.

From a Biblical perspective, in our English language, we have the word "faith," used as a noun, and the word "believe," a verb. There is no distinction between these two words on the surface, as we commonly use the words "having faith" and "believing." However, one of the three original languages of the Bible is Greek, and there is no distinction between the words at all. *Faith* in the Greek noun is known as the word "pisitis." For the verb *believe*, the Greek word is "pisteuo." Therefore, they share the same Greek root word, p-i-s-t. So, both terms are really the same.

Therefore, as Dr. K.P. Yohannan puts it, "The faith we need to see our prayers answered only comes and develops from God's Word: *"So then faith comes by hearing, and hearing by the word of God"* (Romans 10:17).[82]

He shares a story about when Jesus was on the Earth on His "Healing Tour," as I call it.

Jesus was walking along with His disciples when he was confronted by two blind men who had heard that Jesus was nearby.

Dialog:

Jesus: What do you want me to do for you?
Blind men: We want to see again.
Jesus: Do you believe that I am able to do this?
Blind men: Yes, Lord.
Then He touched their eyes, saying, "*According to your faith, let it be.*" And they were able to see again.

Do you see that Jesus used the two words "faith" and "believe" interchangeably? To God, there is no difference. We all have heard the following term, "Seeing is believing," but with Jesus, it's the other way around. *Believing is seeing!*

Therefore, faith requires us first to believe, then you will see. (*if you are a scientist, this will be particularly challenging for you, but will change how you see everything!*)

See what?

You will see life the way God intended, not from a worldly viewpoint, but a divine viewpoint. If God created you, then He has done so with a purpose. Therefore, believing He will guide you into a life that He created you to live is done through having faith.

How much faith do I need? Actually, you just need a very tiny amount of it. Jesus told His disciples this about faith:

I tell you the truth, if you have faith as small as a mustard seed, you can say to this mountain, 'Move from here to there' and it will move. Nothing will be impossible for you. Matthew 17:20

Dr. Yohannan explains that a mustard seed is the smallest seed of all plants. In short, faith is powerful! That's a huge comfort when you consider the 'mountains' in your life. Maybe you are going through a divorce. Maybe you are a college student with final exams coming up. Maybe you have a lot of financial debt. Maybe you wronged someone you care about, or they have wronged you. These are mountains, and we all have them.

You can always use your human intuition to figure things out, or you can have faith in God that He will guide you through it all. Again, it can't be both, and you must choose "my way" or "His way." Utilizing His way is performed by having faith in Him to carry you through your circumstances, and helping you live above them!

I have had the privilege of speaking in ministry circles at numerous youth camps and churches. It amazes me that so many attend seeking God have never heard about Jesus except when His name is used in the media (usually used in vain). Therefore, a little background on Jesus that puts *believing* and *faith* into perspective for all of us.

I hope you are ready to expand your faith right now because so much confusion exists about Jesus outside the Bible; it's time to go back inside the Bible to get the story of Jesus straight.

In the book of Genesis, God unfolds the story of Creation. He created the entire universe, and our world, in just six days, and rested on the seventh day. He created man on the sixth day, Adam, and then created Eve for them to procreate and basically start up all of mankind.

God longs and desires for us to Love Him and obey Him, but love involves free will. Think of countries where there are arranged marriages versus non-arranged marriages. You are basically expected to love your mate in an arranged marriage, although you didn't get to choose. That's not love at all! The marital relationship's beauty is that you get to choose your partner because you love each other dearly. God loves us dearly too, but love involves choice, and He gave Adam and Eve the choice to obey and love God or go their own way and basically do whatever they wanted to do, called *sin*. Well, they chose the latter. God placed a tree bearing golden fruit and said, "Eat of any tree in the Garden, just not this one."

What did Adam and Eve choose? To eat of the one tree God said not too, and thus said to God, "We will do it our way."

Therefore, God and man were separated, and it became impossible for man to dwell with God for all eternity because God is holy and man in unholy and tainted with sin. Punishment was now the only option for all men, which involved eternal separation from God on Earth and all eternity.

So, what did God do to solve the *sin* problem? Due to His wrath, we all deserve the punishment of eternal separation, *but* because of His Love, He chose to save us from His own wrath.

Enter Jesus, the Son of God. Basically, God became one of us, in the form of Jesus. He was 100% God, *and* He was 100% man. He was both and lived a perfectly sinless life. Literally, God became a baby, from the virgin Mary. God had to have His diapers changed. God had to learn His ABC's and 123's, just like all of us. God had to study, go to sleep, and eat his vegetables. Amazing.

If you have noticed, I have been using "Jesus" and "God" as if they were the same person. He WAS the same person. Anytime you say the words, "Thank God!" you are really saying, "Thank Jesus!" because, in nature, they are 100% the same.

Consider the following attributes of God, knowing that every attribute is of Jesus and the Holy Spirit (*more details on the Holy Spirit to come*)

Attribute #1: Omniscient. All-Knowing (past, present, and future)

Remember the former things, those of long ago; I am God, and there is none like me. My purpose will stand, there is none like Me. Isaiah 46: 9-10

God knows everything you and I do, which can be scary, but in light of His other attributes of goodness and love, we can find comfort in this truth.

Attribute #2: Omnipresent. He is anywhere and everywhere at the same time, but not in human form.

> *Where can I go from your Spirit? Or where can I flee from your presence? If I ascend to the heaven you are there; If I go down to the depths you are there. Psalm 139: 7-10*

How can God be literally everywhere at the same time? *Ligonier.org* explains, "He exists on a plane wholly distinguishable from the one readily available to our five senses."

God can be everywhere at the same time. He never sleeps or slumbers and can be everywhere we are, so there is no hiding from God.

Attribute #3: Omnipotent. All-Powerful – Nothing is too hard for Him.

> *By the word of the Lord the heavens were made, their starry host by the breath of His mouth.*
>
> *Psalm 33:6*
>
> *[God] is able to do immeasurably more than we can ask or imagine. Ephesians 3:20*

Attribute #4: Sovereign. God as Most High, above all of creation. King of Kings, Lord of Lords.

> *My purpose will stand, and I will do all that I please. Isaiah 46:10*

Sovereign refers to God being in complete control as He directs all things—no person or government can keep Him from executing His purpose. What is His purpose? That all men will come to know Him and love Him. (*Don't worry, ladies, He means you too!*)

Attribute #5: Immutable. God never changes. He doesn't change His mind or go back on His word.

> *I the Lord do not change. So you, the descendants of Jacob, are not destroyed. Malachi 3:6*
>
> *Jesus Christ is the same yesterday, today and forever. Romans 8:35*

Attribute #6. Holy. He is perfect and without sin, even in human form as Jesus.

> *Holy, holy, holy, is the Lord Almighty. Revelation 4:8*

This basically means that God is infinitely perfect. The word "Holy" means sacred, set apart. He is unlike anything else in all creation. John MacArthur writes, "Of all the attributes of God, holiness is the one that uniquely describes Him and in reality is a summation of all His other attributes."

> *Therefore be perfect as your Heavenly Father is perfect. Mathew 5:48*

Yup, right now, you are not liking that verse. You are probably thinking of all your sinful ways and how convinced you are disqualified for Heaven. That's why you and I need Jesus. As you are about to read, He traded His perfection for our imperfection when He died on the cross. Therefore, as a Believer, God the Father only sees His perfection in you. In other words, God sees Christ's holiness in you, not your sinful mess-ups. That's why it's also called "The Good News!"

Attribute #7: Veracity of God. He is truth. He will never lie and is worthy of our faith in Him.

God, who does not lie. Titus 1:2

It's hard to have faith in someone who has a reputation for lying to others. We are fallible, but God is infallible. We can trust Him in whatever He says. That's why we find tremendous comfort in reading the Bible, His truth. We can rest assured He loves and cares for us, and He will never let us fall.

Attribute #8: Faithfulness. God is faithful. He does what He says He will do.

If we are faithless, He remains faithful—for He cannot deny himself. 2 Timothy 2:13

A.W. Pink Tozer writes, "God is true. His Word of Promise is sure. In all His relations with people, God is faithful. He may be safely relied upon faithfulness is an essential part of His divine nature."[83]

This is a huge comfort for those who are Believers. We can take comfort in knowing His attributes when we suffer and go through hard times. God is always unchangingly faithful, good, loving, wise, and with us. He is never against us, even when we majorly mess up!

Attribute #9: Love. He will always love you, for you are His child.

Beloved, let us love one another, for love is from God, and whomever loves has been born of God and knows God. Anyone who does not love does not know God, because God is Love. 1 John 4:7-8

Tozer writes, "It is a strange and beautiful eccentricity of God that He has allowed His heart to be emotionally tied with men. Self-sufficient as He is, He wants our love and will not be satisfied until He gets it. Free as He is, He has let His heart be bound to us forever. God's love is active, drawing us to Himself. His love is personal. He doesn't love humanity in some vague sense. He loves humans. He loves you and me. And His love for us knows no beginning or end."[84]

If you know the story of Jesus, right after I explain His attributes, you will see everything He did was for you and me. Not for Himself.

Attribute #10: Infinite. He is Self-Existing and without Origin.

> And He is before all things, and in Him all things hold together. Colossians 1:17

All these attributes are shared between the Father, the Son, and the Holy Spirit.[85]

I recall I famous hit song by Joan Osborne titled, *One of Us.* It was a catchy tune, and I always loved the song's melody, but the lyrics come from a perspective that God may exist, but He has no idea what it is like to be human, to be one of us. Joan, have you ever been told about Jesus? I mean the real story of Jesus! Because He was one of us! God knows what it is like to be lonely, afflicted, wrongly accused, and even physically beaten and nailed to a cross. He felt every pain (beyond what any of us will ever endure) that you and I can experience. Read on.

Jesus had to earn a living, like all of us do, so He became a carpenter. He worked until he turned about 30 years old, then set out to retire, playing golf and watching TV. Okay, I added that last part!

At the age of 30, Jesus began His ministry, with twelve disciples, or followers. Here we have the first real call to action for FAITH. Jesus walked up to twelve men, and simply said the following words, "Follow Me." Every one of these men stopped what they were doing and followed Him. They left their jobs, their homes, literally everything they have ever known, and followed a total stranger. They didn't know He was God in the flesh. They really just heard about Him, but they knew there was something special about Him before He ever performed any miracles.

Consider just a few of the miracles you will read in any of the four gospels: Matthew, Mark, Luke, and John. Here was a man of flesh and blood, turning water into wine, healing the sick, walking on water, giving sight to the blind, feeding thousands with one boy's lunchbox, bringing the dead to life, and the most important—resurrection. If you are new to all of this, go straight to the book of Mark. This is the action-packed Gospel listing all the miracles Jesus performed. It's easy and fun to read too!

Three years from when he started His ministry, He was whipped, beaten, and nailed to a wooden cross, and hung to die. Why? Well, His own people rejected Him as anything else but a mere man and major interruption to their religious thinking. But He was not just a man; He was God. The same God who spoke the entire Universe into existence, now hanging on a cross covered in His own blood.

Since one of His attributes is Omnipotence, what could He have done? He could have annihilated everyone by merely speaking it, taking Himself off the cross while unleashing fury over all mankind. But that's Hollywood, and there was a purpose for all the blood, the beatings, and all the torture He endured.

You. He did it all for *you* and *me*. He did it for the same Roman guards with their whips of torture in their hands. He was taking your punishment and mine, and paying the debt of our sin, our lies, our mess-ups, all of it.

If you ever heard the words, "Jesus paid it all," that is what it means. Jesus paid with His own blood the penalty of *sin* so that we can be holy, just like He is holy.

He exchanged his perfection for our imperfections, making us as perfect as God Himself. This is also known as the imputation of sin, through which He imputed upon himself every sin you and I have ever done. Again amazing.

He loves you more than you can imagine.

> *There is no greater love than to lay down one's life for his friends.* John 15:13
>
> *For as high as the heavens are above the Earth, so great is His love for those who fear Him.* Psalm 103:11

That's attribute #9. Love. And God is love.

Well, if you believe all that stuff. That requires a *huge* amount of faith, doesn't it? I know many of you reading this may be thinking, "Hold on! I learned that the Earth was formed over millions of years, and you are saying a Creator formed it in just six days. Really?"

Yes.

"Well, I thought I could just be a good person, and that will be good enough to go into Heaven, or into whatever awaits me. And you are saying I have to believe all that stuff about Jesus to get there?"

Yes.

John 14:6 says, "I am the way, the truth, and the life. No man comes to the Father, but by me."

"But I'm religious because I go to church!"

Well, does going to McDonald's make you a chicken nugget? Plus, what part of the chicken does the nugget come from anyway? *Sorry, side thought there!*

I'd like to make a clear distinction here. The word "religion" is found in no place in the Bible, but the word "faith" and the word "believe" are mentioned numerous times in *every* book. In the King James Version, the word "faith" is mentioned 247 times and "believe" 143 times. Religious people do not go into Heaven, but those who simply believe *do*. Therefore, I refer to those who do believe, "Believers," and to those who do not believe, "non-believers." - Christianbiblereference.org

Believe in what? To believe in one thing and only one thing.

You see, this verse printed on cardboard in the crowd of every football game. John 3:16 which says,

> For God so loved the world that He gave his only Son, that whoever believes in Him will not perish, but have everlasting life.

Then there is the following verse, which most people do not know, but equally as important

> For God did not send His Son into the world to condemn it, but to save the world through Him. John 3:17

What if I still believe in evolution and that the Earth was never created, it just formed together on its own the way evolution teaches us?

Go ahead, believe in that! I'm not going to argue about whether Creation was real or if Evolution was true. I loved science in high school and college, and the best grade I ever got was a B. However, this chapter is not about creation vs. science since I am definitely not qualified to be extremely scientific here. But it isn't necessary either. You can believe in the theory of evolution all you want because really, it doesn't matter.

I can see you shaking your head now, "What!?!?"

Seriously, you can believe that dogs came from trees and unicorns still roam the Earth. You are still a *believer* if you believe that God's love for you is so abundant that He literally died for you and wants to be in your life. Just believe in those two little verses, John 3:16-17, and you are destined for Heaven!

This is faith in *action*. Never in the world before or after has a man been able to miraculously heal another, and these men believed that this man called Jesus could heal their blindness. They were blind, and now they see. Just like those two blind men, once you become a Believer and start reading God's Word, your eyes will be opened too!

I apologize for every scientist out there, again. God doesn't use logic to make us believe. He uses the simple things to show that He exists, and faith is the only requirement on our part to have a relationship with Him.

I love Bill Nye, the Science Guy, and so does every child, parent, and schoolteacher. The man is brilliant, as he knows how to simplify the complexities of science in which any child can understand it. He is not a *believer,* though, just a strong believer in science. I really do believe that God and science go together like peanut butter and jelly, almonds and dark chocolate, butter, and popcorn. After all, God created science! Yet, in his book, *Undeniable: Evolution and the Science of Creation,* Bill questions the Creationist viewpoint as he challenges his readers to show him one proof that God exists.

My answer to him, if he were standing in front of me, would be "No."

Why?

Simply because Bill has already seen all the proof, he needs to believe that an Intelligent Designer is responsible for all of this. Just like you and me, Bill has seen the sunrise and set. He has seen flowers bloom, caterpillars turn into butterflies, and babies being born.

Look what Psalm 19: 1-2 says:

The heavens declare the glory of God;

The skies proclaim the work of his hands.

Day after day they pour forth speech;

Night after night they reveal knowledge.

Here is my question for you. When was the last time you witnessed a sunrise or sunset?

Right now, I want you to put this book down and wait until the next sunrise or sunset. I know you have seen one before, but this time I want you to say a little prayer before it happens. It may be cloudy or even raining outside, so you must see it when the sky is either clear of clouds or even partly cloudy. Partly cloudy is even more beautiful than clear skies because you get colorful reflections that are breathtaking.

Go outside moments before the sun rises or sets, and simply pray to God and ask Him, "Lord, show me your glory." Then say no more. Let Him speak to you. He paints the skies every day, and we rarely appreciate the glorious display He lays out for us.

I do this frequently because it is a powerful reminder that He is in control, and He still loves me despite all the dumb mistakes I make every day. He speaks to me, and He will speak to you.

Listen to Him because that moment can and will change your life. Possibly for all eternity.

Putting Things in Perspective

Recently I heard a marvelous story that helps put Christianity into perspective. There lived long ago a prince. He was next in line to be the king of his country and knew he had to find his queen. He also knew of the traditional royal rule: royalty marries royalty. So, he went to all the royal galas and met many well-qualified women to be his queen, but he never took an interest in anyone at the royal events.

On the way to one particular gala, the usual route was flooded out by a sudden storm, and they chose to go an alternative route through the local village. The village people were very poor and sometimes dangerous. The prince mounted in his chariot with several beautiful white stallions and rode through the village on the way to the gala, and everyone in the village ran outside to see the spectacle. The prince noticed in the line of faces one very beautiful one. A girl that had beauty beyond anyone he had ever seen. He arrived at the gala and made his rounds meeting all the other royals, but all he could think about was the village girl.

He asked his chariot driver a peculiar request. He wanted to leave the event early and ride back through the village so he could see that girl again. As they rode through at a much slower pace, he noticed her again but chose not to get out of his carriage. The village could be a dangerous place for a man of his wealth to be on foot. Besides, he didn't want the news to travel back to the palace where he had taken an interest in a village girl.

The following day he rode through again and noticed her hard at work making things she could sell for a living. He did this for several days, riding through the village just to see her face, but she had never once seen his. He wanted desperately to get to know her, but there existed a problem. She was poor. And royal never marries poor; royal marries royal.

There was another reason why it would be hard to bring her into his royal family. He wanted to make sure she wanted to be with him with true love, and not for his money and stature. "How can she love me for *me*?" he wondered. "I want to spend the rest of my life with her and our love to be *real* and uncluttered with intentions for what I have and who I am." Then he had an idea—one that shocked the entire palace.

He laid aside his royal robes and his chariot and became poor, just like her. He left everything he had, walked out of the royal palace, put on rags, and lived among the village people. He chose to work alongside her and make small items to sell for a living. He became good friends with many of the villagers and became happily acquainted with his new love. However, he never revealed who he was until he knew that she would want to marry him.

He knew he had to become one of his own people to communicate and earn their respect and to marry his bride. He had to become poor so that the one he loved could become rich.

Although it's a fairy tale marriage, the story has so much significance in what differentiates Christianity from Religion. Yes, these are very different from each other and are commonly mistaken, yet they are not the same.

My former youth pastor, Scott Crenshaw, once said, "Religion is man's attempt to reach God; Christianity is God's attempt to reach man." From a logical perspective, every religion is basically man's interpretation of what is written. However, what is important is God's perspective that His love for us is so great that he sent his only Son to become one of us so that we can become more like Him.

My father died in the summer of 2015 of congestive heart failure. The week that he was rushed to the hospital, I was asked to speak at a youth camp in Colorado, far away from any airports that could have gotten me quickly to Houston where he lived. I called him while I was driving out to Pagosa Springs, Colorado, to see how he was doing. He was feeling great and so proud that I was on my way to minister to some youth that needed to hear God's good news. Little did either of us know he was just a couple days away from major medical complications that would take his life.

On the night of his death, I was asked to deliver the message of God's salvation to the youth. Here is what made that a tough speech. I knew that while I was speaking at that very hour, he was dying. I've never exercised so much faith as I did that night, faith that I would be focused on my speech delivery, yet prayerful that God would take my father to Heaven peacefully.

I started out my message with the following words

"There are two kinds of people in this world. But everyone has their own guess as to what they are.

Some say that those two kinds of people are:

Successful and non-successful

Rich and poor

Famous and infamous

Extroverts and introverts

Positive and negative

The "have's" and the "have-nots"

But from God's perspective, there are only *believers* and *nonbelievers.*

I shared with them the same Gospel story I just shared with you but ended it with this:

"My father will be entering the kingdom of Heaven before any of us go to sleep tonight. For over 50 years, he has had the comfort and peace of knowing that he will be with Jesus when he does pass on into Heaven. How about you? Are you ready to have the same amount of faith as he has, right now?"

At that moment, more than half the room of youth gave their lives to Christ, just as my father was meeting Christ, face-to-face. I broke down in tears with the gravity of the moment. I'll never forget it, and neither will any of the youth and other pastors who packed the room that night. It was just so surreal!

You *have* got to read on to the next chapter. The Ergonomics of Death discusses all we need to do to prepare for death itself, so we can have the peace which only God can give us while we are alive on this Earth, just as my father had in his life. What is Heaven like, anyway? There's no way to describe it since we do not even have the words in our language, or the languages of the Bible to describe it, but the next chapter will give you a good idea!

The Ergonomics of the Believer

Being a Believer has its privileges. In fact, Dr. Robert B. Theme lays out 39 things that happen as a result of placing your faith in Christ.

Here is just a few of my favorite:

1. Your place in Heaven is sealed. Forever. You are Eternally Secure. Ephesians 2: 8-9
2. You belong to the Royal Family of God. (no street sweepers in Heaven!) 1 Peter 1:9

3. You share everything Christ is and everything Christ has. Romans 8:17
4. He fights for you and is for you, not against you. Romans 8:31
5. He supplies all of your needs. Philippians 4:19

Of all of these promises of God, here is one that is not promised.

Life will be easy! Just believe in God, and all of your problems will go away. False!

In fact, your problems may even increase based on your situation. Saint Paul's life is an example. His life was easy before he encountered Christ and tremendously difficult after he became a Believer. Yet God carried him through all of his trails, and Paul learned how to live above his circumstances. He taught us what he learned in all the books of the New Testament that he wrote.

It's worth keeping the faith. Here's a little background on Paul. He was formerly known as Saul, a Roman citizen and Jewish Pharisee who was ordered by the Romans to persecute and kill those who were called Christians. He was a threat to anyone who followed Christ—until Christ, Himself showed up. He simply appeared before Saul and said, "Saul! Why are you persecuting Me?" Then Saul went blind for three days before he could see again. When he was able to see again, "scale-like" things dropped from his eyes, and he was really able to "see" but, for the first time, from a Divine perspective.

Henceforth, he repudiated his Jewish name, "Saul" and became known by the Roman name "Paul," as he began a ministry of telling others about Jesus. (en.m.wikipedia/Paul the apostle)

Paul's message was not received warmly by all those he used to call his friends. They beat him repeatedly and threw him into prison over and over. He was visiting churches and trying to

245

help them by showing them in plain terms how to be followers of Jesus. This was the early days of the church, only about 30-50 years after the death and resurrection. Persecution rose to new levels for Christians and the church, especially for Paul.

He must have been so frustrated! He just wanted to tell churches what was on his mind, but how could he when he was repeatedly beaten and imprisoned? All he could do was write and write and write. Obviously, God had much bigger plans for Paul's messages. Paul wanted to share his thoughts with the people standing in front of him. Little did he know he was writing not only to the churches of his day but also for our day too! He had to write to the churches of Corinth, so now we have 1 and 2 Corinthians. He had to write to the churches of Thessalonica, so now we have 1 Thessalonians. Paul wrote more than half of the New Testament book. And at the time of his writings, he never imagined that his writings would end up in the best-selling book of all time, The Bible.

Even Paul was a flawed man, just like all of us. He called himself "The chief of sinners," even more so than you and me. And yet, God chose him, a man whose mission was to kill Christians, to be the chief of Christians.

So, what kind of things did he write? Only things that God Himself would want all of us to know, such as this verse right here:

"For our light affliction, which is but for a moment, is working for us a far more exceeding and eternal weight of glory " 2 Corinthians 4: 17-18

Translated, this verse means whatever you are going through is life, and no matter how rough, it is not worth comparing to what God has planned for you in Heaven! All that is required is faith.

Faith alone in Christ alone. Period!

Life on Earth will not be easy, especially if you are a Believer. By putting your faith in knowing that He cares for you and will never leave you, you can endure any hardship this world throws at you. The Faith-Rest Technique is a great tool for any Believer and is explained in the following section.

However, salvation by faith is incredibly simple. It just takes belief on your part, and a simple prayer that says, "Lord, I believe in You, and your death for me on the cross. Please come into my life."

Simple. Simple. Simple. One little prayer to God and your eternal destiny is secure. Forever.

That will never change despite what you do or what you endure. You are now a part of the Royal family in Heaven, your new home!

Read Romans 8:38, then let it sink in next time you watch a sunset!

Ergonomics of the Faith-Rest Life

After you become a Believer, you need to learn Bible doctrine. Remember, now you can "see" because you now believe, so reading the Bible will be of high interest to you! It will help you see from a divine Godly perspective, verse what you see on the evening news, and it will bring you comfort, peace, and joy!

When adversity strikes, you need to remember that God is in control. He has so many promises that He fulfills in us, but we need to know what those promises are to claim them in our prayers to Him. Speaking of prayer, what is it? Well, it's communication to God Himself. He wants us to talk to Him every day, continuously! He loves to hear from His children, and you are now a child of God! Just as an earthly father loves to hear from his own child, so does God with you.

Remember these three attributes:

> God is immutable, unchanging. Faithful to His Word. Lamentations 3:21-22

> God is omnipotent. All-powerful and able to perform everything He promises. Romans 4:21

> God cares for you. He wants you to dump all your problems on Him. I Peter 5:7

Those are just three facts that you learn when you study God's Word, the Bible. When you internalize these truths, you start learning how to live above your circumstances, in what is known as The Faith-Rest Life.

I'm sure every person has heard the story of David and Goliath, found in I Samuel 17. David was a teenage boy, about 14 years of age, confronting an intimidating giant standing over 9 feet tall, with 125 pounds of armor, and carrying a 15-pound spear. He was the Arnold Schwarzenegger of his day, versus a scrawny teenage boy. The giant scoffed and laughed at his little opponent, but David was serious when he told the giant what would happen. David said, "I'll strike you down and cut off your head for the battle is the Lord's, and he will give you all into our hands." I Samuel 17:47

Here is an example we can all live by in trusting the three qualities of God I just shared with you. God is unchanging in His love for you, He is all-powerful, and he cares deeply for you. Therefore, when you give Him a problem, the problem is no longer your problem, but His problem! If He can create the world by merely speaking it into existence, making something from nothing, is anything too hard for Him?

In this story, he used the most unlikely contender, David the teenager, to take down a trained warrior with a black belt in manslaughter. Yet, the battle was over in less than two minutes. That's even faster than a Mike Tyson fight! Just ask Evander Holyfield!

You should memorize the following verse; it's one of most Believer's favorite verses in times of trouble:

> *"Casting all your anxiety upon Him, because He cares for you." I Peter 5:7*

What's required in giving your giants to God? Your troubles, heartaches, debt, struggles, doubts, etc.? Just ask Him to take them upon Himself by saying,

"Lord, I have this issue, and I'm unable to deal with it as it is just too big for me, but not too big for You. Please take it! I love you, Lord!"

Then breathe. Relax. Rest.

And don't take your problem back. Just trust in Him, let God do the fighting for you. He will win. He always does!

That is the Faith-Rest Technique. It's like the Texas Two-Step:

One: Give it to Him by asking in prayer.

Two: Breathe. Resting in His might, not your own.

This same formula applies to when you sin or mess up. Before you became a Believer, you probably lied, cheated, and stole things out of the grocery store. After you become a Believer, you will still probably lie, cheat, and steal things out of the grocery store. However, now you have a Guide to help change you into who God wants you to become. This is referred to as the

Holy Spirit, who is God in the Trinity, when He speaks to us. Think of the Holy Spirit as that "still small voice" who speaks to your conscience, just as a Guide and/or Counselor.

Nothing catches God by surprise. God knows that Believers will still continue to sin, but His desire for you and me is to change us from the inside out. However, you cannot grow spiritually in Him when you are in your sinful thought patterns and stuck in your own ways. Therefore, God gave us another tool in the Faith-Rest Technique.

I John 1:9 says:

> *"If we confess our sins, He is faithful and just to forgive us and cleanse us of all unrighteousness."*

When you fail, and we all do every day, here's the formula:

One: Confess your sin to God in prayer, reciting to Him 1 John 1:9 as you speak to Him.

Two: Thank Him for His forgiveness.

Three: Breathe. Enter the Faith-Rest Life.

Again, so simple, but only if you Believe and decide to spend time with Him in prayer and reading the Bible to grow consistently.

Also, get into a good church. Going to church is not necessary for salvation for Heaven, but it is necessary to make new friends. It's necessary for fellowship, which you must do to grow as Believers encourage one another.

> *Proverbs 27:17 says, "As iron sharpens iron, so does one man sharpen another."*

Translation: You grow as you spend time studying God's Word with others. You receive comfort knowing that no sin, no struggle, *nothing* is too hard for God to handle! Plus, He is for us and *not* against us. He will never be angry with you or place His wrath on you. He wants to bless us. He wants to bless you. What is required?

Faith and devotion. That's puts the wheels in motion!

Ergonomics of P-L-A-N T-R-E-P

Before concluding this chapter, I want to end it on a positive note—a very positive note. Here is another one of my favorite verses in the Bible, and it brings everything I have explained in this chapter together. I love acronyms. Why? Because I have a terrible memory. Also, I'm severely directionally challenged.

Has this ever happened to you? You are driving down the highway, and you need to get gas, but the gas station is on the other side of the highway. So, you exit off the highway, turn left under the underpass, and arrive at the station to fill up the tank. You get back in your car and get back on the highway, going the *wrong* direction. You drive a few miles before you realize you need to turn back around and return to the right direction for your destination. It happens to me almost 99% of the time!

In life, we will all get "turned-around" and go in the wrong direction. Our *stinking-thinking* kicks in when we get upset with someone or turn to fantasies that have destructive paths. As a Believer, you need to tap into the power of positive thinking God's way.

How? He teaches us how to do that, in the following verse written by Paul:

> *"Finally, brothers and sisters, whatever is true, whatever is noble, whatever is right, whatever is pure, whatever is lovely, whatever is admirable—if anything is excellent or praiseworthy—think about such things."*
> *Philippians 4:8*

251

Sounds great, Gunnar, but how am I to memorize that one?? If you are like me, let's tap into some acronym power!

We need to re-arrange some of the keywords from this verse, but here's how it plays out:

Say to yourself, "I should shift my thinking unto things that are

Pure – P
Lovely – L
Admirable – A
Noble – N

True – T
Right – R
Excellent – E
Praiseworthy -- P

What do you do before you go somewhere? You plan your trip there, right?

Welcome to the Game of Life, and here is how you play it God's way. You PLAN TREP every single day.

In my previous chapter on leadership (Chapter 5), I shared with you The Four-Way Test that all Rotarians recite at every meeting. Here it is as a recap:

In all we think, say, or do:

1. Is it the truth?
2. Is it fair to all concerned?
3. Will it build goodwill and better friendships?
4. Will it be beneficial to all concerned?

Mix that with PLAN TREP, which you are already doing if you do one or the other, and your outcomes in this life will be extremely positive, *regardless* of your circumstances. This is the "secret sauce" of living to your potential and beyond what you can do if God was not in your life. True, you can live out the Four-Way Test even if you are not a Believer, but you cannot practice PLAN TREP unless you are a Believer. Why? Simply because you need God to do it! He is your foundation, and PLAN TREP is impossible to practice in your human strength. You are simply not strong enough to think from a Divine perspective.

PLAN TREP is an outpouring of spiritual growth. With Christ as your foundation, practicing Philippians 4:8 will guide you into the man or woman God intends you to be. It's highly contagious, and it will affect every person you come into contact with. It will not keep you from getting lost on highways, though!

• BREAKING IT DOWN •

Application for the Ergonomics of Faith

1. When was the last time you prayed, asking God to help you through a tough time in your life?

_____

_____

_____

2. Watch a sunset. What was the experience like? Did God speak to you?

_____

_____

_____

3. How do you believe the Faith-Rest Technique will work for you? Have you already used it in dealing with an issue or a struggle of yours?

_____

_____

_____

4. How does PLAN TREP look in your life right now? Are you ready to apply it to your life right now?

_____

_____

_____

5. Are you eternally secure? There is either YES or NO to this question. If you are unsure, ask Jesus into your life right now. You only need to do this once in your life. It's irreversible!

CHAPTER TEN

The Ergonomics of Death

DEATH. WE ALL love talking about this topic, right? Surprisingly we do talk about it all the time; we just don't realize it. How many times have you said something like, "I love you to death!" In every wedding, it is said by both parties, "Till death do we part." And you recite a joke you think is funny, and your friends claim, "I just died laughing!"

In retrospect, death is not just a part of life that we all accept; it's the most important part. My objective for writing this chapter is to give every reader peace. I'm not talking about a tranquil peace you may feel when sitting next to a flowing river. I'm talking about abundant, amazing peace.

I have a good friend who always tells me that it terrifies him when he thinks about his own death. He always asks me when this lively topic comes up, "Gunnar, doesn't it cause you any anxiety whatsoever that one day you will die?"

Great question, and it's one that we all think about, doesn't it?

Let me ask you that question. You will die one day. It's inevitable. The last time I checked the record, the ratio still stands 1:1. Just as everyone was born, everyone will die. Does it cause you any anxiety when you think about death?

What was my answer to my friend? And what is my answer to everyone reading this? I looked my friend straight in his eyes and said, "I'm looking forward to it!" His reply, "How?!? How can you have that amount of confidence and peace about dying?"

That's where this chapter goes, my friends. I want to provide a level of comfort about death that you have never known. That comfort comes not from me, and not just from experts (like all other chapters) but from our Creator Himself, the Lord God Almighty.

You see, death is not the end for the person who believes (Believer) in Christ's death on the cross; it is merely a transference from this life into the other. And the other life? What's really on the other side anyway? What awaits for the Believer? And what waits for the non-Believer?

Great questions that will be tackled in this chapter.

Just as we need to prepare for our death spiritually, we need to prepare for our death physically. The formalities of preparing a Will and planning out your funeral are extremely important. Unfortunately, many simply don't prepare a will before they die, and therefore it is left to the state to decide what happens to your estate. That is not the last memory you want to impress on your loved ones!

I remember someone said, what I think is the very superficial statement: "When you are born, you want everyone smiling, and when you die, you want everyone crying."

Those may not be the exact words, but the underlying purpose of the statement is clear. Sure, your loved ones crying when you die implies that you were so well-loved on this Earth that no one wanted to see you pass, but you would hate those tears of love to turn into tears of anger and resentment when your loved ones realize you didn't formally prepare a will.

Therefore, the Ergonomics of Death is divided into two sections—the physical and the spiritual. The first section will help you prepare for your death in the correct legal way. You want to take care of your loved ones, and you want to minimize negative surprises. The second section will help you face the reality of death spiritually. I intend for you to have the same confidence and peace about death as I do, which is God's intention for every living person!

The Physical-Readiness of Death

On April 27, 1998, *The Kerrville Daily Times* front page reported the death of one of my friends, Mike Davidson of Trinity Baptist Church in Kerrville, Texas. He was the youth pastor and extremely well-loved and respected in all of his circles. He was a tremendous leader with his youth group and with his elders. He actually resembled Rod Stewart, the rock singer. He was young, early 30's and so full of life. The church's pastoral staff reported following his death, "Mike was a respected youth leader throughout his community. He was a great guy."[86]

He had a beautiful wife who was just two weeks prior to the due date for twin girls, in addition to two other young daughters already. With everything going on with his life—leading a solid youth program, fulfilling major obligations with the church, vibrant marriage with children on the way, nevertheless, he thought about his own death. One night he sat down with his wife and wrote out how he wanted his funeral to be. He carried life insurance policies that would take care of his family if anything should happen to him, and formally prepared his will. Just a short time later, he died.

He was on a twin-engine plane headed from Grand Prairie to Fredericksburg, Texas, with one of his friends and the pilot. Upon their return, the plane lost control when it flew into powerlines and killed all three passengers on board. The bodies of all three men were so mangled and burned; the only way they could be identified was by their teeth' DNA. The news was devastating, and when I visited the church, it was obvious how incredibly loved Mike was by everyone there. Just two months after his death, all the youth went to their regularly scheduled summer camp in Alto Frio, Texas. I also attended the camp as one of their keynote speakers. I visited with all the youth and his wife, with their new twin girls. The kids from his youth program were more somber than usual, still mourning and having a tough time finding fun at that camp. His wife, however, was joyful.

That's right. His wife was *giving* comfort to others rather than receiving comfort. Why? Because Mike was both spiritually and physically sound in his death. In that one evening he had everything planned out in the event of death, and his wife and two kids were well taken care of monetarily. Mike's preparation helped give his family peace of mind to go along with the spiritual joy that only God can give in such extreme circumstances of dealing with the loss of a loved one.

Regardless of the size of your estate, each person should plan to leave it to someone you love. According to *verywellhealth.com*, there are four things you should do in preparation for your own death:[87]

1. Plan ahead and make your wishes known. Prepare your Will and choose an Executor whom you trust will be legally responsible for making your Will known to everyone and choosing a probate attorney unless one is already appointed by you. More important than choosing an Executor is choosing guardians for your kids. There is a guardian of the person and a guardian of the finances. Ideally, this is the same individual.

2. Plan your own funeral. Sit down with your spouse or closest relative and write out your funeral event. Funeral planners are a great resource to help you do this adequately.

3. Allow yourself to grieve. In Chapter 2, I listed the most stressful events one can have in life, and the loss of a loved one ranks highest. It is never easy. I lost seven relatives in ten years, and I still grieve over each one of them. They all died too young, except my grandparents, who lived into their nineties. I'll expand on how I got through the grieving process later in this chapter.

4. Review your life. Have you seen the movie *Saving Private Ryan*, starring Tom Hanks? It's intense, especially the opening scenes of the Invasion of Normandy. However, the movie opens with Private Ryan as an elderly man standing over his commander's grave [Tom Hanks]. He has tears in his eyes as he turns to his wife, with his family in the background, and asks her, "Tell me I led a good life, tell me I'm a good man." She replied, after looking at the grave and seeing their loved ones behind them, "You are."

His commander gave his life so that Private Ryan could live. In turn, Ryan didn't want that act of heroism to return void. He wanted his life to count and to mean something. If you are young and reading this chapter, you have your whole life in front of you. Don't live it selfishly but live as unto others. Always give, and life will give back to you. Jesus said,

> "Whomever wants to keep his life shall lose it, and whomever loses his life for Me will find it." Matthew 16:25

If you are old and walk around with a cane in your hand, but you are reading this, it's not too late. One of the most respected church leaders of our day is Rick Warren, pastor of Saddleback Church, who once said, "If you are alive on this Earth, God still has a purpose for you." Moses was 80 years old before he led the Israelites out of Egypt. Col. Sanders was 62 years of age before he first franchised the Kentucky Fried Chicken name. Leonardo de Vinci painted the Mona Lisa was in the latter part of his life as well. The Bible refers to grey hair as a sign of wisdom, so bestow your wisdom unto someone else. They will want to hear from you and learn from you, so give your wisdom away generously!

The preparation of your will is no easy task, and it's very tempting to put it off for another day. Then the day of your death comes sooner than you thought, and it's too late. As Reebok's famous slogan says, "Just do it." Wait was that Reebok? Anyways

That's what happened to the Queen of Soul, and an American Icon, Ms. Aretha Franklin. She just passed in September 2018 with seemingly no formal will in place. According to the New York Times, Aretha Franklin left behind her entire $80 million estate to be determined by the state of Michigan as to what happens. This varies from state-to-state, so you should check on what happens when someone dies without a Will to your estate. We get an idea of how the laws work in Ms. Franklin's hometown of Detroit, Michigan:

According to Michigan law, the assets of an unmarried person who dies without a will are divided equally among their children. Ms. Franklin had been married twice but was long since divorced. Though wills are public records in Michigan once a person has died, the document itself often does not contain the kind of financial details that may become public as an accounting of her estate proceeds.

High-profile probate proceedings can drag on for years and lead to infighting among families, lawyers, and others. Such estates can become especially complicated when it comes to issues like music rights. The case of Prince, who died two years ago and left no Will, has led to numerous family disputes and even the revocation of a multimillion-dollar music deal.[88]

Regardless if you are in your twenties or eighties, you need to prepare a formal Will. You know the date of your birth, but you do not know the date of your death. Having a Will signifies peace that your loved ones will be blessed with your monetary possessions. It also signifies those you want to leave out of your Will, for whatever reason. In Aretha's case, it turns out she was attempting to write a Will for her multi-million-dollar estate, according to scribblings found in a spiral notebook. The discovered Will was submitted to the probate court for determining what happens to her estate, in which she is survived by her four sons and no spouse.[89]

Therefore, let's review three main things you need to do to plan for leaving this Earth:

1. Prepare a Will

2. Plan your funeral
3. Carry a good life insurance policy

It's very tempting to procrastinate in getting these things done. You would have every excuse in your favor if you knew your own expiration date, but you don't. According to the Nations World Population Prospects report, approximately 7,452 people die *every day* in the United States. That means a person dies in the U.S. approximately every 12 seconds![90]

How many knew they would be dying the day they actually died? I imagine only those told by a medical doctor in ICU would know, but even then, it may be too late. We can all get run over by a steamroller on our way home today. Therefore, be like Mike, the Youth Pastor. He set aside the time to get it all done with his wife, and when he departed from this Earth, no *guesswork* was involved. Plan your death today, because you may not see tomorrow.

Just as it is hard to talk to your children about the birds-and-the-bees, it is much more difficult to have an end-of-life conversation with your loved one. The Conversation Project is a wonderful organization to help you have such talks! The numbers are staggering about how many avoid these important discussions. Their research concludes:

> While 92% of Americans say it's important to discuss their wishes for end-of-life care, only 32% have had such a conversation. 95% of Americans say they would be willing to talk about their wishes, and 53% even say they'd be relieved to discuss it.[91]

This service offers "starter kits" to help guide you with the discussion of planning the end. They are available in many languages and even offer special kits for those with dementia or even seriously ill children. This is a great tool for you if you feel inadequate to have a conversation without external help. The most important thing is not to put this off until tomorrow, as tomorrow may never come.

Therefore, include the following when mapping out your day (from Chapter 6) today:

1) Prepare a Will. This is actually an easy thing to do, and even though you don't need an attorney to do it, I advise you to hire one. It will cost you a little more money to hire an attorney to prepare your will, but you can also have greater peace knowing that you will have someone to call if things go wrong. If you choose the do-it-yourself route, many legal platforms are available to you. I personally like *Legal Zoom* as a good source. Just be sure to sign and notarize your hard work. An unsigned Will is unenforceable.

My ergonomic take is to keep it simple. The more complex the Will is, the better idea it is to bring on a hired attorney specializing in Will & Probate. There are two important questions of a Will:

The first question is, "Who gets to be my executor, and who shall be my appointed guardian?"

The second question is, "What happens to my possessions when I die?"

You will have peace of mind knowing someone you trust will be in charge of your money and possession distribution. Wills assign a place for cars, jewelry, art, your vintage vinyl but NOT your bank accounts and retirement accounts. It's not just a legal document; it's peace of mind for you and everyone around you! You definitely do not want your passing to be any harder than it will be, so having a solid will in place will make the entire process much, much easier!

2) Plan your Funeral. You are doing this for your loved ones because you will not be attending this event yourself. Where do you want your service? What pictures do you want displayed? Do you want an open-casket service or just flowers displayed? What music do you want to be played? Who do you want to give your eulogy? You get to plan your order of service, and it's performed so that you are remembered well. That's the best gift you can give to your family!

Also, what happens to your remains? You can choose to be buried, which can be expensive. A more cost-friendly means of disposal is cremation or donation. You can donate your body to science, just as my grandfather Gunnar chose to do. This means that those who practice medicine can practice on your cadaver. Medical schools love to see healthy cadavers, as well as unhealthy ones. If you were a life-long smoker, your cadaver will be a great tool for future doctors to examine and study. The same goes if you died of cancer, substance addiction, or just physically unfit. In short, your remains can help save lives for those who practice medicine. Those who strive to help others may choose this route, knowing that your remains will serve a good purpose rather than decomposing in a casket. Or your body can be cremated, as my father was, and choose where you want to spread your ashes. Believe it or not,

I haven't died yet, but when I do, donating my body to science will be the route I'll choose.

I recommend choosing a funeral planner to help you lay it all out for when that last day of your life comes. You definitely want to leave your loved ones some instructions about what to do with your body when you pass. Then the funeral experience will be organized by you, and no one can change that.

3) Carry a good Life Insurance Policy. There is so much confusion over life insurance policies, but they sure are popular on Law & Order episodes as motives to murder someone! Life insurance is a contract between an insurance policyholder and an insurer. Upon the policy holder's death, or you, the insurer promises to pay a beneficiary a determined amount of money in exchange for a premium.

One great benefit of having a life insurance policy is that you can designate the expensive costs of the funeral within the policy you choose as one of the benefits. To prevent an impending murder from a greedy beneficiary, you can write in specific exclusions to limit the insurer's liability, such as fraud, suicide, civil commotion, and yes, even murder. Life-insurance policies usually fall into two major categories:

- *Term Life*. Term Life Insurance provides coverage for the insured or the beneficiaries involved for a specified amount of time: 10 years, 15 years, or whatever timeframe you determine. The financial responsibilities covered may include consumer debt, mortgage debt, and even funeral costs. This is usually a lower-cost option, even if you are not in good health. I suggest you do your research on what term life policies are the best fit for you and your loved ones.

- **Whole Life**. Whole Life Insurance policies are guaranteed to last a lifetime, provided the premiums are paid regularly. The insurer can designate the lump sum of the "death benefit" of the policy to the beneficiary once the insurer dies. This is a more costly option yet can pay more on the end for the beneficiary.

Tackle the Big 3 today! You will feel better that it's done and share with your key relatives or beneficiaries that your Will has been prepared and where they can find it. That's the job of the designated executor of the Will. After your day of death, no one can call you and ask where you placed your Will. It's funny, but I sometimes hear stories of the "misplaced Will." The Will was prepared and hidden because information on it was not to be known until it needed execution, but then lost because no one could find it!

The bottom line is your loved ones will be blessed with financial peace of mind when your fateful day comes. Funerals can be very expensive, so that's an excellent reason to carry a life insurance policy to cover those expenses. Your departure from this Earth will be hard enough for your loved ones, and you don't want the added burden of funeral costs and the final medical expenses as well. These medical expenses can be more than a funeral, depending on how much intervention was done in your final days, as well as the length of the illness itself before the day of death.

By the way, if you never liked any of your relatives and have no one to leave your possessions, make me your beneficiary! I'd love to take very good care of your money, house, cars, stocks, etc.! No complaints from me. Scouts honor!

The Spiritual-Readiness of Death

I believe everyone knows about the story of Cassie Bernall. She was one of the students killed in the Columbine High School shootings on April 20, 1999. The gunman pointed the gun at her head and asked her the question, "Do you believe in God?" She said, "Yes." With the first part of that gunshot ringing in her ears, she was in Heaven the very next moment. That is the confidence and spiritual-readiness I want you to have. Cassie had no will in place nor a life insurance policy, but she was spiritually ready to meet her Maker.

I encourage you to read *Jesus Freaks* by DC Talk. The book contains many stories of those who stood death in the face and died for the name of Christ. *Jesus Freaks* opens with Cassie's story, which has impacted millions to be spiritually ready for death. What is fascinating about Cassie is that most of her life she was a rebellious teenager. She was into drugs, drinking, and partying. She was even suicidal at one point and threatened to run-away numerous times. Yet, one day at a summer youth camp, she heard about the incredible love of Jesus, the fact that every sin she had ever committed would be permanently erased and that she could spend an eternity in Heaven. All she had to do was to decide to follow Christ, and her eternal destiny would be permanently secured, forever. Like all of us, Cassie planned to live a long life, have a stable career, and raise a family. She never thought a massacre was coming her senior year of High School, and that she would be one of the many killed that day. No one knows their day of death, so waiting to be *spiritually ready* is a really bad idea.

I already mentioned the fact my mother died on December 15, 2007. She was too young to die at just 63 years old. She was feeling good that day and in relatively good health. She spent the day with her close friend JoAnn. They went Christmas shopping together. She got her hair done. They had a wonderful lunch together. My mother was excited about seeing all of her three kids over to the house for Christmas. She went to bed, and the Lord took her home to Heaven. She had a blood clot that traveled to her heart and took her life. She died the way she wanted to die. She always told us, "When I go, I want to go in my sleep. I want to simply wake up in Heaven." God granted her request, but the timing sucked! It was a mournful Christmas for us all. The toughest part of this Christmas was her absence. She was always the cornerstone of every Christmas holiday. As kids, we all unwrapped presents as she sat back with a huge grin on her face, taking it all in. Heck, nothing changed when we all became adults! She still wanted us all together, sitting by the Christmas tree, unwrapping all of her gifts that she acquired cheaply at Walmart and Marshall's. But that Christmas in 2007, unwrapping gifts was extremely difficult for all of us. She bought me a really ugly button-up shirt with buzzards all over it, which was too large. But I kept that shirt all these years, and I even wear it occasionally on Christmas in remembrance of her.

Most of us have a story of a loved one who has passed. It's tough. In the Life-Event Stress Test (Chapter 1), the death of a loved one ranks #1 as the most stressful event you will face in your lifetime.

However, time heals. I know we have all heard those two words when we lose a loved one, and it's true. Many Christmases have gone by since my mother's death, and now I'm around all the family members we really enjoy the holiday again. Sure, we all think about her, but we also have spiritual peace that she is in a much better place. She loved the Lord, and now she is with Him forever. Plus, we know we will all see her again. With that peace, *time heals.*

"Okay, Gunnar, great, but that didn't help me!" I can hear you saying. It's tough when you lose a parent, but immensely harder if you are a parent who lost a child. In her book, *Ambiguous Loss,* Pauline Boss explains the grieving process is very difficult, but it makes us stronger as human beings. As a family therapist, she works with families dealing with a close relative or friend's loss.

She recommends increasing your physical activity and inter-action with others as a better route than being passive and alone in your grief. Although passivity is also a part of the healing process, there needs to be a balance. Boss encourages individuals to do anything physically and socially to become active again, rather than sitting in isolation, which can lead to depression. Prayer is essential to this process of coping with a recent loss. When I lost my mother, the pastor let us know that he grieved over the loss of his father for more than six months before he was able to be as functional as he was before the loss. It took a lot of prayer to help him cope with the fact that his father simply was not around anymore.

Another remedy encouraged by Boss is laughter, even for just a few moments. This can be accomplished through open communication with family members and close relatives, re-membering humorous moments shared with the one who has passed. Laughter relieves our bodies' cortisol levels and replaces it with serotonin and shows appreciation for our loved one's life as a celebration.[92]

When my mother passed, it took our family several months to do this, but it really helped us accept the new normal without her presence in our lives. One of the funniest moments of my mother's life was one my sister shared with us all. When she was just a teenager, she went to see a movie with our parents. Of course, our mother ordered a large Coca-Cola and a large tub of popcorn. In the middle of the movie, she went off to the restroom, and upon returning, she got confused as the theater was very dark. She sat down next to a large man who resembled her husband; she didn't notice that to his left was his wife and children. She nonchalantly started eating his popcorn and even took a sip of his drink. That's when his wife asked her what she was doing, and my poor, embarrassed mother apologized and rejoined her real husband. After that incident, movies with our mother were never the same!

I believe all the above can really help with anyone suffering from the loss of a loved one, but in my opinion, the Bible gives us comfort at a whole new level. Think about this absolute truth **God is transcendent of time.**

Here's what I mean

I love the following verse, and it really helps in times of grieving over a loved one. Here it is:

> *A thousand years in your sight is like a day that has just gone by, or like a watch in the night.*
>
> *Psalm 90:4*

This truth is repeated in 2 Peter 3:8,

> *But do not forget this one thing dear friends: With the Lord a day is like a thousand years, and a thousand years is like a day.*

We have a short life here on Earth when compared to eternity. You see, in Heaven, time doesn't exist. To put it into an Earthy perspective of time in Heaven, God says that 1,000 years is like a 24-hour day on Earth. However, it's even shorter than that! The verse says, *"or like a watch in the night."* In those days, thousands of years ago, a "watch" was regarded as a three-hour period that a soldier or guard would have to stand guard, fully awake and alert in the event of an enemy attack. Even today, in our armed forces, soldiers would have to take turns taking a watch while the others slept for about the same time. Therefore, what God is saying is that 1,000 years is like three hours to Him!

How does that comfort us? I lost my mother in 2007, and I lost my father in 2015. I'm in my 40's at the time of writing this book, with hopefully another 40 years of life left before I die. It will be another 40 years or so (*hopefully*) until I see them again in Heaven, but it will be just a few more moments, even seconds, before they see me again.

Did you lose a loved one? Maybe your parent, friend, or worse yet, a child? It may be years or even decades before you see them again *but* not to them! That loved one who departed Earth will see you in just a matter of a few moments!

I don't know about how you feel about what I just wrote but knowing that promise of God has helped me overcome seven recent deaths of family members!! Of course, this only applies to the one who believes in Christ.

Everyone who calls upon the name of the Lord will be saved. Romans 10:13

You may be thinking, "Oh, no! My loved one who just passed was an atheist, agnostic, or believed in something else!" Have no fear!! Why? Because my question to you is this, "How do you know?"

How do you know that your loved one didn't believe at any point in their life that Jesus died for them? They may have decided to keep it in the privacy of their own soul, never telling anyone. Or, they may have secretly prayed to believe in Christ just moments before they died themselves. Once you place your faith in Christ, it's ironclad. Regardless of when you believed-- whether it was in the beginning or at the very end, you will be forgiven and saved!

> *For I am convinced that neither death nor life, nor angels or demons, neither the present nor the future, nor any powers, neither height nor depth, nor anything else in all creation, will be able to separate us from the Love of God in Christ Jesus our Lord. Romans 8:38-39*

You cannot spiritually save someone else, but you can pray for your own salvation, right now!

How do you do it? You simply say the following prayer. There is no formula as much as a request to God. Remember, my mother thought she would be alive for many more years, and she died unexpectedly. Someone will die in the next 12 seconds, unexpectedly. Do this now, and change your eternal destiny forever:

> *"Dear Lord, I am a sinner. I believe that you loved me so much that you died on that cross. Save me from my sins and come into my life. I want to spend an eternity with you in Heaven and make you my Lord and Savior."*

That's it. Once you say those words and sincerely mean it, you are saved from the eternal damnation of Hell. Speaking of Hell, it was never meant for any person. It was created for Satan and his demons. They chose to rebel against God, and God just created a place for them to face their punishment. God loves you, though, and wants you to be with Him forever, but He will not make you into His puppet. He wants you to choose Him, willingly. Once you do that, you become His child. Essentially, you are "born again." You now have a new life, and you are now a new creation (Galatians 5:17).

Get ready, because after you say that prayer, God begins His work on you. He wants to change you into the person He created you to be. You will develop what I call the *spiritual thirst*, which can only be satisfied by going to a Bible-based church, reading the Bible, praying, and fellowship with other Believers. You will also want to get baptized as He himself modeled with John the Baptist. These things are new desires that will develop in your soul and not prerequisites for getting into Heaven. There is only one prerequisite for going there, and it's agreeing that Christ's death on that old rugged Cross was for you.

Once a Believer in Christ, there is nothing you can do to lose your salvation. Sin won't make you lose it, because now sin is no longer a Believer's issue. Suicide won't do it either. Romans 8:38 is true for any Believer because Christ's death has washed away our sins and disabled death itself. There are religions out there that claim suicide is an automatic ticket to hell, but C.S. Lewis challenges that belief. In C.S. Lewis book, *The Problem of Pain*, suicide is just another sin that has already been paid for on the Cross. People talk about death as if it ends it all. And people often rationalize that if this life becomes too painful, one can always commit suicide for an early escape. In reality, the horrible thing about Christianity is that it offers no such escape. It assures each person that he is going to live forever.[93]

I once saw a picture book of many headshots of random people. These individuals were all still alive and regret the day they decided to commit suicide. Each one took a gun to their own heads and fired but did not die. Their faces were mangled and very deformed. The act itself only made the issues they were trying to escape much worse. For not only could they not show their faces in public due to their disfigurement, but they had the emotional abuse from family and friends who were in disbelief that they would attempt suicide at all. I've heard many stories of people trying to take their own lives, only to live the remainder of their lives in regret. In short, only God can allow such an act to even happen, because if you are alive, His purpose for your life on Earth is not yet complete.

Remember, friends, although life serves us big problems, we serve a big God. He is always there for our comfort and time of need. Did you know that God has a phone number? It's three 3's in a row, and an easy verse to memorize.

> *Call to me and I will answer you with great and mighty things you did not know. Jeremiah 33:3*

That is what prayer is all about. Instead of jumping off a bridge, pray. God has an answer, and He is the answer. He is all you need. Listen to the song from 7eventh Time Down, titled *Just Say Jesus*. It's a powerful song for us in times of adversity, and it's helped me through some hard times as well.[94]

Here are some of the lyrics of this song. They can easily become your prayer with anything you are struggling or going through. It's a catchy song, and I love it when it just starts playing in my head. You will like it too!

Just Say Jesus, sang by 7eventh Time Down

> *Life gets tough, and times get hard*
> *It's hard to find the truth in all the lies*
>
> *When you don't know what to say*

Just Say Jesus

There is power in the Name
The Name of Jesus

If the words won't come
Cause your too afraid to pray
Just say Jesus

I Peter 5:7 says this, "Cast your anxiety upon Him, because He cares for you." Remember, you are more than His creation; you are His child. Just as you care for your own children (*assuming you have one or two, or the national average of 2.5 children*), He cares for you and wants the best for you. He loves it when you talk to Him, and you are never a bother. He calls us His children and his friends, so talk to Him as you would your own father or best friend. He is always for you, not against you!

> *What shall we say in response to these things? If God is for us, who can be against us?*
>
> *Romans 8:31*

The Ergonomics of the Death and Resurrection of Christ

Do you understand the digestive system and how it works? Most of us do not, yet every day, we eat and drink. Our bodies receive nourishment through what we eat, and yet we do not have a single clue as to the physiology of how it all works. Just as we have a very limited understanding of our digestive system, we can have a limited understanding of what Christ has done on the cross, and still receive salvation. According to C.S. Lewis, the death of Christ on the cross is where "something 'unimaginable' breaks into our world. Somehow, Christ's death puts us right with God and given us a fresh new beginning. Lewis simply encourages all of us to simply accept Christ's sacrifice because "Christ's death has washed our sins and disabled death." Remember, Christ died but resurrected from His death three days later, something only Deity can accomplish. I love what Lewis writes concerning the death of the King of Death. He explains the importance of the resurrection:

> *Achievement in rising from the dead was the first event of its kind in the whole history of the universe. He has forced open the door that has been locked since the death of the first man. He has met, fought, and beaten the King of Death. Everything is different because he has done so. This is the beginning of the New Creation: a new chapter in cosmic history has opened.*[95]

All you need to do is accept that truth, and you will be saved from eternal damnation. Unbelievable that Christ's love for us is so immense that he would step out of Heaven, become a man and die a horrible death, just to exchange places with us. He took on all of our sins when He died on that cross so that we can be completely and totally 100% forgiven by taking on our punishment. Unbelievable that all you have to do is believe, as no one can earn salvation themselves.

My father's closest friend, Mr. Wallace, sends me an email blog full of spiritual truths that enlighten my soul. One particular blog was so perfect for this chapter that I just had to share it. Read it carefully, as it clearly explains the whole picture of death:

Our Sovereign LORD reigns: Righteousness and Justice are the foundation of His throne:

> The LORD is the supreme ruler of the universe and Righteousness and Justice are the very foundation of His Kingship. (see Psalms 89:14 & Psalms 97:2)

Before man ever existed on earth, there existed an angelic civilization. The LORD God created Lucifer as the highest angel in God's Angelic Kingdom. Lucifer was the anointed Cherub. He was full of wisdom and perfect in beauty, and he had the freedom and power to act at his own discretion and self-will. At some point, he chose to rebel against the Godhead and take over heaven as the sovereign ruler; He longed to be served and worshiped as God. The betrayal and uprising included one-third of the heavenly host joining in the revolt against the LORD God.

The rebellion was short-lived, and Lucifer, also called Satan, was put on trial along with his rebellious cohorts. They were found guilty and sentenced to the lake of fire forever. But there was an appeal of the verdict. The argument was that the sentence was unjustly harsh and unfair. Satan, which means accuser, attacked the Justice of God. He claimed that God had given freedom of choice to each angelic creature, and therefore when that gift was freely exercised against God, it was unfair and unjust to eternally condemn those who chose to go their own way. (see Isaiah 14:12-14 & Ezekiel 28-11-19 & Revelation 20:7-10)[96]

Mankind was created to resolve this angelic conflict. First, God brought Adam and Eve into the trial's appeal phase and gave them the same freedom of choice. In the center of the Garden of Eden were two trees. One was the tree of life, and the other was the tree of the knowledge of good and evil. They could eat of every tree in the garden with only one exception.

The tree of the knowledge of good and evil was forbidden to eat from, and the consequence of doing so was death.

Satan did a job on Eve and convinced her that God withheld the forbidden tree from being eaten because it was a fruit that would give them knowledge to be like God when eaten. Eve bought the deception and ate of the tree and then gave it to Adam. Eve was completely deceived, and while Adam was not deceived, he chose to go with Eve in rebellion against God.

The LORD God then sets up one positive tree. To bring many sons and daughters into an eternal relationship with himself, he chooses to become flesh and dwell among mankind. The cross becomes the One positive tree to embrace or reject. The LORD God himself becomes flesh to die for all mankind while we were yet his enemies. This so great salvation was announced while Adam and Eve were still in the Garden of Eden. He killed an animal and dressed man and woman in skins to cover their fallen state. They had lost their glory covering and were naked. The blood of an animal had to be shed to provide a covering for them. It is written in Hebrews 9:22:

> *"For without the shedding of blood there is no forgiveness."* - *no sins can be forgiven unless blood is offered.*

Jesus, who is the visible image of the invisible God, shed his blood for us on a cruel Roman cross that we might be forever forgiven of every sin, past, present and future. He who knew no sin was made sin so that we might be made the righteousness of God in him. (2 Corinthians 5:21) – "but now once at the end of the age hath he appeared to put away sin by the sacrifice of himself." (Hebrews 9:26)

The gift of righteousness satisfies the Justice of God. The atoning sacrifice by God himself for us, forever exalts His supreme Justice and forever disproves the argument that God is not Just. When we make one positive decision to believe and receive this saving grace, we become a cloud of witnesses that refutes the argument made by Satan in his appeal against God's Justice. As the cloud of witnesses grows in number, the evidence becomes overwhelming that the foundation for the LORD God's throne is Righteousness and Justice. He gives us his righteousness through Christ Jesus to satisfy his Justice. This is why Jesus said In John 14:6-9, "I am the way, the truth and the life: no man cometh unto the Father but by me, He that hath seen me has seen the Father."

In conclusion: Once we have accepted the gift of His Righteousness, which satisfies His Justice, we are positioned under the New Covenant of Grace to reside in Christ Jesus. At the cross, we were crucified with Christ. He died for us and as us. It is no longer we who live but Christ who lives in us. And the life we now live in the flesh, we live by the faith of Jesus, who loved us and gave Himself up for us all. (Galatians 2:20)

Life in Christ Jesus is designed to be a foretaste of glory divine. It is a process that, as we behold Him as the Living Word and the written Word, we are transformed into his image with ever-increasing glory from the LORD, who is the Spirit. And where the Spirit of the LORD is, there is freedom. (see 2 Corinthians 3:17-18)

It is a work in process, so don't be discouraged when you stumble. There is no condemnation to those who are in Christ Jesus! We have been made right with God through the death, burial, and resurrection of Christ Jesus. His righteousness satisfies God's Justice. It is a gift of God, not of works lest anyone should boast.

One positive decision for Christ Jesus and we join a cloud of witnesses that forever condemns Satan and his fallen angels.

Satan is the chief principality of darkness behind the powers of this corrupt world system, and the invisible power of darkness behind all the evil rulers that have come and gone in human history!

Adam and Eve made one negative decision, and by God's amazing grace and mercy, He reverses One negative into One positive decision for Christ Jesus. This is why we are here in time to freely choose for or against Christ Jesus, who paid it all. Sin had left a crimson stain, but He washed it white as snow. To Him be the glory forever!

Jesus is LORD

Blessed be the Name of the LORD - His Mercy endures forever!

-Mr. Wallace

Two more of my favorite verses that give us comfort in times of loss, as well as comfort concerning our own death, are found in I Thessalonians and I Corinthians.

Brothers and sisters, we do not want you to be uninformed about those who sleep in death, so that you do not grieve like the rest of mankind, who have no hope. I Thessalonians 4:13

No eye has seen, no ear has heard, and no human mind has conceived the things God has prepared for those who love Him. I Corinthians 2:9

So here is what I can safely conclude as what these two verses point to Heaven!

The Ergonomics of Heaven

What is Heaven like? I have a story that will shed some light on Heaven.

There once was an old married couple who spent most of their lives together. The wife made sure her husband ate bran muffins every day because they were nutritious and healthy. They didn't have much money, but they were both Believers in Christ. One day, they both died and went to Heaven. St. Peter greeted them and showed them around Heaven. They were both in complete awe in this majestic place. St. Peter took them to their mansion in Heaven, more beautiful and larger than any mansion on Earth.

The man said, "Is this place really ours?"

St. Peter said, "Yes, it's all yours!"

Then St. Peter took them to a huge buffet feast, with unlimited portions, featuring better food than anywhere on Earth.

The man asked, "You mean we can eat all we want and never gain weight or get heart disease, diabetes, cancer, or anything?"

St. Peter laughed and said, "Yes, of course! Your bodies are eternal now. You will never get sick or even get fat."

Then St. Peter showed them the largest, most beautiful golf course they have ever seen.

The man asked, "This course is amazing! What are the club fees?"

St. Peter just laughed and shook his head and replied, "Sir, you can play all you want, and there is never a fee."

Then the man turned to his wife and said, "Geez Helen! If you hadn't made me eat all those tasteless bran muffins, we could have been here a lot sooner!"

Sounds nice, doesn't it? We can always try to imagine Heaven with some of our memories of snow-capped mountains, green grass fields with bright yellow sunflowers blooming throughout, or even staring at the clear night sky watching for falling stars. But heaven is much, much more beautiful than the most beautiful scenery imaginable on Earth. When I was a youth pastor,

I would always try to paint the picture of heaven by telling the youth, "You see how much bigger the night sky is than our world? That is what Heaven is to outer space." And then I'd follow it up with, "Scientists say we use only 2% of our brainpower. It would take the remaining 98% just to conceive Heaven!"

How do I know? Well, I don't. I just have *faith*. Immense faith. But somehow, I know I'm right when I say that there really is a place called Heaven waiting for me when I die, as it is for every Believer. We have all heard of near-death experiences from people that claim they saw heaven. It's always some crazy story that they were traveling down some dark tunnel towards a bright light, and then right before they came into the light, they would wake up.

Don Piper was not one of those people. He *did* die! And he came back to life 90 minutes after a tragic car accident caused his heart to stop beating. He wrote a book called *90 Minutes in Heaven,* in which he describes what he saw and experienced. I will share some of those details here, and it really adheres to what I Corinthians 2:9 says,

> *No eye has seen, and no ear has heard what God has prepared for those who love Him.*

Don Piper does his best to describe what he saw, with enormous difficulty:

> *"As I try to explain this, my words seem weak and hardly adequate, because I have to use earthly terms to refer to unimaginable joy, excitement, warmth, and total happiness. Everyone continually embraced me, touched me, spoke to me, laughed, and praised God. This seemed to go on for a long time, but I didn't tire of it."* [97]

He said this as he was immediately surrounded by family and loved ones who had passed in his lifetime. He recognized every one of them, and he refers to his arrival into Heaven as "the greatest family reunion of all."

Then he writes about the beauty of Heaven itself.

> *"Everything I experienced was a first-class buffet for the senses. Heaven's light and texture defy earthly eyes or explanation I could hardly grasp the vivid, dazzling colors." Basically, the best way Jon could explain all of it was like entering "another dimension."*

The Bible also says, "He will wipe our tears." Tears of what? I believe it may be tears of regret, as we will all have them when we behold the beauty of Heaven, then think about those whom we never told about the wonderful love of Christ. We may also have tears of remorse over things we have done in the body that could negatively influence others. But God promises to remove those tears. Don echoed this as he wrote,

> *"I wasn't conscious of anything I'd left behind and felt no regrets about leaving family or possessions. It was if God had removed anything negative or worrisome from my consciousness, and I could only rejoice at being together with these wonderful people."*[98]

I've often wondered and even asked, "How old will we be in Heaven? Will we be the same age that we die?" That is a great question, and Don explains what he saw in his great-grandmother, someone he has not seen since he was a child. He remembered her as slumped over with osteoporosis, and an extremely wrinkled face and no teeth. But in Heaven, she stood tall, no wrinkles, and a beautiful smile of sparkling white teeth. Don explained, "As I stared at her beaming face, I sensed that age has no meaning in Heaven." Remember, time doesn't exist in Heaven, so no one grows *older* there.

Here is my favorite part of Don Piper's experience in Heaven. He felt loved. Immense love. A love so perfect that he felt "more loved than ever before in my life." This world we live in doesn't emanate love at the level it resonates in Heaven. So many of us are unloved, even by our closest relatives. That ends completely and totally when you die because in Heaven the love never ends. That makes sense as God continually reminds us in His word, "God is love." I John 4:8, 16

Don writes,

> *"I get frustrated describing what Heaven was like, because I can't put it into words what it looked like, sounded like, and felt like. It was perfect, and I knew I had no needs and would never need again."*[99]

It's hard to believe that God would allow a man to return to Earth to tell his story of his trip to Heaven, but God has a purpose in all He does. I believe God wanted to give us all *reinforced* hope. He gives us a lot of hope in His Word, but it sure supports our faith in knowing that He really has prepared a magnificent place for you and me when we die. In fact, the moment you become a Believer in Christ, Heaven is now your new home!

> *Let not your heart be troubled. Believe in God and believe also in me, for in my Father's house are many mansions. I go there to prepare a place for you. John 14: 1-3*

God's love for you is so huge; He wants you in a huge mansion inside His house. That must be some house! Inconceivable, yet undeniable, He wants you to be with Him forever in Heaven, your new home.

Right now, my hope for you is hope restored. It takes just a mustard seed of faith in the love of Jesus to qualify you for citizenship of Heaven. You no longer need to fear death, as death has lost its sting.

> *Where O death, is your victory? Where O death is your sting? I Corinthians 15:55*

C.S. Lewis described the event of death itself in comparison to an evening meal. Suppose you order a nice T-bone steak dinner with two sides and dessert. The meat represents all the important relationships and wonderful events of your life. The sides represent your work-life and hobbies. The dessert, however, is your death. No, I'm not referring to Death by Chocolate (*to die for!*) or New York Cheesecake (*because that would be cheesy!*). Death is like the dessert at the end, a sweet ending to a fantastic meal. Death is actually something to look forward to because Heaven is waiting for you on the other side.

My mother's name was Karen Armer, and she wrote a book entitled *C.S. Lewis on Death & Dying*.[100] If you are not aware of C.S. Lewis, he was the author of *Chronicles of Narnia: The Lion, Witch and the Wardrobe*. C.S Lewis loved to write allegories illustrating the Biblical story of God's love and Heaven itself. Have you seen the movie or read the book? You should! It's a fun book to read and well-illustrated with Aslan, the Lion representing Christ, and the three children who entered his kingdom through a wardrobe.

Spoiler alert! Aslan dies at the end as a sacrifice for the youngest of the three children, taking on her punishment. However, the witch failed to read the inscription on his stone table, which read,

"If a willing Victim that has committed no treachery is killed in a traitor's stead, the Stone Table will crack; and even death itself would turn backwards." -Deep Magic

As a Christian allegory, the Stone Table symbolizes the Mosaic Law of the Old Testament. The Mosaic Law regarded every form of treachery (sin) to be punishable by death. Just as Aslan, the Lion transcended the rule of Deep Magic by sacrificing himself; Christ transcended the Mosaic Law by dying on the Cross willingly, allowing forgiveness of sins to be possible.

Just as Aslan raises himself back to life and restores the kingdom as it once was, Christ was resurrected three days following His death, restoring us unto Himself.

Here's how it all applies to you and me. As I quoted earlier, God is Love. And because of His love for us, He provided a way for us to have eternal life in this wonderful place called Heaven, and that was only through His own sacrifice. He gave up His life so that we could *have* life. He says this in His word,

Greater love has no man than this, that he lay down his life for his friends. John 15:13

God calls us His friends. And He calls us His children. Yes, parents can love their children and be their friend too, and I believe this is vital to a great parent-child relationship. Why? Because friends want to be with each other, willingly.

Now you can see both sides of the coin, so to speak. Don Piper tries to explain the enormous amount of never-ending love he was experiencing in Heaven, and yet here is God-in-the-flesh displaying His love for us by spreading out His arms and dying on a rugged cross.

I can hear you possibly saying, "He did it for all humanity, but not just for me." You are right and wrong at the same time. If you were the only living person on Earth, He still would have gone through all the torture of the cross and death just for you. You may feel inadequate at this moment, but that's not how the God of the Universe sees you. He doesn't see your sin and mistakes; he sees you as His child. He loves you despite what you have done, as Romans says,

> *But God demonstrates His love for us in this: While we were still sinners, Christ died for us. Romans 5:8*

Therefore, you are loved. You are God's creation. His death for you is a gift, and it's up to you to accept it. I hope you do accept it because it is a decision you will not regret. Your life will have a new purpose, and your eternal destination in Heaven is secured.

My mother wrote her book in 2007 and died the same year. Ironically, she wrote about death just before experiencing death herself. It took me years before I could read her book because so much of her personality resonates throughout her book. She was an amazing person, and I miss her dearly, but I'll be with her again in just a few moments.

So dear reader, how do you feel about the subject of death now? My prayer for you is that you have a peace you never had before reading this book. Billy Graham was probably one of our greatest preachers of all time. His crusades have resulted in millions of people becoming Believers. Just like Aretha Franklin, he also died at the time of writing this book. When asked about his own upcoming death, he replied, "I'm just trading one home for another." Exactly. But consider your next home a major upgrade!

• BREAKING IT DOWN •

Application for the Ergonomics of Death

1. Let's get you thinking about the Big 3:

   A. Your Will: List five things and the people you want to inherit your money, possessions, etc.

   a. _____

   b. _____

   c. _____

   d. _____

   e. _____

   B. List five things about your funeral that would best represent you for your loved ones.

   a. _____

   b. _____

   c. _____

   d. _____

   e. _____

   C. Your Life Insurance Policy. Have you found the one you like? Who is your designated recipient?

   _____

   _____

   _____

2. As you review your life, are you the person you always wanted to be? Why or why not?

    _____

    _____

    _____

3. Do you have peace about where are you going when you die?

    _____

    _____

    _____

Conclusion and Services

IN THE BEGINNING of this book, I stated that its purpose is to help you maximize your life while living on this planet. My goal is simple, to assist you as if you were an alien landing on planet Earth not knowing anything about life as we know it. As an alien life form, your questions while visiting here might include:

What is this body I'm in, and how do I take care of it?

What is the best way to spend my time while I'm here?

How do I lead others into action and productivity for a worthy cause?

What's the secret of getting along with others and making new friends?

How do I manage my money, so it doesn't manage me, and what are my real chances of winning this lottery thing?

Is there more to life than this? What's beyond this life when I perish?

Well, I think I covered all those topics (and more). I hope you enjoyed the ride through the chapters. I hope you have been entertained with many eye-rolls, groans, and chuckles, and have been encouraged to live your life to the fullest!

And you can enjoy each day if you apply what you have learned. From health management areas to time management to money management, there are proven techniques that can really destress every area of your life. It's your <u>attitude</u> through all of the twists, turns, and speedbumps of life that determines the <u>altitude</u> of how high you can go. Remember, life is 10% what happens to you and 90% how you react. Besides, 90% of the things we worry about never come to pass, so stop worrying and start living! Look ahead of you, not behind you, and you won't run into trees or other things!

The end result really can be a life filled with abundance—in joy, relationships, and productivity in work and private time. Your attitude will reflect how you handle your stress level, and that is the factor in the equation that is entirely up to you. The key in all of this is to learn to live above your circumstances, not under them. You can't do it on your own strength, but you can on God's strength. He is willing and able to help you in any event in your life. All you have to do is pray and believe He can.

I come that you may have life and have it to the fullest. John 10:10

Gunnar T Speaks Speaking Engagements

I would be honored to share principles from the *Ergonomics of Life* with your workforce or next event! My fee structure changes depending if you are a non-profit organization or youth-oriented event. Plus, if you have a church-related event, I would love to come and share the love! You can always visit my website and book me by filling out the request form, <u>Ergonomics of Life Interior 10212020.docx</u>.

Here are three of my favorite keynote speeches that may perfectly fit into your audience needs:

Keynote: The Ergonomics of Wellness: Work/Life Balance

In this talk, we examine healthy choices that are research-proven to boost your productivity in every area of your life. We examine three areas where we can make easy adjustments: your food, your time-management, and your work relationships. This talk reveals the healthy habits of centenarians worldwide and what they do to live happier, more productive lives that matter.

Includes

In-Office Exercises & Stretches to Reduce Chronic Stress

This workshop teaches effective exercises and stretches that employees can do in the workplace to reduce chronic muscle aches and pains associated with stress. We examine stretches and exercises compiled in a study led by Washington University and proven to reduce chronic stress.

Keynote: The Ergonomics of Wellness on the Road

Are you a road warrior? Whether you travel domestically or internationally, you will want to know how to stay well, prevent sickness, and keep things simple. This is a talk that's perfect for your sales team! In this talk, we discuss travel insurance, how to reduce jet lag, and staying fit on your travels. These are tips that will surprise you!

Includes

- Best travel insurance options that will cover you.
- How to quickly overcome jetlag.

- Nutritional Advice that will keep you energetic and thin.
- Illness Prevention.
- How to get flight and hotel upgrades for nothing!

Keynote: The Ergonomics of Entitlement

This talk is centered on understanding the Millennial generation and building productive, meaningful relationships. Today too many are job-transient, unstable, and lost. They need to be *rescued* by work environments that give them a sense of purpose and security. Together we uncover the history leading to the parental philosophy in raising Millennials and five tactics to develop them into effective leaders. This talk is research-based with proven strategies that work!

Gunnar T's Coaching Program

I've helped thousands of individuals just like you to become *ergonomically* healthy. It's powerfully intimate and tailored based on your current fitness level and personal stats, combined with the most up-to-date techniques to help you either lose or gain weight. Unlike most programs that focus on the *quantity* of clients, such as large app platforms, my coaching program focuses on *quality and results.* You are the most important person that I coach because I will know you. You will love your whole-body transformation and become more optimistic about how you look and feel because you will have a solid nutrition and exercise regimen that fits you perfectly.

My Mission Statement to You:

I create a customized program specifically for you that's ergonomically fit for your lifestyle.

Translated

I will make you look good, feel good, and help you make more money.

Imagine this: Where do you want to be 12 weeks from now? How about one year from now? Anything is possible! That's where we begin. It's all about the *present* you and the *future* you!

I've helped people lose as much as 100 lbs. in less than a year! I can help you lose the weight you want to lose without sacrificing all the foods you love to eat. We will virtually meet to discuss your progress every two weeks, and I will give you advice and update your nutrition and fitness program. The program usually begins with a body detoxification plan, then a blood analysis by my board of physicians, followed by an ergonomically designed coaching program that is tailored just for you. You will know what to eat and how to exercise to reach your desired goals.

But it goes beyond nutrition and exercise. This is Life Coaching too! I'll help you rise to the next level or to chase that dream you have always had but never pursued. I've been "stuck" in life many times, and it is not a fun place to be. You should be doing what you love to do. Whatever that "dream" is in you, I believe God put it there. Let's rise up together!

All you need to do is sign-up on my site, https://www.gunnartspeaks.com/gunnar-t-coaches, request a free 30-minute consultation. You will also need to have your bloodwork results (within six months) as much of our assessment for you is based on it and a short "All About You" Intake Survey.

You can also subscribe to my site for updated content via my blog posts and video feeds, and join my Facebook page, Facebook/gunnarisms.

My blog posts have ties to every chapter in this book. Every day I find best practices in managing time, money, and stress to keep you up on the latest thinking. Plus, I'll always inspire you with memes and quotes. Best of all, you will be better at well—just being you. The *best* you! We are all in this boat together, so start paddling! Let's pursue excellence together!

See you soon, friends!

For booking Gunnar to speak at your next event, or to sign up for my wellness life coaching program, go here: www.GunnarTspeaks.com

Facebook/gunnarisms

Instagram: @gunnarisms_live

LinkedIn: https://www.linkedin.com/in/gunnarthelander/

Twitter: @gunnarisms

YouTube: GunnarT

Notes

Introduction

[1] "Why we are paying more for coffee?" Erin Meister Counter Culture Coffee, May 10, 2019, https://drinks.seriouseats.com/2011/02/why-coffee-will-and-should-cost-more-coffee-price-increase.html

Chapter One: Ergonomics of Stress

[2] "Social Media Statistics and Facts" Statista, September 4, 2019, https://www.statista.com/topics/1164/social-networks/

[3] "42 Worrying Workplace Stress Statistics." American Institute of Stress, September 25, 2019, https://www.stress.org/42-worrying-workplace-stress-statistics

[4] The Holmes & Raye Stress Scale, https://www.mindtools.com/pages/article/newTCS_82.htm

Chapter Two: Ergonomics of Your Body

[5] Tesh, John. "Intelligence for Your Life," Thomas Nelson, 2012, p.68

[6] "9 Charts That Show Why America is Fat, Sick, and Tired," Kathlene McCoy, June 13, 2017, https://draxe.com/health/charts-american-diet/

[7] National Institute of Diabetes and Digestive and Kidney Diseases, Data 2014 https://www.niddk.nih.gov/health-information/health-statistics/overweight-obesity

[8] "Facts and Statistics," December 2018 https://www.hhs.gov/fitness/resource-center/facts-and-statistics/index.html

[9] Tesh, John. "Intelligence for Your Life," Thomas Nelson, 2012

Chapter Three: Ergonomics of Work

[10] "Burnout at Work, Can We Prevent It?"
https://www.bakkerelkhuizen.com/en-us/knowledgecenter/burn-out/

[11] "Job Stress," American Institute of Stress, January 20, 2011,
https://www.stress.org/42-worrying-workplace-stress-statistics

[12] "What Are the Risks of Sitting Too Much?" Edward R. Laskowski, M.D.,
https://www.mayoclinic.org/healthy-lifestyle/adult-health/expert-answers/sitting/faq-20058005

[13] "Sitting Positions for Good Posture," Written by Jennifer Huizen, May 21,
2013, https://www.medicalnewstoday.com/articles/321863

[14] "How Many Colors Can a Computer Screen Represent?" by Stephen
Westland, April 23, 2019, https://www.quora.com/How-do-computer-screens-affect-vision

[15] "Four Simple and Effective Ways to Avoid Digital Eye Strain," Occupational
Health & Safety, by Hanish Patel, April 1, 2019,
https://ohsonline.com/articles/2019/04/01/four-simple-and-effective-ways-to-avoid-digital-eye-strain.aspx

[16] "The Snowball Effect of Healthy Offices," CBRE, by Elizabeth C. Nelson,
https://www.cbre.nl/en/healthy-offices-research

[17] Oppezzo, M., & Schwartz, D. L. (2014). Give your ideas some legs: The
positive effect of walking on creative thinking. *Journal of Experimental
Psychology: Learning, Memory, and Cognition, 40*(4), 1142–1152.
https://doi.org/10.1037/a0036577

[18] Verkinos, Joan. "Sitting Kills, Moving Heals." Linden Publishing, 2011
www.joanvernikos.com

[19] "If You Work On Your Feet," Healthline.com, Written by Kimberly
Holland and Valencia Higuera, January 10, 2017,
https://www.healthline.com/health/workplace-health/if-you-work-on-your-feet

[20] "How To Achieve the Best Standing Posture," Physioworks,
https://physioworks.com.au/FAQRetrieve.aspx?ID=44668

[21] "What is Vanna White's Salary on Wheel of Fortune?" by Karen Gardner, December 22, 2018, https://careertrend.com/what-is-vanna-whites-salary-on-wheel-of-fortune-12398543.html

[22] "Stanford Study Finds Walking Improves Creativity," by May Wong, April 24, 2014
https://news.stanford.edu/2014/04/24/walking-vs-sitting-042414/

Chapter Five: Ergonomics of Leadership

[23] "5 Facts About 'Miracle of Dunkirk'" by Joe Carter, July 20, 2017, https://erlc.com/resource-library/articles/5-facts-about-the-miracle-of-dunkirk

[24] Churchill Has Mastered a Stutter and a Lisp to Become an Orator," in the Kansas City Star, February 6th, 1941

[25] Hitler had Jewish and African Roots," by Heidi Blake, August 24, 2010, https://www.telegraph.co.uk/history/world-war-two/7961211/Hitler-had-Jewish-and- African-roots-DNA-tests-show.html

[26] Gates, Bill. "The Road Ahead." Penguin Books, 1996, p.181

[27] Blanchard, Ken. "The Heart of a Leader." Eagle Publishers, 2000

[28] Leadership Qualities of Steve Jobs," by Beth Hendricks, www.study.com

[29] Blanchard, Ken. "The Heart of a Leader." Eagle Publishers, 2000

[30] Maxwell, John. "Becoming a Person of Influence." Thomas Nelson Publishers, 1997

[31] Walsh, Bill. "Reflections on Coach Wooden, Wooden: A Lifetime of Observations On and Off the Court." McGraw Hill, 1997

[32] Ibid.

[33] "Eight Suggestions for Succeeding," Wooden: A Lifetime of Observations, McGraw Hill, 1997

[34] "Successful Leaders," Fast Company, Issue 222

[35] Blanchard, Ken. "The Leadership Pill." Simon & Schuster, 2003

[36] "10 Major Accomplishments of Ronald Reagan," by Anirunh, February 11, 2017, learnodo-newtonic.com/ronald-reagan

[37] Sinek, Simon. "Leaders Eat Last." Penguin Random House, 2014

[38] "Corporate Culture, Evidence from the Field," National Bureau of Economic Research, K. Hodes, March 2017, http://www.nber.org/papers/w23255

[39] Maxwell, John. "Today Matters." Center Street, Hachette Book Group, Inc, p.64

[40] Keller, Gary. and Jay Papasan, "The ONE Thing: The Surprisingly Simple Truth Behind Extraordinary Results," Bard Press, 2013, p.103 www.the1thing.com

[41] Lachlan, Paul, "Freeway to Work and Wealth," Harmony Press, 1982

[42] "Freud and the Unconscious Mind," by Saul McLeod 2015, https://www.simplypsychology.org/unconscious-mind.html

[43] Ballantyne, Craig. "Perfect Day Formula." p.72

[44] Tracy, Bryan. "Eat That Frog!" GABAL, 2002, p.7

[45] Allen, James. "As a Man Thinketh." LN Fowler, 1964

[46] "The Great Train Robbery," MoMA article of movie made 1903, https://www.moma.org/learn/moma_learning/edwin-s-porter-the-great-train-robbery-1903/

[47] Will $10 Million Make You Happier? Harvard Says Yes-If You Make it Yourself and Give it Away," by Nuezd, December 14, 2017,

[48] Dweck, Carol S. "Mindset: The New Psychology of Success." 2006, pp. 217, 223

[49] "Household Income 2018," By Gloria G. Guzman, September 2019, https://www.census.gov/content/dam/Census/library/publications/2019/acs/acsbr18-01.pdf

[50] "US Home Prices & Values," https://www.zillow.com/home-values/

[51] "Auto Loan Statistics 2020," by Jen Jones, January 10, 2020, https://www.lendingtree.com/auto/debt-statistics/

[52] "69% of Americans Have Less Than $ 1000 Savings: How to Save More for the Future," GoBankingRates, December 2019, https://www.forumdaily.com/en/opros-69-amerikancev-imeyut-menee-1000-sberezhenij/

[53] "U.S. Credit Card Debt Begins to Slide in Tandem with Confidence," by Robert McKinley, October 2019, https://cardtrak.com/2019/10/09/debt/u s credit-card-debt-begins-to-slide-in-tandem-with-confidence/

[54] "U.S. Average Student Loan Debt Statistics in 2019," by Natalie Issa, June 2019, https://www.credit.com/personal-finance/average-student-loan-debt/

[55] "Auto Loan Statistics 2020," by Jen Jones, January 10, 2020, https://www.lendingtree.com/auto/debt-statistics/

[56] "How to Create Ray Dalio's All Weather Portfolio," by Aron Vesper, September 2019, https://nine-thrive.com/how-to-create-ray-dalios-all-weather-portfolio/

[57] Financial Peace University, by Dave Ramsey, https://www.daveramsey.com/fpu/#in-progress=0

[58] Webster Dictionary – *Fortitude, https://www.merriam-webster.com/dictionary/fortitude*

[59] "Happiest Place on Earth," Les Brown Quotes https://www.goodreads.com/author/quotes/57803.Les_Brown

[60] "Be the Change," Mahatma Gandhi quotes, https://www.goodreads.com/author/quotes/5810891.Mahatma_Gandhi

[61] Planning and Progress Study, 2015 Northwestern Mutual, https://www.northwesternmutual.com/insurance/

[62] Maxwell, John. "The 21 Irrefutable Laws of Leadership." Thomas Nelson, 2007, pp. 48-49

[63] Northwestern Mutual Claim data 2008-2013

[64] Northwestern Mutual, Monthly Budget Sheet (Figure 7.1)

[65] Simon Sinek, "Millennials talk," https://www.youtube.com/watch?v=hER0Qp6QJNU

[66] Generation X, GenX, Wikipedia.org/wiki/Generation_X

[67] "Generation X, GenX," by Julia Kagan, June 25, 2019, Deloitte report/Investopedia.com/terms/g/generation_X

[68] "Marriage and Divorce," American Psychological Association, https://www.apa.org/topics/divorce/index

[69] "Household spending by single persons and married couples in their twenties: a comparison Bureau of Labor statistics," by William Hawk, 2011, https://www.bls.gov/cex/anthology11/csxanth6.pdf

[70] "A Rising Share of Young Adults Live in Their Parents' Home," Federal Reserve Bank of Atlanta, August 1, 2013, https://www.pewsocialtrends.org/2013/08/01/a-rising-share-of-young-adults-live-in-their-parents-home/

[71] Bruneman, Steven W. "Winning the Marriage Gamble." 2012, https://stevebruneman.com/

[72] "9 ways millennials are approaching marriage differently from their parents," by Shana Lebowitz of the Business Insider, November 2017, https://www.insider.com/how-millennials-gen-x-and-baby-boomers-approach-marriage-2017-11

[73] "America's Generation Gap in Extramarital Sex," by Nicholas H. Wolfinger, July 5th, 2017, Institute for Family Studies blog

[74] "Millennials are killing marriage — here's why that's a good thing," by Kari Paul, Marketwatch, February 16, 2018, https://www.marketwatch.com/story/millennials-are-killing-marriage-heres-why-thats-a-good-thing-2018-02-08

[75] "What is Agape Love? (And What Does it Mean for Me?)," by Rachel Dawson, *Crosswalk.com*, May 18, 2018, https://www.crosswalk.com/faith/spiritual-life/what-is-agape-love-and-what-does-it-mean-for-me.html

[76] Centennial Heritage, Power of Faith, *Is Christianity in the US almost dead?*

[77] "New Harvard Research Says U.S. Christianity is Not Shrinking, But Growing Stronger," by Glenn T. Stanton, Harvard/Indiana University, January 22, 2018, https://thefederalist.com/2018/01/22/new-harvard-research-says-u-s-christianity-not-shrinking-growing-stronger/

[78] Centennial Heritage, *Power of Faith* by Joel Osteen, p.10, "Sometimes spell faith R-I-S-K."

[79] Centennial Heritage, *Power of Faith* by Rick Warren, p.26, "Purpose for your life far greater…"

[80] "The Incredible Design of the Earth and Our Solar System," by Rich Deem, http://www.godandscience.org/apologetics/designss.html

[81] "Einstein and Intelligent Design," by Stephen Caesar, January 16, 2008, https://biblearchaeology.org/research/investigating-origins/3446-einstein-and-intelligent-design

[82] "Believe Jesus When You Pray," by Dr. K.P. Yohannan, https://www.gfa.org/kpyohannan/5-minutes-with-kpyohannan/believe-jesus-when-you-pray/

[83] "The Attributes of God," by A.W. Pink Tozer, http://www.godrules.net/library/pink/249pink1.htm

[84] "The Existence of God," by A.W. Pink Tozer, http://www.godrules.net/library/pink/252pink_a1.htm

[85] "15 Amazing Attributes of God: What They Mean and Why They Matter," by BST, August 2019, https://www.biblestudytools.com/bible-study/topical-studies/15-amazing-attributes-of-god-what-they-mean-and-why-they-matter.html

[86] "Youth Pastor Dies in Plane Crash," The Kerrville Daily Times, April 7, 1998

[87] "How to Prepare for Death in Your Own Home," by Angela Morrow, March 2020 https://www.verywellhealth.com/preparing-for-death-1132516

[88] "Aretha Franklin Died Without a Will, and Estate Issues Loom," by Ben Sisario, August 2018, https://www.nytimes.com/2018/08/22/arts/music/aretha-franklin-will.html

[89] "3 Wills Found At Aretha Franklin's Estate," by Anastasia Tsioulcas, May 2018, https://www.npr.org/2019/05/21/725345750/three-wills-found-at-aretha-franklins-home

[90] "How many people die a day in the US?," by IndexMundi Blog, https://www.indexmundi.com/blog/index.php/2018/03/05/how-many-people-die-a-day-in-the-us/

[91] "The Conversation Project," http://theconversationproject.org/about/

[92] Boss, Pauline. "Ambiguous Loss." Harvard University Press, 1999

[93] C.S. Lewis. "The Problem of Pain." 1940, p. 121

[94] 7eventh Time Down, lyrics to song "Just Say Jesus"

[95] C.S. Lewis. "Miracles." 1947, pp. 148, 150, 151

[96] Wallace Rutland, Blog

[97] Piper, Don. And Cecil Murphey, "90 Minutes in Heaven." Revel Publishing, 2004, pp.70, 76, 88

[98] Ibid.

[99] Ibid.

[100] Armer, Karen. "C.S. Lewis on Death & Dying." Xlibris Publishing, January 2007

Suggested Readings

Great Wellness Sources

- *Intelligence for Your Life* by John Tesh, https://tesh.com/
- *Sitting Kills, Moving Heals* by Joan Verkinos www.joanvernikos.com

General Wellness Tips for Home and Work

- https://www.mayoclinic.org/healthy-lifestyle/adult-health/expert-answers/
- *The Snowball Effect of Healthy Offices*, CBRE, by Elizabeth C. Nelson https://www.cbre.nl/en/healthy-offices-research
- Verywellhealth.com Blog, https://www.verywellhealth.com/
- *As a Man Thinketh* by James Allen, https://asamanthinketh.net/
- *Mindset: The New Psychology of Success* by Carol S. Dweck https://www.amazon.com/Mindset-Psychology-Carol-S-Dweck-ebook/dp/B000FCKPHG

Great Sources for Your Workplace

- *Sitting Kills, Moving Heals* by Dr. Joan Vernikos https://www.joanvernikos.com/pages/sitting-kills-moving-heals.php
- *Stanford Study Finds Walking Improves Creativity*, by May Wong, April 24, 2014, https://news.stanford.edu/2014/04/24/walking-vs-sitting-042414/
- *How To Achieve the Best Standing Posture,* Physioworks, https://physioworks.com.au/FAQRetrieve.aspx?ID=44668
- *If You Work On Your Feet,* Healthline.com, Written by Kimberly Holland and Valencia Higuera, January 10, 2017, https://www.healthline.com/health/workplace-health/if-you-work-on-your-feet
- *The Snowball Effect of Healthy Offices,* CBRE, by Elizabeth C. Nelson, https://www.cbre.nl/en/healthy-offices-research
- *What Are the Risks of Sitting Too Much?* by Edward R. Laskowski, M.D., https://www.mayoclinic.org/healthy-lifestyle/adult-health/expert-answers/sitting/faq-20058005

Great Sources for Your Leadership Development:

Works by John C. Maxwell: https://www.johnmaxwell.com/
- *The 21 Irrefutable Laws of Leadership*
- *Becoming a Person of Influence*

Works by Ken Blanchard: https://www.kenblanchard.com/
- *Heart of a Leader*
- *Everyone's a Coach*
- *The One Minute Manager*
- *The One Minute Manager to Work*
- *Power of Ethical Management*
- *Consumer Mania!*

- *The Leadership Pill*

Works by Bill Walsh and John Wooden: http://www.coachwooden.com/bookstore
- *Wooden: A Lifetime of Observations on and Off the Court*
- *Reflections on Coach Wooden*

Works by Simon Sinek: https://simonsinek.com/
- *Leaders Eat Last*
- *Start with Why*

Great Sources for Your Time Management:

- *Eat That Frog!* By Brian Tracy, https://www.briantracy.com/
- *Today Matters* by John C. Maxwell, https://www.rich-business.com/today-matters/
- *The One Thing* by Gary Keller, https://www.the1thing.com/
- *The Perfect Day Formula* by Craig Ballantyne, http://www.earlytorise.com/perfectday/

Great Sources for Your Money Management:

- *Financial Peace University* by Dave Ramsey, https://www.daveramsey.com/fpu/
- *The Total Money Makeover* by Dave Ramsey, https://www.daveramsey.com/store/product/the-total-money-makeover-hardcover-book-workbook
- Planning and Progress Study, 2015 Northwestern Mutual, https://www.northwesternmutual.com/insurance/
- *How to Create Ray Dalio's All Weather Portfolio*, by Aron Vesper, September 2019, https://nine-thrive.com/how-to-create-ray-dalios-all-weather-portfolio/

Great Sources for Your Growing Your Relationships:

- *Winning the Marriage Gamble* by Steven W. Bruneman
  https://stevebruneman.com/winning-the-marriage-gamble/
- *Marriage and Divorce*, American Psychological Association,
  https://www.apa.org/topics/divorce/index
- *The Four Loves*, CS Lewis

Great Sources for Dealing with The Loss of a Loved One:

- *Ambiguous Loss* by Pauline Boss,
  https://www.ambiguousloss.com/
- *90 Minutes in Heaven* by Don Piper,
  http://donpiperministries.com/
- *C.S. Lewis on Death & Dying* by Karen Armer,
  https://www.amazon.com/Karen-Armer/e/B001JS1CZE%3Fref=dbs_a_mng_rwt_scns_share

Great Sources for Your Growing Your Faith:

- *The Purpose-Driven Life* by Rick Warren,
  https://store.pastorrick.com/books.html

Works by C.S. Lewis: https://www.cslewis.com/us/books/
  - *The Lion, Witch and the Wardrobe*
  - *The Four Loves*
  - *The Problem of Pain*
  - *Miracles*

- Crosswalk.com Blog by Rachel Dawson,
  http://www.racheladawson.com/crosswalk
- The NIV, NKG Bible, https://www.zondervan.com/
- Biblearchaeology.org Blog, https://biblearchaeology.org/

- Christianbiblereference.org Blog,
  https://www.christianbiblereference.org/
- Works by Dr. K.P. Yohannan,
  https://kpyohannan.org/books/
- Works by A.W. Pink Tozer, https://awtozer.com/about/
- Biblestudytools.com/15 Amazing Attributes of God and
  Why They Matter, https://www.biblestudytools.com/

ABOUT THE AUTHOR

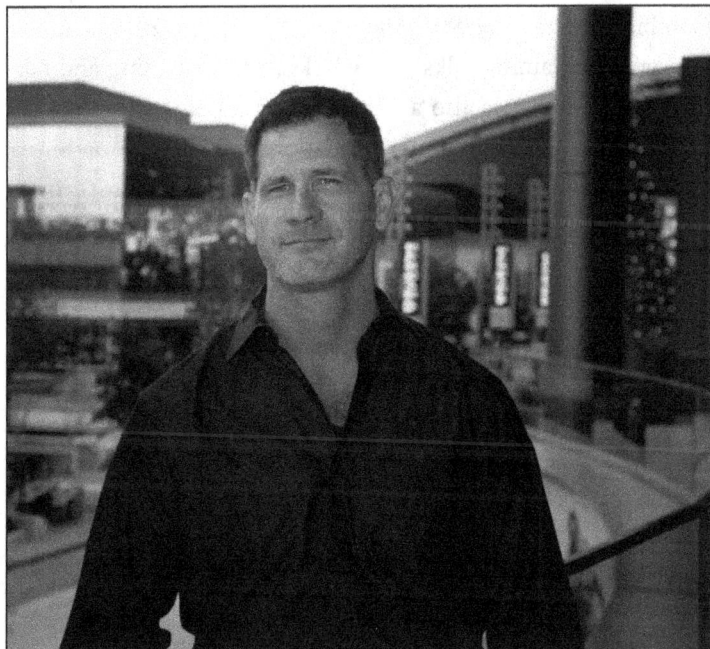

Gunnar K. Thelander, who earned his Master's and Doctorate in Exercise & Sports Science and Organizational Leadership, is a dynamic Speaker and Coach helping others live healthier lives that are "ergonomically-fit" for their lifestyles. Whether you are trying to improve your game at work, home, or traveling, this book is perfect for you. Gunnar is also a Certified Life & Wellness Coach through *The Professional Coach Academy* and *A.C.E.*, which has already helped approximately 8,600 clients in his wellness practice in the past twelve years.

The practical insights he shares in this book are easy yet effective for a total body, mind, and spirit transformation. He has been a school teacher and sports coach for over ten years before becoming a professional speaker and personal coach for thousands of individuals just like you. Nominated "Best Up and Coming Speaker" by *Star Marketing Summit* in 2019, Gunnar delivers entertaining talks that will keep you laughing and taking notes. Gunnar is also a Rotarian and loves sharing ideas to give back to the community. For more information or hiring Gunnar, "Gunnar T" to speak or coach, contact him through gunnarTspeaks.com.

www.ingramcontent.com/pod-product-compliance
Lightning Source LLC
Chambersburg PA
CBHW050456270326
41927CB00009B/1768